Sunnyville

RICKO DONOVAN

Wild Card Press

ISBN: 978-0-991-18821-5

ALSO BY RICKO DONOVAN

The Broken Promised Land

Sun of Sunnyville

ACKNOWLEDGMENTS

I would like to express my profoundest gratitude to The Nashville Writers Meetup for all the valuable critique and encouragement, to Wildacres Writers Workshop for providing a foundation for learning the elements of crafting a good story, to my editors Charlotte Muñoz and Sherry Wilds for guiding me through the door to the mind of the reader, and to anyone who lent an encouraging word or two on the initial drafts.

1

Marion Legrand and her daughter Elise arrived at last to Sunnyville. The two French women were dead on their feet after shuffling hurriedly around train stations and airport terminals, checking and re-checking themselves for tickets and passports. Sunnyville- a spread of marshland just south of Tampa Florida encompassing about twelve square miles, roughly three of which comprised Sunny Glen Palms. It was established for the exclusive development of retirement communities in an area populated for millions of years mostly by alligators- those giant reptiles by now reduced to a minority, emerging from the shadows every now and again and crawling out onto the golf greens to the vexation of their human invaders. For many of those twenty thousand human inhabitants over age fifty-five, Sunnyville Florida would prove to be the final stitch of life's tapestry.

While her daughter Elise made small talk with the shuttle van driver in hesitant and methodical English, Marion craned her neck this way and that at the moving panorama. What her eyes met was a landscape mostly alien to her- unremarkable with its overabundant signage, parking lots, strip malls, convenience store gasoline stations. No hint of sand. The van raced along a four-lane divided by the meridian strip of neatly trimmed grass, palm trees and azalea bushes, then at last a sign emblazoned with fancy bronze letters- Sunny Glen Palms. At the entrance was an arched facade covering the roadway and a gate with a uniformed guard. While the guard carefully matched their information to a manifest the two women exchanged puzzled glances at the formality of the protocol. Marion fetched her fine leather handbag and began to rummage around. From among a paperback edition of Gore Vidal's *Inventing A Nation*, a French-English dictionary rife with dog-eared pages, and a battered copy of Le Monde, she fished out the flimsy airmail envelope. She carried Mimi's letter like a talisman. It was, after all, what had brought her here. She opened the letter once again as the guard waved them on- inviting them, somewhat hesitantly and without fanfare, into the domain of Sunny Glen Palms.

My dear sister,

I write you not from the poolside but the bed, where I have been lying awake all night with my mind wandering here and there from one dark forest to another and I cannot stop it. The sun shines so brightly behind the blinds and yet I am caught here like a prisoner to my own fears. The past seeps through the walls of this, the very first brand new house I have ever lived in. In spite of its fresh paint, its shiny new fixtures and the modern conveniences, the past creeps in and shadows me, haunts me.

The minivan drifted over a speed bump. Marion pushed a strand of hair from her eye and glanced out the window, as if she just might spot her sister on the lawn of one of the cookie-cutter houses that lined the road.

You have often visited me in my dreams. Do you remember when we were little girls in pigtails, kicking up the sand beneath our feet as we sprinted along the beaches of Biarritz in those summers before the war? When we got ourselves overheated, how we ran- I stopping short at the water's edge to watch you plunge headfirst into the phantom sea. I always had to feed the cold sea one piece of me at a time. You took it all in one breath. Do you remember how you used to splash at me from the chilly waters?

The van circled around a fountain and from there entered the main road, a big green sign announced it as Sunset Boulevard. To the right lay a large building skirted by palm trees, behind that was a pool beside a man-made lake. To the left lay a long stretch of shuffleboard courts, fenced-in tennis courts and a volleyball court with a sagging net.

From the time Bobby took me to America I felt so much that I had exceeded your courage by venturing not just the few yards into that ocean but halfway across the world. I've gone through the years believing it was I who held the mightiest courage but now I see it was you. You were courageous enough to stay there and make a life on your own terms. The only danger I faced here was an exuberant culture that believed prosperity could fill that unspeakable void into which we are born.

Elise tugged at Marion's elbow and pointed at an elderly couple trolling along the side of the road on a golf cart. They were dressed from head to toe in white- Elise nodded at her own colorful blouse, bright red jeans and flowery headscarf. Marion pinched her daughter's ear lightly and then returned her attention to the letter.

> *Robert has left me un-wanting in my old age, the pension and my social security make it feasible to retire. But it was never a life I would say was built on my own terms. I raised two sons with the full expectation of pride and perhaps a certain reward for my efforts. Even when I caught young Steven in the bathroom with those dirty magazines, even when Tom disappointed us with his spell of substance abuse, I never faltered in my pride as a mother nor my belief in them. Now they have forsaken me for their respective corporate dramas, the stock market, they have forsaken me for football, they have forsaken me for their silly home improvement schemes, their frivolous home equity loans, their status-symbol timeshares, the spoiled brat grandchildren I never get to see.*

The van continued to make an interminable amount of turns through winding streets for which a 15 mile-per-hour speed limit applied. After the villa structures, the houses were modest bungalows with carports. Then they came upon a newer development and the yards took on a different standard of grooming- neatly trimmed lawns, well-pruned shrubs, colorful flowerbeds.

> *Oh maybe I'm just feeling sorry for myself. I think loneliness has infected this continent like a disease. Everyone looks so confident but there is so much danger now they say. We are more at risk with each passing day and you never know who's going to do what. Now the danger I face comes not from the world around me but from inside myself. Oh my dear Marion, this last leg of my life has been fraught with a loneliness that nudges with the dull ache of a rock to the ribcage. My dear Marion come at once, I believe I am dying.*

*

The operation was going to get a little hairy. This was the portion of the manufacturing process he'd anticipated with a combination of eagerness and dread. Joining the wings to the fuselage entailed precision adhering at multiple contact points.

Frank Alsatian removed his vapor solvent respirator mask and wiped his brow with his shirtsleeve. Frank had close-cropped hair gone almost fully gray, a significant set of jowls that somewhat lent him the look of a boxer, and a suntan which lent a handsome factor to a face which otherwise held no distinguishing features. On his body all the weight went upstairs and left him with a set of chicken legs to support it.

There was a breeze outside, beyond the screen doors that ran the full length of the garage door. Inside the garage the air was close. Frank had moved their Ford Explorer out into the driveway to make room for the large-scale model airplane surgery. He'd elevated the airplane parts on horses so as to place the job at waist level. Beyond the diameter of his immediate work area the garage was tidy, sparse, and ordered. If one were to enter the Alsatian household from the garage, they might reasonably assume the house beyond was immaculately clean and furnished in a sensible manner. In the Alsatian garage, the golf clubs were stacked neatly in one corner next to the golf cart. A sheet metal tower of shelves stood next to a tidy workbench and held various tools and implements neatly ordered, bearing numbered stickers as if for inventory purposes. One might practically eat off of a cement floor unblemished by even the teeniest oil stain. From a small transistor radio that sat on the workbench, the squawking voice of a talk show host who was extremely pissed off about one thing or another reverberated against the bare walls of the garage. Frank covered his face again with the mask, waving the duty knife like a magic wand. With the other hand he steadied the wing and prepared the glue dispenser. Just as he laid it to the plastic piece a voice sounded from over his shoulder in the driveway.

"Hey buddy, watcha up to?"

It was the easy tone of Gerry Hagoden, rocking back and forth on sandaled feet, scratching at the slight paunch beneath his Bermuda shirt abstractedly. It was Florida and he was retired and by god he would flaunt it.

Frank peered over his shoulder with a good measure of indignation, masked by the vapor solvent respirator. He wanted to ignore his neighbor and return to the project at hand. *He* didn't go around sneaking up on people at inopportune moments, after all. He didn't go around anywhere unless invited or if attendance was expressly required. Instead he lowered the torch to waist level and once again raised the visor and wiped at his brow, not at sweat but at some impulse to evince a certain rankling at his neighbor's intrusion. With no small effort he managed to summon a minimum of social decorum.

"Hello Gerry."

Gerry scratched at sandy hair just beginning to go gray at the sideburns. This and the regular rounds of tennis and golf had kept him fit and looking younger than his sixty-seven years. "Looks like another beauty," he said. "Is she gonna be ready for a flight test before the sun goes down?"

"Maybe. Maybe so."

Gerry sniffled, glancing around as if he'd lost something and expected it to turn up from any direction. He sniffled every waking hour due to allergies as yet unidentified. Gerry didn't care to know their origin or their category, such awareness would hardly cause them to disappear into thin air. "We still on for golf tomorrow?"

"Seven o'clock, pardner."

The somewhat familiar form of address would have made Gerry Hagoden wag his tail were one attached.

"Guess I'll shuffle off, leave you to it."

"Okay pal, see you tomorrow."

Gerry shuffled off somewhat reluctantly to the house directly opposite the Alsatians. Attached to the light post hung the black shingle with gold lettering, *Gerald and Geraldine "Shirley" Hagoden*. He wished he were out on the links today, or that there were some other excuse to leave the house.

He re-entered through the screen door at the side of the house. His house was the same model with the identical floor plan as the Alsatians. One entered the house from the front only through the garage. It was the first house in his life that placed the front door at the side of the house. It struck him as odd when they'd picked it out five years ago, he didn't give the matter much thought anymore. It was his wife Shirley who rushed excitedly to sign the papers in the offices of Windmere Properties after they'd extended a brief visit to her sister Alma and her husband Mike. *Buy one of the new developments* was Alma's mantra for the entire duration of the visit- *you can get one for a song*. Gerry didn't need much cajoling- he'd sing a song a million times for the lush green manicured landscaping with palm trees baying in the wind, the pool, the amenities, the opportunity to pay a reasonable fee for golf courses that were a mere stone's throw away to be utilized at a moment's notice. They went back to Michigan determined to unload their house and sort through a lifetime's accumulation of possessions to determine what was irreplaceable and what could be chucked. Immediately upon returning from Florida he was beset by daydreams of long afternoons lounging by the pool in anticipation of cocktail hour at the neighbors or on their own screened-in porch at the back of the house. Daydreams of hours plying himself undistracted to lengthy thriller novels. Daydreams of tooling around the sand traps and water hazards in between machismo-laden drives and crowning-touch putts on a golf cart laden with personalized touches. Scorecard stationary pinned to the dashboard with Elvis-décor bordering, a Playboy Bunny rear-view mirror ornament, a mock Rolls Royce grille at the front, a Michigan license plate attached at the back. But alas, since the move pleasure was not administered in the steady dispensing of his daydreams, but in small irregular doses. Time didn't crawl along through lazy afternoons but was flying by much too fast since they'd retired- he from the GM plant and Shirley from both the Ann Arbor public school system and a paralegal career spread between several employers.

The screen door he kept forgetting to oil screeched when he pulled it open and diverted his wife's attention from their next-door neighbor Mrs. Norton. Shirley Hagoden, to her credit controlling a weight that needed monitoring due to unwelcome genetic inheritance. What you might call stout, with what you might call a cute face framed by salt and pepper hair that fell in natural curls just to the point where her neck began.

"Oh there you are, back already."

His wife turned from her place on the sofa near the sliding doors at the back of the house. With their retirement came the nagging sense his movements were monitored and remarked upon ad nauseam.

"Yes, dear."

He addressed his wife always with terms of endearment, however laced with sarcasm, due to their shared name. Geraldine. Gerry. It was a dilemma that hadn't eluded him on their first date. It presented itself immediately as a matter to be ironed out among all the other items that would come to be ironed out over the years. While his addresses ran the gamut of affectionate terms- *darling, dearest, beloved one, cupcake, honey, sugar, my sweet, sweetheart, baby, light of my life-* it was initially Shirley who got to stick with the name Gerry. On the heels of the more formal stage of their courtship, she became Shirley for reasons Gerry never probed. All he knew was that he didn't like the name- not the ring of it to his ears nor the play of it to his eyes did he like the nomenclature that she, and he by association, was stuck with.

A dismissive glance sent him wandering abstractedly into the kitchen. Mrs. Norton cocked her head towards Shirley to indicate her ears were still available.

"So *any*way…" a deep intake of air and she resumed a monologue that was becoming all too familiar to him, "I think this new therapy is going to help a great deal with the overeating, maybe the smoking, my bad temper. I got a bad temper you know. Yes! Oh I got a bad temper sometimes. You know I don't know where I got it from but my son Jimmy, phew! He definitely didn't get it from his father. My hubby's as meek as a lamb, oh dear."

"Where did you get your place settings Shirley," asked Mrs. Norton so as to divert the focus away from Mrs. Hagoden's shortcomings.

"Oh those," said Shirley peering over her shoulder to the dining room table and the placemats Mrs. Norton referred to.

"Walmart honey," she shrugged with a dismissive wave of the hand.

"How about that?"

"Well, you never can tell what you'll find in that place. My son's always chastising me for shopping there. Costing American jobs, they get all that stuff from China, so forth and so on. But really, they provide jobs and how can you beat their prices?"

"Well," said Mrs. Norton.

"That son of mine. Honestly he gets stirred up over the craziest things. If I lost any sleep over those things in my lifetime, I'd- why I'd surely be a basket case by now."

"Well," said Mrs. Norton.

"Are you going to the Club tonight," she grabbed Mrs. Norton's hand, imploring.

"Why, I- I don't know, I hadn't thought of it…"

"Oh, *do*! Do come to the Club tonight, you can ride over with me and Gerry."

The announcement from the next room that he and his wife were going to Thursday Happy Hour and Pub Night at the South Club tonight was news to Gerry Hagoden. But he never objected to the idea- his wife liked to dance, he didn't mind to. There was alcohol to be had, even if it was only cheap house liquor and rather bland lager. A few drinks and the selection of contemporary popular music blended with songs they'd dated to in the fifties took years off his life for a few precious hours.

"Well, I guess I might," said Mrs. Norton. "What time are you planning on heading over?"

"Oh, I don't know, we'll call you."

"Do, and I'll let you know if I feel up to it."

"Oh no! You're coming Edna Norton whether you like it or not!"

Mrs. Norton shrugged, balancing thoughts of indignation against appreciation at being made to feel wanted and somehow associated with Shirley Hagoden's immediate future happiness.

She said okay Shirley I'll go.

*

Gerry soon tired of the house and vacated it once again. He didn't return to his neighbor's garage, he averted his eyes both from it and the sidewalk to his left and the golf course greens that it led to. Instead when he reached the end of the short concrete driveway bordered by clipped grass, he turned right and headed for the Coco Palm Circle cul-de-sac. In the middle of the cul-de-sac was an island in a dead sea of blacktop, a well-groomed little oasis of grass and mulching from which tall palms sprouted. Gerry was enamored of his surroundings, delivered as he was from bland and nondescript Michigan suburbs to a faux tropical oasis. This was indeed a haven of calm, if only for the occasional passing car- it seemed to him not enough people took the opportunity to walk and enjoy these idyllic surroundings. These were the thoughts that regularly accompanied his many walks. And Gerry liked to walk, oh how he liked to walk. He would leave the house often, he would just leave that house and walk.

He passed house after house and when he reached the corner of Normandy and Chaplin, he spied Alice McLaughlin pruning her rosebushes and waved. She waved back and glanced at the spade clutched in her hand as if the gardening implement itself beckoned her to resume the work at hand.

Gerry made up a tune in his head and he began at first to hum and then whistle it. Presently he came upon an obstruction to his fitting use of the sidewalk and the right portion of the street. A van sat there in front of him, and beyond it at the curb a flatbed truck. Interrupting the steady flow of groomed and sign-posted front yards, a tar-stained white tarp, old discarded shingles littering its surface. From up on the roof came the sound of heavy hammering and loud chattering back and forth. A crew of Mexicans laying a new roof in the hot sun. He waved at them and they waved back. With an instinctive respect for good honest labor Gerry diverted his path to the other side of the street while surveying the work site. In doing so he nearly collided with a Buick Regal that came screeching to a halt inches from him. The hood ornament entered his field of vision with an alarming abruptness and he stared down at it, then up the hood to the windshield, behind which a face registered shock and alarm that quickly turned to the crimson of anger. The face turned to that of the person sat next to it and the two seemed to have an exchange that ultimately led to the driver lowering the electric window and peering out of it with no small effort, her face in a grimace while she bellowed, "What the hell is wrong with you!"

Gerry threw up his palms, gesturing with a measured affability. "I didn't…"

"You didn't. I'll damn sure say you didn't! Why don't you watch where you're going? This is a street mister. Got it, a street!"

Gerry stood speechless. He went neither right nor left. He just stood there in front of the car, because he sensed a significant event had transpired and its abrupt end left it suspended, somehow frozen in time.

The driver seemed to be momentarily distracted by her passenger, whom to Gerry lent the potential of an arbiter, a levelheaded peacemaker who didn't go around hollering at complete strangers. But the driver was already out of the car and demanding personal information with a rapid fire diatribe from a taut wrinkled face that seemed most at home in a scowl.

"There's too many people out walking around here who needn't be out walking," she declared, striding to the other side of the car in a pantsuit that appeared a size too small, ordering her passenger to fetch a pen and paper from the glove box.

"It is not in this man's best interests to be out walking the streets," she announced. "Somebody needs to alert the homeowners association."

Suddenly a voice from up on the roof, coarse, gentle but firm no less. "Hey lady, I thinking you no bother this man."

She wheeled around, incredulous, shielding her eyes from the sun to locate the source of this new cause for vexation. "Why don't you go back to work and mind your own business?"

"Hey lady, take easy, make peace."

She shook her head, clearly determined not to engage any further with this dark sweaty man who had a reckless disregard for the English language.

"Give me that." She took the pen and a crumpled piece of paper from the passenger.

By then Gerry had recovered and met her at the sidewalk on the other side of the street. "Now listen," he said, "I'm sorry I wasn't watching where I was going, but I–"

"What is your name sir?"

"Oh no," he said, "I'm not giving that."

The man on the roof kept hollering down and by now his fellow workers stood beside him, fully captivated by this new diversion and its prospects for entertainment. Gerry stood his ground, hoping for a swift and proper resolution to this disruption serving to unravel his peaceful life. Surely no harm had been done to anyone's person or property and civilized people, in Gerry's estimation, had better things with which to occupy their time and effort. But this woman didn't see it that way, in spite of the half-hearted protestations of her passenger who remained in the large Buick, which seemed to embody the same intimidating presence as its owner.

She lingered, they seemed for the moment at a standstill, Gerry uncomfortable with the close proximity. He backed up a step and the woman seized this retreat as a chance to advance her attack. "Look," he said, "enough said. Return to your vehicle and I'll return to my walk. I don't want any trouble here."

This seemed to slow the woman down considerably, and her passenger lowered the electric window and spoke evenly.

"Janet get in the car. We'll be late for Bridge for godsakes. Let's leave this man to his walk. It was an accident."

"You nearly hit me," said Gerry. "I'm the one who should be taking information."

No sooner had the words left his mouth he immediately regretted them. But fortuitously a commercial van now came to a stop behind the Buick and loomed... blocked, waiting. Janet, part of her own personal information revealed and perhaps conscious of the legal aspects of the situation, backed up and turned on her heels, her booming voice reduced from yelling at Gerry to merely muttering to herself. She yanked the door open, settled herself inside and slammed it shut. She didn't give the men on the roof so much as a glance as they gazed down upon her with a collective bafflement. When she drove off slowly, her lips were still moving and Gerry met her eyes for a moment and decided to refrain from any further remarks.

"You did the right thing. Better not to argue with people like that."

Gerry's consolation came from a young girl with boyish features. She had her hands balled into fists and planted to skinny hips, she wore a tee shirt and jeans cut off just below the knees with no socks under a pair of Converse high-tops. He hadn't seen her approach the scene from the yard behind where he stood.

"Are you okay," she asked, scratching at her knee and then toying with medium-length hair dyed a rust-red with natural brunette showing at the roots.

"*I* am," he replied.

The men on the roof shook their heads and resumed hammering at shingles.

The girl said, "That woman was totally out of line."

"Well, I'm just glad she didn't hit me."

A trebly voice boomed from behind them. "Hello, how are you young lady?"

The speaker was a stout woman holding a broom, taking a break from sweeping the clipped grass at her feet.

"Oh fine." The young girl shuffled her feet and stared at the ground.

"How's Flora getting along?"

"She's fine."

"Let me tell you kid, your uh... great great-grandma, is it?"

"Yep."

"Well, she is one of the kindest people there is to know."

The girl lowered her head, kicking at the neat trim of the grass. "I won't argue you there."

"She'll keep us all forever young. A hundred candles, shoo-wee! It's gonna be one birthday party *I'll* sure never forget."

Gerry's skirmish now over, he turned his gaze on the roof and the Mexican interlocutor.

"Hey meester, that lady she crazy."

"I know."

"She crazy."

"Yessir. Don't much care for the likes of her."

"Que? What?"

"Me," he stabbed a finger at his chest then pointed in the direction where the car had driven off, "no like her."

"She crazy."

With a nod and a wave he continued his walk down the sunny side of the street, his spirits somewhat afflicted.

*

She slept the sleep of the dead. The commotion outside had stirred her out of it, and when her eyelids fluttered awake she lay flat on her back with her arms over her chest. *Like a vampire*, she thought to herself, *or like a corpse laid out to wake.* She studied her hands. With each passing year, the anatomy presented itself through the skin with greater definition- the tendons, ligaments, bones and oh yes, the veins all seemed to be jumping out of her skin. Her knuckles bulged slightly with the long-awaited and unwelcome onset of arthritis. She pushed herself up on an elbow, raised herself sideways and dropped her feet to the floor, hitching up her silk pajama pants to reveal a set of spindly legs. Pushing herself from the bed to a standing position she raised her arms and stretched a body that was just a week shy of a hundred years old. She threw a shawl over a bony set of shoulders and a body cruelly riddled with aches and pains- her medicine chest however, was curiously free of prescription drugs.

Flora Wheeler stared at the mirror above the sink in her bathroom, playing with her face, pulling at the leathery skin.

I don't want to be a bother to anybody became a sort of mantra for Flora Wheeler after the death of Earl. Earl just five years out of working the power lines and then in the offices of that utility company. Him just two weeks out of Pennsylvania and down to Florida to enjoy the golden years. That event of some thirty odd years ago seemed, for Flora, to mark the onset of old age. But an old age oddly spared of any major physical ailments. There was no cancer in remission, no organ transplant, no coronary seizure, no triple bypass. One afternoon a calm sunny sky was suddenly overtaken by one of those tropical storms that doesn't announce itself and she fell flat on her face rushing towards the South Club building. Upon x-ray, hip replacement surgery was suggested. She reckoned a few more mild winters in Florida would make it bearable with ibuprofen. She got more winters than she counted on, but managed. Her bladder was weak. Some years ago a kidney infection. A cerebral aneurism almost ten years ago. But nothing revisited her, and nothing hung around like an unwanted guest, and so three generations of her progeny had been spared any deliberations over the necessity for long-term care, assisted living arrangements, home health services or any other such burdens. Regular phone calls yielded not even the slightest evidence of a confused or greatly distressed mind.

There was little money to worry about, she had inherited nothing but her progeny and all her life was about living within her means. And those means were diminishing rapidly, but who on earth expected to reach the ripe old age of one hundred? No amount of financial planning could have predicted nor prevented it. First, Earl's pension was wiped out by a merger with the power company shortly after she'd closed on the house she now woke up in. After that, she had set up a trust for her children and grandchildren with what Earl left her, and drew a small allowance to supplement social security and leave her living in the manner to which she'd grown accustomed- paycheck to paycheck. By the dawn of the computer age she was already part of an older demographic that was naturally disinterested. So as the stock values in her accounts tumbled, as Earl's pension fund was obliterated by corporate wheeling and dealing the news arrived to her in paper statements that she chucked in the garbage as fast as she received them. Whenever her great-grandson Nathan went to great lengths to explain these things to her it went in one ear and out the other.

She had buried a husband, three sons, two daughters, five grandchildren, a great-grandchild. One of the living descendants was curled up on the futon in the guest den just off the main area, her discarded red converse high-tops and a pair of flip-flops scattered on the shag carpet, her laptop cast aside once again in favor of a book. She peeked in.

"That story any good?"

"Yep. But the real excitement was outside. Just now."

"Really."

"Yep. Some dingbat lady yelling at some poor old guy. Out front. On the street."

"Ah, marriage."

"I don't think they were married."

"Right out front?"

"Yes mam."

"Oh I wish you'd... stop calling me that."

The girl looked up from a dog-eared paperback. "It's only out of respect."

"You have never shown me..." Flora methodically lowered herself into the recliner, "any lack of that, my curious little grandchild."

"Great great-grandchild. And I'm not so little anymore."

"When you get to be my age, I reckon everyone's little."

The girl frowned.

"Don't you mind it. You think too much and too hard on things. Watcha reading?"

The girl closed the book and held it aloft.

"On the Road," she said. "Jack Kerouac."

"Good story?"

The girl nodded. "People," she said, "were so noble then, they lived so passionately, as if every day might be their last."

"Yes. You'd have thought the same of our lot, growing up in the mountains of West Virginia."

"Was it rough?"

Flora drummed the arm of the recliner. "Winters," she said, "were dark and seemed to take forever to get through. You spent all the rest of the year preparing for it. She tugged at her ear and said, but sometimes we found ourselves foraging for food well into December."

"Why'd you leave?"

"Earl, that'd be your great great-granddaddy, came back from the First World War. After a few years in the mines, one of his army buddies had a business idea back there in his neck of the woods. That'd be up in Pittsburgh. Earl didn't see much to do around Thomas, that'd be our parts, and so he took his ambition and me to the big city," she sighed, "and we never looked back."

"Nana?"

"What."

"Do you think I could be free to travel. When I'm eighteen I mean."

"Well honey, I guess when you reach the age of consent you can do whatever's in your mind. Or heart, or, or whatever. But don't tell your parents I told you that. I know they'd like for you to go to college."

Flora thought, there I go again, compelling this teenager to keep a vow of secrecy for something that is so fundamentally human. Do what's in your heart. College– with each generation she had observed the educational standards rising and rising, yet why did young people seem so less fundamentally smart? She as a rule tried not to meddle in the affairs of her children, theirs, and theirs. But it seemed the level of parental worry and protection had reached unreasonable extremes.

"What did you do when you grew up in the mountains?"

"Phew, let me see. Had babies mostly. I was pregnant with my first child just before Earl went off to fight in the war," Flora said, squinting at her lap as if scanning it for memories and then looking up sharply at the girl. "Now don't you go get pregnant."

The girl laughed at this and then leaned in. The years had diminished the power of Flora's speech, but in volume only.

"So there I was, all of sixteen and holding my own while my sweetheart went over to fight the Kaiser in Europe. Daddy worked the mines. Your great great great-grandad that is, Ned Boothe. Guess I was just a little girl like yourself, not knowing too much. Just finding out about the world, one lick at a time. That was right before what they call the Great Depression set in. We were so durn poor we didn't know the difference. My folks, they were... homesteaders. They worked the land and that's about all. Little banjo music and moonshine in between. Am I boring you?"

"No, quite the contrary."

"*No, quite the contrary,*" she mimicked, "where'd you learn to talk like that?"

The peculiar girl merely shrugged.

"Anyway, he worked the mines, and the mines worked him. Worked him to death."

"Nana," said the girl. "I want to travel."

"Oh? Where to?"

Melinda shrugged her shoulders and glanced around the room. "I think just until I find a place that suits me. Where I feel like people, I don't know, look out for each other more. Everyone here seems so, so busy all the time. Everything moves so fast. I just want to go to a place where people care."

The girl often switched gears so quickly from muteness to an unbridled talkativeness, leaving Flora stunned.

"Oh Nana, I feel like I can talk to you about anything. You listen, that's what kind of place I want to live in, where people just listen. And care about each other, aren't so lonely. Oh Nana, I just don't care about the things the other girls care about. I don't care about getting a car, about celebrities. I hate the mall," she tugged at Flora's shawl, "you understand me don't you Nana? You didn't have all this when you were young, I mean I like the technology stuff. Don't get me wrong, I feel so attached to my laptop, it's like a pet! But sometimes I feel like there's too much around me and it makes me want to scream at somebody. Just scream."

They remained silent a good while, then Flora returned to her story. "I had young ones, she said, and more than my share of housework. We didn't have washing machines until I was too old to get much benefit from them, my dear."

"I wish I grew up when you did."

"I'm not so sure you do."

"Or the sixties," she plied with fresh eagerness, "what were the sixties like?"

"I was too old... to be a hippie."

"Well, did you know any hippies?"

"I had more than... my share of hippie grandchildren. You want to know the truth? I sometimes thought what some of them were wanting, driving at... well- you might as well have called us hippies. Way back in our day."

Flora closed her eyes and once again the room fell quiet.

The girl was having problems. At school, mainly. When her mother Sharon called it was with a measured reluctance. As the conversation wound its path, her panic made itself known. Her fourteen-year-old daughter was not applying herself at school said the report cards. She was drawing in, avoiding others, she was devouring books. A dwindling attention span. Sharon said, 'The other kids make fun of her. You know how awful kids can be. She seems distracted, aloof. The divorce, the divorce, the divorce. It was hard enough for me to go through, Nana, but I think I left her in the lurch. Yes, yes I did, whether I meant to or not, that's beside the point. I left my little girl in the lurch. And I can't seem to make it up to her in those few moments we have together. I work long hours. We eat in silence. She stays glued to the laptop. Or the TV. Or the books. But I don't mind them so much, at least she's, I don't know, engaged somehow.'

'Sharon,' Flora had said, 'I want to suggest something. I want Melinda to come. To stay with me. The next school break. By herself.'

'But wouldn't that be an imposition on you?'

'Nonsense. Why are visits such an imposition these days.'

'I just thought at her age–'

'Nonsense. I've been around children all my life.'

'This one's a handful.'

'You were a handful yourself. So was your mother. And her mother, come to think of it.'

Sharon sighed audibly into the phone.

'Her next break is at Christmas. They're doing repairs at the school– they don't start back until the end of February. How do you want to do the arrangement?'

'She gets tired of me she leaves. I get tired of her she leaves. Same way it always worked between folks. Except in marriage of course. Worked that way, I'd have been single by eighteen. Sorry.'

'That's alright. Times are different.'

'They sure are.'

'I'll have to go over the particulars with you. She's got certain meds to take, for example. Are you sure you're up to this, Nana?'

'*Meds*. What meds?'

The conversation about hippies resumed and followed them into the kitchen, where Flora poured them each a cup of coffee. They sat down at a round table with a plaid tablecloth. At the center, beside the wicker basket of fruit sat two brown prescription bottles, one fat and one skinny. She saw them and they looked out of place on her kitchen table.

"Melinda," she said when they'd settled in and the hippie talk had run its course. Flora was shifty, restless, kneading her bony knuckles and looking around in every direction. The girl leaned forward and propped her chin on her elbows, readying herself for Nana's soft and deliberate manner of speaking.

"There is something I have been… going over and over in my mind… since you arrived… and I have been wondering…" She cleared her throat. "I have been wondering. About these."

Flora held the brown plastic bottles, considering one and then the other in the manner one might in choosing a piece of fruit at the market.

"Mm hmm," Melinda twirled her hair abstractedly. "What is it Nana?"

"When did you start taking these… the medications."

The girl shrugged. "Two years ago. Maybe three."

"Are they supposed to make you happy?"

"That's the idea I guess."

"Just seems kind of strange, to an old gal like me."

"Nana, I. I've been thinking about quitting them. Just stop taking them altogether."

Their eyes locked, they sensed each other's apprehension. And intentions. At last Flora said, "I'm not a hundred percent on this."

"Are you any percent for it?"

"I don't know nothing about it."

"Because you never had to deal with it."

"I don't know if that's a good thing or a bad thing."

"I started taking less."

"You what?"

"Since I got here. I started cutting back."

"And?"

"I'm not getting as many panic attacks."

"Well…"

"And I'm sleeping much better."

"Are you happy here?"

"Oh yes! Sure Nana. I really truly am. I mean the people can be weird sometimes, like that old guy Boris at the pool that swims in his underwear, or that mean old lady out in the street a little while ago. But it's the same anywhere."

"I'm glad to have you here. I really mean that. It gets awful lonesome sometimes."

Nothing more was said on the matter. They finished their coffee and Melinda stood up and returned to the den, forgoing Kerouac for the Dostoevsky novel.

Flora stood at the sink scrubbing at dishes and silverware. The dishwasher only stole space, she never had tried to figure out how to run it, and she had no use for it anyway. Thoughts of the brown bottles, the girl's prescriptions, now weighed heavy on her mind. Was it out of line to circumvent the wishes of a parent, the advice of a medical practitioner– was it placing the girl in some sort of physiological or psychological jeopardy? She didn't think so. Anti-depressants, anti-anxiety, she shook her head wringing the dishcloth and setting it on the countertop. Zoloft zombies. Whatever the girl's problems, she certainly didn't exhibit them here. Weren't ups and downs a part of life? Why did everyone seem to want to neutralize their feelings? And as for attention deficit disorder, was it any wonder younger people had trouble concentrating when they had so much stimuli? On the computer, hypnotized by games. At home, at school. Everything was going too fast and no drug was going to slow it down any. She stood at the counter and looked at the bright sun blazing its light into the living room and pondered whole afternoons laying on her back among the haystacks looking up at clouds drifting over a blue sky and making up stories. Spending Sunday afternoons after services with her young nippers picnicking in the West Virginia woods with little more than hide-and-seek for entertainment. There was little to distract her at the home she kept while Earl was toiling away in the mines and then the new business, coming home dog-tired with nothing but lovin on his mind. And her obliging most nights, pushing him away on others. Nobody had attention deficit disorder, at least nobody she knew of. But still, was it the right thing to do, with the meds, would her great great-granddaughter suddenly be vulnerable to a euphoria she might not recognize, only to be followed by an emotional crash that could kill her? Well, she couldn't spend her whole life on drugs, could she? Flora had lived through almost a hundred years of bad days and good days, off years and on years, and she once again carefully placed herself into the recliner with a grunt of satisfaction at the fact she'd made it without the aid of any mood-altering substances, unless you counted the moonshine. What brought her down to Florida was that she had a mind to add years to her life. They weren't painless, but there was a kind of comfort in predictability. Bad news only came over the phone mostly. New friends are older when you meet them and when they died, well it somehow just got a little easier to swallow.

The girl peered at her from over the book.

"Nana?"

"Hmm."

"How are you?"

Flora let go a sigh and said, "Tired."

Melinda looked at her imploringly.

"It's nothing to do with you honey," Flora said.

"What is it?"

"It's something to do with being one hundred years old. You'll get to be more tired when you're my age."

The girl brought the book down, marking her place with a finger while drumming the cover. "I don't think I'll get to live that long."

Flora shook her head slowly. "Tell you what, keep thinkin so hard on things, you just might quickly worry yourself to death."

"Nana?"

"What?"

"Are you afraid of dying?"

These questions seemed to come out of nowhere. Flora considered it, studying her fingernails.

"'Course I am, Mel. Just a little bit."

*

They let themselves in with the spare key Mimi's neighbor had left at the guard gate. The house was stuffy and they opened every single screened window. On the kitchen counter Marion found a detailed note from Mimi's neighbor Louise, whom she'd spoken to briefly on the phone last week about the particulars, including directions to the medical facility where Mimi now was. A telephone listing and guide to Sunny Glen Palms.

Once inside the gate, Marion had contrasted that which her eyes met against her anticipative imaginings. What her mind had conjured up was a tropical oasis of sorts, a spa with elderly people taking in the sea air sipping at juice-laden cocktails, with calming ocean views to assuage the aches and pains that arrived unannounced to aging bodies. What her eyes met instead was a very ordered and tidy neighborhood, people out washing cars, walking dogs, Alice McLaughlin fashioning sculpted rosebushes–absent the palm trees it was just like any other suburb.

A fresh breeze had by now revived a house that was in impeccable order. It was a two-bedroom affair, with a main open area combination living room, kitchen and dining area. Delicate trinkets on high glass shelves ran the length of one wall. The wall-to-wall carpet was free of clutter. The countertops were clear of clutter. In the main room, a television screen took up a good portion of the wall and facing it was a long sofa and a recliner. Between them a glass top coffee table, a teapot and serving set neatly arranged. Marion thought of her own beloved cluttered house on the outskirts of the village. The untidy mess did lend to it a cozy familiarity, in stark contrast to the clinical orderliness with which things were kept here. There was a wicker basket beside the recliner that held month-old copies of the Tampa Tribune and a TV listing. A roll top desk in the corner of the room with a gold desk set but bereft of papers. The austere nature of the décor of Mimi's dwelling only amplified the air of abandonment. Marion imagined that not many days before life had persisted with a certain order and predictability within these walls. Her sister coming and going from this place. How abruptly things can change.

A few days back and a continent away Elise had said to Marion, *I won't have you travelling alone, mama. I've discussed it with Etienne and the children. It's our gift to you.* After Mimi's anxious call from the hospital she said urgently, *we must go at once.*

They were jetlagged and the sun was blazing hot outside. But Marion had momentum and she couldn't bring herself to lie down for a moment with Mimi just up the road and possibly at death's door. "We can lie down later. I want to go see her. It looks like fifteen minutes away."

But after combing the entire house and searching in every drawer and cabinet, Elise and Marion could not find Mimi's car keys. They tried her neighbor Louise's phone and there was no answer. Marion found the automatic garage door switch, the huge metal door rumbled open and sunlight spilled into the darkness. They rummaged around the garage and still no keys. The car was locked. "What to do," said Marion.

"I cannot think of where else to look," said Elise.

"But you're too tired now," her mother said. "Maybe we should rest. First."

They saw a woman in shorts and a sun visor approaching them, waving and smiling. "Hello," she said when she reached the driveway. "Welcome. You must be Mimi's family. Welcome to our little corner of the world."

She extended a hand and Marion grasped it.

"I'm Shirley. Shirley Hagoden."

They would now have to drop their native tongue– Elise would be spokesperson since Marion spoke little English. Elise explained their dilemma with the car keys. She had the directions in her hand and Mrs. Hagoden seized the piece of paper and studied it.

"Nonsense," she said dismissively, "I'll take you in my car."

"Oh, but we don't want trouble you."

"Trouble me? Shoo, honey I'm retired and so practically nothing's a bother. Except my husband, but you get used to it. Forty-five years of it, she rolled her eyes. Only thing on my agenda is Pub Night. All the dancing and drinking you can do between all the gossip. Ah," she said wistfully at Marion, "you must be tired, poor dear."

"Yes," said Elise, "we are, how do you say, jetlagged? But mama insists she can't wait to see Mimi."

Mrs. Hagoden said, "Then let's go see Mimi."

*

Frank Alsatian had one eye on his investments and the other on the Fox News channel. Libby was chatting to herself in the bedroom, or maybe she wanted something. All of his broker statements were arranged neatly on the mahogany table they'd salvaged from the house up north. It was tax time, it was time to get his financial house in order. On the golf links yesterday morning, Gerry Hagoden weighed in, specifically on Frank's long-term investment portfolio. Why wasn't his brokerage house more aggressive on selling short and buying long-term options for under-capitalized startups? Why did they send only summary information, where was the nuts and bolts? Gerry wanted to know. So here he was, considering major changes in investment strategy in mid-stream. Jesus. Can't I just play golf and build model airplanes and go for an occasional swim? Maybe he could get his son Michael to look at this stuff. What was with Hagoden anyway, talking money between holes out on the golf course with such braggadocio, the big bag of wind from Michigan. If he was such a man, where were his balls when it came to his wife?

Fox News had a breaking story on a school shooting, and just when he was ready to take a break from figures, the doorbell chimed. He looked up and saw Gerry Hagoden shielding his eyes from the sun and looking towards the backyard. Frank hollered *I got it* to the bedroom.

"Gerry."

"Hey Frank."

"C'mon in."

"Sure Frank. Finish that plane yet?"

"Nope." He resented the slightest inkling of accountability to this pest for anything.

"Get you a beer or something."

"Uh, sure."

Gerry glanced from the breaking news to the dining room table. "You getting those investments in order?"

"Well, it's tax time."

"Uh huh."

Frank passed Gerry a Miller Lite.

"You going to the Club tonight?" Gerry asked.

Frank sighed and flopped down into the leather recliner in front of the school shooting. "I guess so."

"Well Shirley and I are going soon as she gets back."

"Where'd she go."

"Take them French ladies over to see Mimi Brooks, over at Siloam."

"French ladies?"

"Her sister and niece. Just got here from France."

"Great, Frank huffed, our grateful allies."

Libby appeared at the bedroom door.

"Oh hello Libby," Gerry said.

Her eyes darted this way and that as she strode into the kitchen area, opened the fridge and began fetching items for preparing dinner.

"How is the old gal," asked Frank.

"I-I dunno," said Gerry, watching Libby Alsatian.

"I mean *Mimi Brooks*," said Frank not taking his eyes off the shooting.

What it was, Mimi Brooks had a stroke almost a week ago on the heels of a long bout with pneumonia. Far as Frank could tell, it left her sort of melancholy and who knew but it wasn't the onset of Alzheimer's disease, something for which Frank himself had come to know firsthand over the last year.

Frank's wife was becoming unfamiliar to him. A strange neurological disorder that accompanied an established depression diagnosis endowed Libby with an involuntary twitching. Gerry watched as she puttered around the kitchen counter, all the while muttering some personal dialogue that he could only get bits and pieces of. Throughout their married life she prided herself on her smashing good looks and dressed with a definitive class and style to complement them. She had never succumbed to the lure of shopping on the cheap at outlet stores or Walmart– she built her wardrobe at Saks Fifth Avenue and Neiman Marcus. Now she looked disheveled. She did her aimless sleepwalks around their modest square footage in worn out floppy deck shoes, while her fancy heels collected dust along with the other artifacts in the walk-in closet. Her charcoal black hair was now peppered with gray. Her plain tee shirts bore food stains. She could still prepare dinner, so long as Frank kept an eye on her.

"No need, I'm eating at the Club tonight Libby," said Frank with his eyes glued to the television and breaking news.

"Well," she said, "suit yourself."

Gerry moved away from the blaring widescreen TV and closer to Libby.

"Nice day out there," he said.

She shrugged. "Every day is good weather."

She fixed her gaze on the countertop and the leftovers in sturdy Pyrex cookware. "What does it matter," she said. "What does anything matter?"

"Hmm?"

Gerry was confused– what on earth could she possibly mean? He took a swig of beer and drummed his fingers on one of the tall stools that lined the kitchen countertop.

"I wanted," she said to the leftovers, "to be a good person. Somebody who loved generously."

She looked up and Gerry caught her eye.

"Lived like a fool. A damned fool!"

"Sshh, keep it down," said Frank at the TV.

"All my damned life. Why, oh why!"

That got Frank turned around. "I'm trying to watch this, Libby. Maybe you should go and lie down."

"Lie down," she repeated.

Gerry Hagoden palmed his beer and quickly knocked it back. Set it on the counter. "Well," he said, "better get going," to the back of Frank's head.

Frank gave a small wave without getting up.

"See you at the Club," Gerry said while gently closing the screen door behind him.

*

They arrived at the hospital– Marion and Elise with an excitement tinged by worry at the state they might find Mimi in, Shirley with an anxiety about her unfamiliarity with Mimi's room having betrayed her neglecting to visit her stricken neighbor. At reception they learned they were still within visiting hours but the patients were limited to two visitors at a time. The nurse was kind enough to make an exception without any cajoling, so the three of them trailed behind her. Between the walk and the elevator they learned that Mimi had just finished another session of physical therapy. The specialist would be in tomorrow and they could discuss her medical care and future plans then. The ward had the smell of sanitizers and a young man in blue scrubs was mopping the tiled floor, the yellow caution wet floor signs splayed about the place. They did their best to negotiate the dried portions of floor to Room 327. Mimi sat upright in bed, propped by several pillows. The television was on at a volume low enough so as to be indiscernible.

Mimi was frail enough to allow ample room for Marion and Elise to perch themselves on either side of the bed. Marion stroked at Mimi's gray and brittle hair. The illness and the stroke had aged her considerably– indeed it seemed a different woman altogether whose hollow stare met Marion's troubled eyes. Growing up, Mimi had always been the more lithe of the auburn-haired and brown-eyed sisters. Mimi had a dancer's figure. Over the years on an American diet she struggled with her weight. Now seeing her on the lesser side of her teenage figure, Marion determined to get her back home and cuisine her back to health. Mimi was a year younger but now there appeared a wide gap in years between her and Marion and in the other direction. Marion did the math in her head and it was hard to imagine that Mimi and Robert had visited her and her late husband Martin almost twenty years ago. She remembered Mimi clutching Robert's arm with the eagerness of a schoolgirl and once again pointing out the landmarks of her childhood. An innocuous little town in the French countryside, idyllic and serene in contrast to cosmopolitan Paris with its bustling crowds amidst theatres and cafes where they'd met during the war. The Paris in which all those years ago they danced and dined, far removed from the more rural country the Germans had ravaged and Robert had seen combat in.

"Marion," Mimi said in her native French, "it was good of you to come."

"How are you feeling?"

Mimi's thin lips curled into a smile.

"Better. Better now that you're here."

"Elise also."

Marion nodded over toward the other side of the bed and her daughter, whose broad smile punctuated exotic emerald eyes. She had the plainer features of her father, a glowing countenance.

"Oh," said Mimi, while attempting to push herself from the pillows. "I am so glad to see you."

"I also Auntie," Elise replied in English, leaning in to halt her with an embrace. "I can speak English most perfectly. I want you to know," she spoke slowly, waiting for Mimi to nod her comprehension, "that I can communicate with your doctor. Or nurse, as you need."

Only when she was sure Mimi could keep up with her words did she pick up the pace of them. Then she returned to her native tongue and Marion rejoined the conversation.

"Nous vous aimons," she said while squeezing her sister's hand and throughout their dialogue that phrase kept resurfacing from both mother and daughter at Mimi's gaunt face that seemed to light up more and more with each exchange, as if in challenge to her emaciated frame lying in the bed. Shirley Hagoden looked on through dampening eyes at the reunion that unfolded in a strange tongue before her. Elise and Marion each clutched a hand of Mimi's and stroked her hair and her face while the three of them exchanged words. Occasionally Elise and Mimi would test each other's English and Marion noticed right away how Mimi's accent had faded even more since they'd last met and she'd had occasion to hear it. Then they would revert to their native tongue and she could join the dance.

Nous vous aimons! And Shirley intrinsically understood the words because no matter the language they were universal and solemnly understood as the powerful message of mothers and sisters and they provided the ultimate comfort in a world that regularly dealt harsh blows. Shirley Hagoden *just knew* the meaning of the words and she couldn't contain herself any longer, she was sniffling and reaching inside her handbag for a Kleenex. She walked away from the bed and over to the window, the curtain was drawn and she could gaze upon the parking lot and listen to those words surface out of the ocean of a strange language that was peculiar to her ears, in tones that were familiar to her heart. *Nous vous aimons.* There was nothing as powerful as the affirmation that we are not alone in this world. Nothing else that could better serve to assuage pain, or fear, or despair. There was nothing mightier than the message of love.

*

The staff had to stay late on Thursday nights, because it was Pub Night after all, and Pub Night meant business. More beers were pulled and more cocktails mixed in one night than the entire rest of the month. Windmere Properties had top-of-the-line audio equipment and a willing employee to spare them the extortionate price of a professional DJ. The equipment provided the employee did not include turntables or a vinyl collection. The employee got by with a dual CD player. The employee got by with a stock collection of the greatest hits of the 50s and 60s, and enthusiastic residents gleefully provided compact discs from their personal collections. The party started at six o'clock and went on until eleven. There was of course the regular food preparation capacity– cookouts were common unless it rained. So dinner was there to be had. Fun was also there to be had– Pub Night was gossip central to the regulars, it was a welcome diversion for the chronically shy and introverted types, it was a chance to show off for the more expressive folks, it was the ultimate icebreaker for new arrivals.

Frank Alsatian relished it less for personal and more for abstract conversations that all too often revolved around political ideology. Had Philip or Sugar Gaston ever occasioned to be in the vicinity of the patio table where he regularly held court out there by the man-made lake they would likely have been unable to restrain themselves from letting go some caustic remark or another at his running monologue of contempt at those things for which he did not personally endorse. As it happened no such encounter had transpired until that night.

Frank was particularly verbose, holding court there on the patio sitting at one of the cast iron tables. His audience was Gerry Hagoden, Edna Norton– who'd tagged along with Gerry, Ron Shutmeyer and his wife Vanessa, and his most ardent supporter, the recently widowed Betty Molnar. It seemed the French were at the forefront of Frank's complaints and bore the brunt of his anger. Their failure to support the preemptive strike on Iraq had his blood in a boil. He'd just made a run to the grille and the bar, and was preparing to take a breather from the politically charged discourse that the pro-union GM man Gerry Hagoden had been doing his level best to divert to the more urbane topical territory of the professional golf circuit.

Shirley Hagoden determined to join the boys, and she approached the table with two strange-looking women. Their cotton dresses looked too colorful and out of context. The older one wore a headscarf and the younger one a very unusual felt hat that was colored amber and had talons that gave the impression she had her hair woven in dreadlocks even though she didn't.

"*There* you are," said Shirley at Gerry. "Is there enough room for three more?"

Gerry's attention remained captive for an extra beat to the more striking features of the elder, a woman of years well in advance of the Sunnyville age minimum, something Gerry never would have guessed. Marion Legrand was possessed of a good figure, not the least bit gauche in the cotton dress with a low neckline. There was a calm elegance about a broad mouth, thin lips, high cheekbones and a pair of exquisite brown eyes. Her grey-streaked auburn hair pulled up and clasped in the beret-like headscarf, wisps dangling along the sides of a sleek neck, graceful right through to her wrinkles and age spots— what you might call *a looker.*

Gerry got up to collect another chair. Frank guessed after a brief moment of puzzlement who these strangers were. He rose from his chair to shake hands and smile. Given the chance upon introduction, Frank restrained himself nevertheless from taking a cheap shot at the French. It was somehow different when it was a real person standing in front of you, and not a mere abstraction or TV image.

"This," said Mrs. Hagoden, "is Frank Alsatian. He's the center of attention here at Sunny Glen Palms."

She glanced surreptitiously at Frank while he shook his head.

"No one can quite exceed the queen bee of our proverbial honey hive here in that capacity Shirley."

His grandiloquence was both unexpected and unusual— it took Shirley Hagoden back a little. Nonetheless, jabs thrown, they all shook hands and sat down together absent any further scurrilous remarks. Frank offered to fetch another pitcher of beer for the table but Shirley wasn't having it.

"Nonsense. Wouldn't you ladies prefer wine," she asked presumably.

"My brother defended your country in the Second World War," Frank was quick to inform their guests.

Elise nodded. "We would not be here now had my aunt not fall in love with American soldier. They became sweethearts. She went away with him. Now here we are."

Frank nodded somewhat dismissively at this sentimental fluff.

"I'm very sorry about the circumstances," Gerry offered. Nonetheless, welcome to the Sunshine State. And Sunny Glen Palms. He sincerely hoped Frank wasn't going to let the alcohol take him down the ornery drunk route tonight, he'd have to steer the conversation away from World War Two or else Pub Night might deteriorate and erupt into World War Three. He somehow doubted the two ladies kept up much with the PGA tour. He'd think of something.

Marion and Elise decided to have a look at the bar, and would be sorely disappointed to find only wine of the boxed variety, one pink and one white. They returned to the table contented nonetheless with vodka cranberries. No, they were too tired to eat. Shirley brought an extra hotdog and hamburger back from the grille anyway, beaming and pointing at the plate as if it bore exotic objects. They nodded appreciatively, looking around at the crowd whose gazes fell on them from time to time.

Frank was already five beers in and didn't have anything particularly pressing on his mind, other than a despairing bipolar wife at home but that was right now at the back of it. Marion on the other hand was beginning to feel a tad bit guilty at the welcome but unanticipated onset of pleasant social interaction. What had she expected, she thought as she played with her ring and looked up every now and again and smiled politely at the new faces that surrounded her. Perhaps remaining at her sister's bedside, talking and playing cards around the clock, attending to her every wish and need? She certainly hadn't imagined this– getting drunk and wanting to dance the night away at a quasi night club not long on the heels of her arrival. She glanced every now and again at her daughter who was watching Frank Alsatian carefully as he was doing the bulk of the talking. Marion could make sense out of bits and pieces of the discussion, which seemed to revolve around war, mostly the Second World War. Elise frowned enough for Marion to sense it was not altogether agreeable to her daughter.

Then Frank seemed to come to a resolution of sorts and a lull descended upon those gathered at the cast iron patio table, a silence that seemed natural and necessary as the sun began to set on the other side of the man-made lake and everyone took a breath and watched a group of herons poke their beaks at the water through a veil of mosquitos against a fading blue sky, as if on the threshold of a new chapter of the evening.

Debbie D'Antonio stepped in, slapping Gerry hard on the back. Her husband Tommy lingered in the background and then leaned in for introductions. He asked what the two ladies were drinking, waving a hand at their empty glasses. Elise told him and before they could object Tommy was making tracks to the bar.

"My husband's such a flirt," Debbie sighed, "and now look, we got two beautiful French women on our hands."

Elise translated this to Marion and they both giggled.

Shirley conveyed the unfortunate circumstances that had brought about their visit and then Debbie elbowed her way around the neighboring crowd to lay a hand on Marion and then Elise's shoulder. "I'm sorry to hear that. Mimi is such a wonderful, wonderful lady. We all love her dearly, what's not to love? Oh, please let us know if we can do anything, I mean it." Debbie gave each of their shoulders a squeeze. Public displays of affection were not Frank's cup of tea and he poured himself another beer and sighed. What else to expect, people grew old here, grew old and sick. And died. The music changed from a slow dance to an up tempo Supremes number and he got up then, he got up and out of his chair and he asked Marion across from him if she cared to dance by way of nodding his head at the fracas of dancers in front of the DJ's table. Marion understood and flitted gracefully around the table, took his hand and the crowd opened in front of them and they cut a path to the dance floor. She was an agile dancer, and Frank knew his way around the dance floor. Soon the Hagodens appeared and Gerry did his best to keep up with Shirley, who was an extremely accomplished and enthusiastic dancer. The Supremes faded and *Mony Mony* by Tommy James and the Shondells came on. Frank and Marion broke from each other's arms but remained facing one another on the dance floor. Gerry took the opportunity to do a little solo riffing, freed from the strictures of following Shirley's lead and the risk of stepping on her toes.

The dancing seemed to lighten Frank's mood and Gerry Hagoden was glad of that, because he knew the other potentiality that came into play when Frank Alsatian had one too many, and it was not pleasant. And there were outsiders now, there were *guests* and they were there not from another state or another region of the country but another country altogether, a country that Gerry knew little about but for which Frank seemed to have some special knowledge that caused him to become untethered and haphazard.

Back outside Ron Shutmeyer had two fresh pitchers set up at the table and it was getting dark. Gerry caught his wife's eye and nodded at Frank's back with a worried look. But Shirley was still shuffling and snapping her fingers to the music and merely shrugged. What they stumbled upon was a group embroiled in a conversation about the perpetual state of fear that terrorists had come to inflict on an uncomprehending world. Betty Molnar was clearly monopolizing a dialogue that was dangling precariously on the precipice between healthy ground and the deep plunge into a very unhealthy chasm. Gerry could sense it, he could sense these things. He was ready to go home, he wanted to go home. But he clearly knew he wouldn't. He needed to see this one through. He needed to serve as an arbiter, it was his fate tonight. He needed to reassure the foreigners that Americans were not disagreeable, egoistic and caustic. He wanted to go home.

Betty was saying, the world changed after nine eleven, everything changed, the world has never seen the likes of this. Elise, who'd had a few cocktails by now, was saying no, it's *your* world that has changed. What you call terrorism has plagued *our* continent ever since the dawn of civilization. What about *your* continent, your country and the slaughter of the Native American Indians? Until it arrives at your front door it doesn't exist, this is myopic. "This is myopic," she repeated.

Gerry tried to head it off at the pass, saying can we all just agree to disagree, but Frank was clearly not having any of that. He'd poured himself a beer and was ready to engage. Betty was glad of reinforcements having arrived, more than willing to turn it over to the chief.

"The way I see it," said Frank, "we've all got a part in this—" and for a moment Gerry thought that perhaps his neighbor might be taking a more conciliatory posture, not wanting to step on the toes of the charming and exotic lady with whom he'd just shared the intimate proximity that dancing brings. "We've all got a part in this," Frank repeated for emphasis, "and some of our allies are just not getting on board."

He looked evenly between the Hagodens, Edna Norton, Ron Shutmeyer and his wife Vanessa, Betty Molnar, Debbie and Tommy D'Antonio, avoiding the eyes of both Marion and Elise.

Elise rapped on the table and said, "On board for what? Bombing innocent people without provocation? How is it this is not terrorism? How do you justify such behavior, you seem to give yourself immunity for your own violent actions. The rest of the world does not see it this way."

Elise's face was reddening and this gave her mother some cause for concern. Marion got the gist of the conversation, but not all the nuances. Any hope that Gerry Hagoden held out for salvaging a peaceable evening was slipping away fast. Frank had resumed getting drunk, as if to match the level of inebriation of his perceived adversary.

"Look," he said in the manner of one losing patience with a feebleminded child, "we lost nearly three thousand lives to these lunatics, these fanatics who hate our way of life and would like nothing more that to wipe us off the map. This isn't the time for peace talk, this isn't the time for… negotiating with these nut jobs. They don't think like we do."

"Don't count *us* in your *we*," said Elise while Marion massaged her shoulder and said, "I think we go home now."

Ron Shutmeyer suggested the subject be changed and Shirley was right there with him, if anyone could jump in and take the bull by the horns it was Shirley Hagoden.

"This," she declared, "is absurd and *you*,"– here she stared daggers and pointed her cigarette accusingly at Frank Alsatian– "*you* are completely out of line. Here these poor women come all this way to see a sick relative and all you can do is sit there like king of the world and argue and carry on like a son of a bitch. Can't you see they're jetlagged and tired?"

"It's a free country," Frank retorted, "it's a free country and since when is there an inappropriate time to argue about matters as important as this?"

"It's not that important," Ron Shutmeyer shook his head abstractedly, "it's not life and death."

"Yes it is," said Frank.

Enter Philip and Margaret "Sugar" Gaston, the seasonal Canadians, who'd now insinuated themselves into the gathering– huddled right next to Tommy and Debbie D'Antonio, recent attendees at one of the Gastons' by now notorious dinner parties.

"That's the trouble with talking politics at a party," Philip remarked. "Everyone starts talking out of their ass instead of their mouth."

Frank shot him a dirty look and sneered at them. "Leave your Canadian ass out of any discussion of our great country, the best damn country in the world. If you don't like it why don't you just pack it up and go on back to Canada."

His retort rather startled the Gastons, as Frank Alsatian had up until then addressed no further comment to either of them since the polite poolside introduction upon their arrival two years ago. Not even the obligatory grunt of acknowledgement getting in or out of the hot tub. In fact he harbored quite an unfavorable opinion of the intruders. In fact he resented their mere presence. They were young and had retired earlier than they deserved to, on a fortune he'd made as a dental surgeon in that godforsaken socialized health care system up there. They paraded around the South Club pool barely dressed. That annoying Philip Gaston at his age in a Speedo! These damned people didn't play golf, they played *volleyball* for godsakes. They held outlandish dinner parties in which they and their guests availed themselves of too many fancy cocktails, and he had heard vague rumors about marijuana use on the patio. And, it had been flying around for quite some time that they were *nudists*. They embarked regularly on naked group cruises, and who could guess what scenes of debauchery and moral corruption attended those adventures in depravity— and yet the *Gastons*, how he hated the presumptuous ring of that name or the mere mention of it, had not the requisite discretion to conceal this ugly and savage part of their nature. Their money pockets couldn't go deep enough to compensate for their lack of decorum and dignity. Windmere Properties had recklessly bent the rules to allow these forty-somethings in the gate and yet they unabashedly went about their way to destroy the very reputation of an otherwise stable no-nonsense age-discretionary retirement community. And yet there were some of those people with whom Frank associated who'd swear up and down the Gastons were the kindest, most decent and respectable people they'd ever run into. Well Frank Alsatian was not having any of it.

"Well it's a pleasure to meet you *too*," said Philip, raising his glass of beer at Frank. Sugar had less an air of levity, she glared at Frank Alsatian and his lack of social decorum, his utter disregard for the protocol of manners in a public arena. Indeed his lack of discretion was a breach of conduct, an infringement on a set of social graces that had for her become a religion.

"I just don't like people telling me what I can and can't say. In my own *country*," said Frank to Tommy D'Antonio.

"Please pardon our intrusion," said Philip with a sigh and a broad sweep of his hand at the table. "Everyone looks like they're having *so* much fun."

Sugar looked as if she might have something to add, but Philip took her elbow and the Gastons took their tanned athletic selves to more inviting circles that might better appreciate their company. Mrs. Norton was beginning to wish she hadn't succumbed to Shirley Hagoden's invitation after all. At the same time one of the staff, a young lady with her blond hair pulled back in a tight bun and dressed in the black and white garb of a referee came over and asked if anyone needed anything from the bar. The staff often trailed Philip Gaston because he was very rich, generous to a fault, and was known to regularly buy rounds. With a somewhat affected air of affability and good cheer, peace was promptly restored to the table in the presence of the staff.

"Another round of whatever these ladies are having," said Frank, gesturing at the newcomers. But Elise shook her head, they were tired and it was a long day and they were ready to leave. She got up amidst the protestations of those at the table, all of whom lamented to some degree the untoward behavior, looked on with regret at their guests' all too premature leave-taking, wished the evening might end on a more congenial note. But Elise and Marion had their purses already and thanked Mrs. Hagoden for all her help and for a lovely evening. Gerry got up to shake hands and insisted on driving them home despite their desire to walk, escorting them to the Hagodens' car in the South Club parking lot. He walked in silence while they spoke sparingly in French, but as he pulled the doors open for the ladies he addressed them.

"I'm very sorry for the rude behavior of some of the folks tonight. Please realize they don't speak for all of us."

"It's quite alright," said Elise, and Marion said don't worry Monsieur Hah-go-den.

"No," said Gerry, "it's inexcusable. I want you both to know, that if you should need anything, you need only call myself or Mrs. Hagoden. Do you have our phone number," he wanted to know. Elise shook her head and so he rummaged through the glove box for a pen and wrote it down on the back of a crumpled business card. He drove them right to their door, he put the gearshift in park and before Marion could reach for the door handle he took her hand in his and after a light shake he drew it to his mouth and placed a kiss upon it, because that's what he deemed appropriate in that moment, he thought that's what they do, over there. Elise was out of the car already and didn't see any of it. Marion, unfettered, said thank you Monsieur Hah-go-den for all your kindness and patted his hand goodbye.

2

It was just after seven o'clock in the morning and the sun was blazing and it was already hot. It was January 2004. The Bush Administration was increasing the number of ground troops in Iraq and making inroads in Afghanistan. The deficit was growing but markets were stable. The men were out golfing today. They met at Pioneer Greens, the eighteen-hole course favored by Frank Alsatian and Gerry Hagoden– provided the latter could keep the ball out of the troublesome water trap on the ninth hole.

Frank was golfing poorly that morning. It was the third hole and he was already over par on both of the first two. Gerry and Tommy D'Antonio once again sat side by side in Gerry's golf cart, the canopy roof shading them. Frank was riding his own cart solo since Kenny Fitzroy, their usual partner, had called in sick. Now at last he was on the green with a not-too-bad chip shot. He was a few inches from the hole and he swiped at the ball to drag it in and it curly-cued around the hole and spun out. Frank scowled at the ball and shot a sour glance at his partners.

"C'mon," said Tommy, scrawling at the scorecard with a tiny pencil. I'll mark ya down six.

"Uh-uh," said Frank and readied his stance for the putt. Tommy looked over at Gerry and shrugged. Gerry gripped the windshield and drummed his fingers impatiently. Frank missed the shot and hollered out. "Goddammit! Okay, seven."

Gerry glanced around to see if anyone in the nearby houses bordering the course might be within earshot. He didn't think so, and started the cart towards the next hole before Frank had returned his club to the golf bag at the rear of his own cart. It was going to be a long morning, and they usually had lunch at the club afterwards but if this kept up they stood a good chance of missing it.

When Gerry climbed out of bed at six on the nose that morning Shirley was already up and there was coffee in the pot. She was sitting on the screened-in porch out back reading.

"You're up early," he said.

"Couldn't sleep."

Usually neither of them had many words in the morning. Gerry poured himself a cup of coffee, started for the television remote, then reconsidered. "I'm golfing today," he said.

"I know."

He picked up the remote and clicked on the TV to Good Morning America, notching the sound down and stretching his arms at the ceiling. "I think there's only three of us today."

"Oh, Frank out of commission?"

"No, it's Kenny. Down with the flu or something."

"He was awful rude last night."

"Kenny?"

She rolled her eyes at him. "Yeah right, Kenny. I mean *you know who*."

"That still bothering you?"

"I'll be honest," said Shirley, placing her book on the wicker table in front of her, "sometimes I really don't care to be in that man's company."

"He's just going through a rough time. With Libby."

Shirley sipped at her coffee and stared out the window.

Gerry said, "It can't be easy."

"Doesn't give him the right to act like such a jerkoff."

"Well, you know how he can get when he's had a few."

"Yes I do and it's tiresome."

Gerry sighed. He knew he was about to leave the house and he didn't want to argue with his wife. He stepped down into the patio and sat across from her.

"I can make you some eggs," Shirley said.

"Okay honey pie."

"Some eggs and toast. We're out of bacon. When are you going for the food order?"

Gerry heaved a sigh at the television. "Maybe tonight dear, or later this afternoon. Or tomorrow or something."

"Oh, don't wait until tomorrow," Shirley pushed herself up from the chair, leaned in and slapped at Gerry's knee with her paperback. "I made a list. It's on the countertop."

She set about making breakfast in the kitchen and they sat down and wordlessly had eggs and toast together. When he had showered and was going out the door running late she said don't forget the grocery list.

Things hadn't run quite so smoothly over at the Alsatian household that morning. For starters Frank's head felt as if it had been clamped in a vice rather than resting on a pillow. Libby was snoring again. The alarm clock blared and he felt like chucking it across the bedroom as he groped around for the off switch. His mouth was dry. He was beset by halitosis, had been for years, and even in Libby's better days there were no good morning kisses, no snuggling under the covers, no wake-up hanky-panky. Their mushy talk and intimacy in the past had always involved Listerine and been reserved for the evening hours.

Frank planted his feet on the carpet, yawned fiercely and rubbed at his eyes. He could easily have collapsed back onto the bed, but a deal was a deal and he'd just get on his toes and get on with it. Libby was beginning to stir.

By the time he got out of the shower she was pottering around barefoot outside and she was headed for the pond. He dropped the towel, cursing and hobbling around naked, groping for his bathing suit. One leg then the other and he was still damp, pulling on his trunks and chasing after her as she got near the water.

"What are you doing Libby," he asked. "Come back here."

She turned around and she was smiling, imperturbably, gently going her way and his words seemed to have little effect.

"Come back here," he repeated.

But she walked instead and sat by the water's edge. It was uncommon behavior, and it was an artificial pond after all. It was awkward. People might see. People might talk, and then he'd have a lot of explaining to do.

"Libby, c'mon. I'm not in the mood for this. I gotta go golf."

She glanced over her shoulder at him, still smiling. "Go ahead," she said.

"Libby come back in the house."

"No," she said, "I want to sit here."

Frank had troubled himself with no small effort to pry himself out of bed and into the shower and make it this far and now this.

What followed was a scene and Frank knew it was loud enough for someone to witness a grown woman being taken by the arm and at first cajoled then manhandled back toward the house. Frank swore. Libby cried. It was beginning to get pretty loud out there.

Just as they reached the door and he got his fingers upon the handle, his wife screamed, a bloodcurdling scream that made his ears ring.

"Stop it, *stop it!* Stop it this instant," Frank hollered and with all his might he pulled her along with him inside the door and out of public view. Given the force of his pull, had he released his grip he'd have flung his wife clear across the room. But he didn't, he held on to Libby Alsatian because anything otherwise would have breached an unspoken code between two people. Because he had grown old with her and he could no sooner inflict physical harm on her than he could himself.

They settled themselves on the sofa inside.

"You're mean," cried Libby.

Frank pulled his wife to him. "I don't want you hurting yourself, honey. Don't make me worry."

"What did I do wrong?"

"Nothing."

"Then why can't I go," she said beseechingly, her voice now softer. "I want to get out of here."

"Later, when I get back. I'll take you in the car for a ride. How does that sound? Huh? We can go out to the supermarket. Shopping."

"I want to sit by the water."

"There's nothing to see there."

"Yes there is."

"No there isn't."

Frank looked at his watch. It was getting late. He was too tired to argue anymore. What was so bad about sitting by the water? He guessed there was no harm in it, but he wasn't going to encourage it now. He hugged his wife and stood up. A dizzy spell hit him and he recovered with a deep breath and snatched the remote from the coffee table. He surfed the channels until he ran into TV Land, the oldies station. *I Love Lucy* was on and he said, "Look honey look."

Libby stood up and Frank took her hand and walked her to the recliner, settling her in and asking if she needed anything before he left to meet the guys. But her eyes were glued to Lucille Ball and she didn't respond. He kissed his wife on the forehead and said I won't be too long.

But that was hours ago and here he was now on the fourth hole and he'd never golfed so poorly in his life, at least not that he could remember. He was trying to make another long putt and he was already two under par. He set himself, rocking on his feet and struggling to concentrate. He drew the putter back and just then Gerry Hagoden farted, loud and long. Gerry and Tommy D'Antonio sniggered, standing there leaning against the golf cart and waiting again for the fourth time that morning.

Frank missed his shot.

A round of expletives, and then Frank flung his club and it end-over-ended across the grass and skittered into the nearby pond.

"I'm done," he said when he'd gathered himself.

"What?" Gerry composed himself and looked at Frank, incredulous.

"You heard me."

Frank didn't bother to go fishing in the pond for the discarded club. He just walked straight to his cart and took off like a shot.

"You believe this guy," Tommy D'Antonio shook his head at the vanishing cart in front of him.

"Well," said Gerry, scratching at his neck. "Should we keep going?"

"Hell yeah we should, I'm in the lead."

"Tell you what. Let's go nine and then leave it alone."

"Aw, Jesus Christ. You damn sissy midwesterners. Alright, said Tommy. Nine it is."

*

"Here you go Nana. Take my arm."

Flora rested her cane beside the seat and Melinda took an elbow to support her as she stepped into the golf cart. Melinda had finally talked her great great-grandmother into letting her pilot it. Flora tried to remember when the last time was anyone had run the golf cart. It was back in October with her neighbor Dottie, whom she often ran errands with. Dottie had flown north in November with heart trouble to see her family and specialists at the Mayo Clinic. Flora'd quit driving the Monte Carlo about ten years ago, it sat in the garage and when she had visitors they could use it. She got around very little and only with the help of others, she had a cleaning lady who also did her shopping once a week.

The streets were quiet and Melinda made a practice run on the golf cart and had it down pat in under five minutes. At one point she switched too fast from reverse to forward– there was a recoil and she quickly turned her head towards her Nana.

"I'm sorry, you alright?"

She reached a hand over to Flora, who sat bolt upright, clutching the cane and staring straight in front of her.

"Never felt better in my life."

"Good. I'll try to be more careful."

"Please do."

The old hickory cane Flora folded her hands over was the only remaining keepsake from her grandfather, its shellac finish only beginning to wear. Flora used it on those occasions when her hip and knees flared up.

They were going to the North Club, it was fifteen minutes by cart and some of it was on the main road, Sunset Boulevard, which had a twenty five mile an hour speed limit that the cart couldn't keep up with so cars passed and you stayed to the right always to the right and Nana wasn't looking forward to this particular part of the trip. But Melinda had devoured Kerouac in one evening and polished off Dostoevsky the next morning, and the Library was on the other side of town so to speak, part of the North Club. Besides, Flora had a meeting with the staff regarding her birthday party. And so they hit the road, Melinda enjoying the next best thing to driving a car, which she had two years to wait on. They came to a long stretch of road and she pushed the pedal down to the floor.

"Easy," said Flora, still staring at the windshield.

"Yes mam."

"Stop calling me that."

"Sorry."

Flora glanced over at her great great-granddaughter. "And quit apologizing."

"Okay, sorry."

Melinda laughed and then they faced each other, Flora's bright blue eyes twinkling with mirth. She said, "Keep your eyes on the road young lady."

Just as they got to the stop sign at the main road the golf cart lost power. Melinda fussed with the key but nothing.

Flora said, "Guess we're out of gas."

"This thing doesn't take gas," Melinda frowned.

"I know that, silly."

There they were sitting in front of the stop sign and cars were beginning to line up behind them. Flora rummaged around in her handbag and fished out a cell phone without anyone particular in mind to call. At last someone got out of their vehicle, a jeep it was, with Canadian plates. The driver had initially cussed about the inconvenience, as he often did on those occasions when he was slowed down in Sunny Glen Palms, complaining at his wife next to him. Then he cut the ignition and went to have a look at the obstruction ahead.

"Flora?"

She had her wiry hair pulled back and her features were chiseled and angular like the finest porcelain, her eyes were a sort of blue grey and twinkled. Her bony fingers still wrapped upon the handle of the cane. He leaned in and hugged a lithe frame all skin and bones.

"Why hello there, Philip."

"It would appear you're kinda stuck, eh?"

"Indeed."

Philip Gaston perched one foot on the golf cart. "Well, let's get this thing out of the way, eh? Or else Sugar and I are gonna be late for volleyball," he chided.

"How is your lovely wife?"

"She's great. Where have *you* been, Flora? Haven't seen you around the pool lately."

And so Flora and Philip had some catching up to do, much to the chagrin of the drivers lining up behind them. What the drivers saw was a young guy in togs and bathing suit and Bermuda shirt, Ray Bans on his tanned face, one foot resting comfortably on a golf cart, laughing and gesticulating to the passenger, leaning in to shake the hand of the driver. They didn't realize the cart was inoperable. Somebody sounded their horn behind the jeep and Sugar didn't even turn around, she just shrugged and spread her arms out palms up like whaddya want me to do? Philip and Flora continued bantering back and forth while the cacophony of horns grew louder and louder, and at last got his attention. He motioned to Sugar and she heaved a sigh and got out of the jeep to help him push the cart first back a little and then off to the side on the grass and the sidewalk. By now the horn choir had drawn a man limping out of the house on the corner lot. He walked over to the cart. Melinda was still fiddling with the key.

"She just needs a charge," Philip said.

"Oh, well why not use my charger?"

"You have a charger," said Sugar, "how wonderful."

"Yeah, I got a golf cart, I got a charger. If that doesn't do the trick you can borrow my cart. I'm not going anywhere anytime soon."

"You're a dear," said Flora, who had by now extricated herself from the cart with Philip's guidance. Sugar had by now come alive, hugging first Flora, then Melinda, and at last their rescuer by way of introduction.

"Well," said Philip, "do you have an extension cord long enough to reach out here?"

"I've got enough in that garage would probably reach all the way to the interstate," the fellow chuckled.

"Let me help you," said Sugar, and the two of them shuffled off to the garage.

Flora clutched Philip's hand and patted it. "Are you and Sugar coming to my party this weekend," she wanted to know, "I'm sure you're on the guest list."

"We got your invite," said Philip, "wouldn't miss it for the world Flora."

Flora Wheeler was one of the pioneers of Sunny Glen Palms, having moved into Windmere Properties' new venture back in 1982 on one of the first lots by the North Club. Those glorified bungalows now looked antiquated. Not long on the heels of Flora were the senior Gastons– Fred and his wife Virginia, the now deceased parents of the jovial young man who stood before her. It was by way of his parents that Flora had come to know these younger Gastons, when they were merely occasional visitors. Back then, Philip was building up a dental surgery practice and Sugar was a social worker. They had a son and daughter who were now in their early twenties. It was by way of his parents that Philip had come to buy into what had become to he and Sugar more of a community than their rural property in Canada that enabled him to hunt game through summer, much of which they transported frozen by way of the jeep and ultimately set in the deep freezer in the garage, then doled out regularly through their elaborate dinner parties, the soirees for which they maintained an ever-changing guest list and for which both Sugar and Philip hosted with all the charm, grace and attention to detail one might ever hope for as an invited guest.

Sugar now trailed a string of extension cords towards the golf cart with dogged determination, and the good fellow wheeled the battery charger down the driveway. Philip chattered away at Flora, and when the man at last reached the cart with the charger glanced at it casually as if a mild distraction from their exchange of banter. Sugar and Melinda removed the cover and all the batteries' cells needed distilled water. The man had some of that too and topped them up. They needed to move their jeep, they needed to get going and so Philip tapped the canopy of the cart and he and Sugar were waving at another confused driver behind their jeep, on their way to volleyball.

*

Gerry and Tommy D'Antonio called it a day after nine holes. Tommy won handily. Frank's tantrum seemed to have had the effect of throwing Gerry's game off just a little– perhaps he felt somewhat to blame for it. It was too early for lunch and so he dropped Tommy off at his cart at Pioneer Greens. Unsure of what to do with himself, he trolled around onto Whispering Hills Road and at last headed towards the South Club. He had his bathing suit and a towel in the basket behind the seat and maybe he'd go for a swim.

He squeezed in between two carts. His stomach was still unsettled and he attributed this to the beer last night. He stepped off the cart and left a trail of farts along the brick path towards the gate to the pool, keeping a careful eye out for lizards, they made him anxious. To his left the cool waters of the pool and the steamy hot waters of the hot tub beckoned him. To his right– two shuffleboard decks, a paddleball court and then the volleyball court where a game was in progress. He looked over the fence at the pool to see who was there he might know. He spotted his wife applying suntan lotion to her arms and talking animatedly to her neighbors at either side on the chaise lounges. Something hit him square on the back and he jumped around and broke wind sharply. A few snickers from the court, the volleyball at his feet.

"Nice block," yelled Ron Shutmeyer and Gerry reached for the ball, somewhat miffed at both the offending object and the perpetrators not far away. He doubted anyone could discern the unbidden response of a problematic digestive tract.

"Hey," said Ron, "c'mon! We're down a player, you wanna join in?"

"I'm not very good," Gerry said, "I mean I don't know how to play." He tossed the ball at a cute young blond who must have been visiting her grandparents. She flashed a set of pearly whites at him and said we'll show you how to do it. There were about twenty players and they all faced him, beckoning him to the court as if to smooth over their transgression.

"No," he said, "that's fine. I've got to meet my wife."

"Aw c'mon," said Gaston, who had a pair of large trunks over his Speedo, "we need to even up sides."

The others chimed in and he noticed there were a few attractive young co-eds among the group, beaming, ebullient, visiting on their Christmas holidays.

"Okay," he said. "But I'm warning you, I'm a beginner."

"That's how we all start," said Gaston, "then get hooked."

Gerry hesitated. Ron Shutmeyer approached, the ultimate lure. Ron Shutmeyer, whom he'd met at the Michigan meet-and-greet last spring, was a sort of comrade in arms. A Detroit man, an early GM retiree at fifty-three years old, he and his wife Vanessa another exception to the over fifty-five rule. Real estate was slow and Windmere Properties didn't like empty houses. Vanessa's widowed dad was here, he was lonely and their visits cheered him up and she worried about him. So Ron got pulled along somewhat reluctantly. Ron had toiled at various labor jobs for GM beginning after high school and craved something more adventurous. Ron wanted to hitch a wagon and go west. But here he was at eleven thirty in the morning in a retirement community cajoling a man more than twenty years his senior into a game of volleyball.

How could Gerry say no? Not now. He trailed after Ron and the perky co-ed held the ball under one arm and directed him to a position on the court. He would be on her side today. They usually knocked off at noon. He'd give it a try. It was the middle of a match so it was learn by doing. The first miss came when he and the short lady in bright neon trainers standing beside him watched a ball drop between them, a moment of hesitation where neither of them committed. Then, rotated to the front, he drilled the ball right into the net. Philip Gaston burst out laughing across the net from him on the other side. The ball was delivered to the server, a svelte middle-aged man in a tank top and an expensive pair of trainers, who drilled one by one the winning points. Everyone started gathering up their belongings and most headed for the pool. Turned out the cute co-ed was Ron Shutmeyer's daughter. She and Vanessa started towards the South Club and the gym. Gerry and Ron trailed after them, talking about General Motors and Ron's early retirement which Gerry marveled at. I'll tell you one thing, Shutmeyer was saying, those thirty-five years flew by like nothing. One minute I'm eighteen years old making out with Vanessa in my muscle car and next thing you know we got two grown daughters and woop there it is.

"You ever miss it," Gerry asked.

Shutmeyer paused at the end of the path and turned to face him. "You mean the plant? He-ell no. Damn, he shook his head, I don't know myself sleeping in till ten on a weekday. And what's a weekday? The days just seem to run into each other don't they."

"Yes. Yes they sure do."

Ron headed for the showers to rinse off the sweat and prepare for a soak in the hot tub. Gerry continued to the main entrance and the South Club front desk upon recalling his promise to Shirley he'd ask security about new procedures for guest passes, because their son Jimmy's family would soon be escaping freezing weather and snowdrifts in Michigan for the promise of more agreeable temperatures and the balmy breezes of Florida, joining the other snowbirds who turned up pasty white and eager for the sun. Between their guest room and the pullout couch for their two young grandchildren, everyone could stay under one roof and Gerry tended to hang around the house more.

Having received instructions on the updated procedures and attendant protocol for purchasing and obtaining guest badges, which seemed to him unnecessarily complicated, he proceeded along a corridor towards the men's locker room to change into his bathing suit. On the way, he passed the modest auditorium where functions were regularly held. He cupped a hand above his eyes and pressed his face to the window of one of the closed double doors. Inside a yoga class was in progress. On a mat at the back of the class and nearest to him and the double doors Sugar Gaston had herself twisted up pretty good, one leg tucked snuggly behind her ears. The rest of the participants matched the pose of the instructor at the front, mat for mat perched on palms and toes, face down. Pressing an ear to the door he could hear the yoga instructor beckoning them to calm and peace and encouraging them to focus on their breathing and to enjoy the pose she referred to as downward dog. She said in soft tones that if they visualized their quiet breaths like water over stones in a river which lay way deep deep deep into the forest, their negative thoughts would disappear in the current and return to the dark void from which they'd emerged. He contemplated this briefly. He backed off from the glass, calling a halt to his eavesdropping. Just a few doors down was the workout room and he checked in there— Vanessa Shutmeyer and her cheery daughter were going about their fitness regimen, bound with the others to the treadmills, eyes glued to the CNN business report, stock values travelling in a red band at the bottom of the screen. He waved to them.

Back outside it was still hot and he shielded his eyes from the bright sun and combed the deck surrounding the pool for familiar faces. It was beginning to get crowded. Shirley waved at Gerry and compelled him to meet the two ladies on either side of her whose ears she held captive. "They're Mrs. Beasley's twin daughters, she informed him, they're visiting from Seattle Washington and..." here she looked quizzically at the woman on her left.

"Rochester. New York." She reached out a hand demurely and Gerry took it obligingly.

"How far families spread themselves these days," Shirley noted. "Well, where have you been?"

"Oh here and there," Gerry shrugged.

"I thought you were golfing."

"Clocked out early."

There was nowhere for him to sit and Gerry glanced around. It was a busy time for relatives visiting and pool furniture could get scarce fast. He wanted to shed his shirt and shoes and plunge into the cool water just behind him. Shirley pointed to an empty chair a few tables down. At the risk of appearing rude he said, well I'm just going for a quick dip, nice to meet you both, and headed for a chair on the other side of the pool by the hot tub to drop his things and join those who dipped and bobbed, swirling their arms under the crystal clear aqua blue water that enticed the overburdened to a purging of worries, away from an often muddied unpredictable world outside, an inviting haven where lines of sunlight shimmered, glistening among shadows in the depths of the floor at their feet.

"Wait," he heard Shirley call from behind. "Don't forget to put some of this on you." She waved the bottle of suntan lotion at him. "I don't want you getting burned."

*

The first son to come down was Steve. His first point of contact was Mimi's neighbor, who was out of town but reachable by cell. Then Siloam Hospital where he was unable to speak to his mother. He'd had to place several important commitments on hold, and his wife and a teenage son and daughter remained behind while he begrudgingly went about tending to his familial obligations. He would pack his laptop and stuff his briefcase with all necessary documents. He would have to teleconference to a not very understanding regional vice president. He'd be extra mindful to include his cholesterol, thyroid, blood pressure and anti-anxiety medications. He would have to put on a good face.

When he turned up at the house the garage was open and his mother's car was gone. The door was locked. The next-door neighbor was back home and found him going this way and that about the yard in his suit peering into each window around the house. She introduced herself and informed him in a casual manner about Marion and Elise. Steve had no notice that his aunt and cousin had been summoned and their unexpected appearance somewhat unnerved him. He knew them only by photograph.

The structures in the newer developments were duplex houses and his mother had a neighbor under the same roof on the adjoining side that she only exchanged brief pleasantries with and they were seldom around and nowhere to be seen now. His mother's neighbor who stood before him was Louise and her mother was on friendly and amicable terms with her. They even played rummy occasionally. Louise gave him directions to Siloam Hospital and he got right back in his rental car and backed out of the driveway. He could sort out the details later.

Not half an hour later he entered the door to Room 327 and once again when he'd fully expected to, he found no one. He decided to call upon the nurse's station for information as to his mother's whereabouts. After a brief wait the nurse on duty, an oriental man in blue scrubs, asked if he could help him. He gave his mother's name and the man typed it at a terminal.

"She's meeting with a specialist at the moment."

"Where?"

The nurse gave him the location of a meeting room one flight up and Steve took the stairs two at a time.

In the room sat a physician wearing a white coat over blue scrubs, clutching a chart to her chest. Across from her sat two women he recognized only from pictures. Between them against the wall in a wheelchair and facing him was his mother, Mimi Brooks. They all turned at his appearance in the doorway. He strode immediately to the doctor and introduced himself with a reserved formality that matched his business attire and greeted his relations in much the same manner. He then proceeded to his mother at the window, bent down to embrace her briefly and receive a kiss on the cheek. He hadn't loosened his tie, not one iota.

"How are you feeling, mom?"

"Not too bad," she cupped his face in her hands and her eyes twinkled at him.

He straightened himself and assumed an empty chair. "Well," he said to the doctor, "what's the verdict?"

The doctor hesitated a moment, studying a clean cut man of medium build with a face going a little chubby at the chin and bearing the onset of a middle age paunch. "I was just explaining to Elise and Marion that your mother has made quite, um, remarkable progress in the few days following what I regard a very minor stroke. I am a little concerned regarding her ongoing pneumonic condition and I've referred her case to a doctor of internal medicine in Tampa."

"When can she go home," Steve cut to the chase.

"I am releasing her to your... aunt's care. In two days. She is progressing well. And she's very fortunate to have such... an attentive family."

The doctor turned back to Elise and they returned their attention to the sheet of paper they each held in front of them regarding the course of medications and physical therapy to be adhered to. They were wrapping up and Steve had the sense he'd turned up late for a meeting. He lingered outside the door and then engaged the doctor on her way out, speaking in a muted tone of confidentiality. "Are there any complications?"

"What do you mean?"

"Is she going to pull through, and how long might I be required to attend to her."

"Your aunt and niece seem perfectly capable. Um–"

"So I'm essentially free to leave? I-I mean I have a brother who can also be called upon in the event you think–"

"You may do as you wish Mr. Brooks."

The doctor turned and there was only the sound of her heels on the shiny linoleum receding as she walked brusquely down the corridor towards the elevator.

He returned to Room 327 by the stairs and found his mother already back in the bed, propped by pillows. He looked from her to the others with the all the gravity of one at a funeral. Marion thanked him for coming and he nodded. They said their goodbyes to Mimi and shuffled out one by one. They stepped onto the elevator together.

"We like it very much... you stay with us. At the house." Marion's rudimentary English suffered when she was nervous.

Steve protested, and insisted on booking a room at a motel nearby but Elise wouldn't hear of it. Steve tried his best maneuvering, he employed his most effective methods of manipulation. His voice had the tone of authority. But Elise met and returned every pitch he served. He was no match. There was no way around it. He followed his mother's car in his rental.

*

There was a modest collection at the Sunny Glen Palms library, housed within the larger North Club on the other side of town. Five rows of double-sided bookcases, and a wall lined with reference materials stacked on glass-encased shelves. A magazine rack beside two round tables in front of the unmanned librarian's station– a small desk upon which lay a stack of sign-out sheets on a clipboard. Melinda sat Indian-style on the carpet in the Fiction aisle, absorbed in a hard cover edition of Carson McCullers' *The Heart is a Lonely Hunter* with the focused attention of a surgeon. She looked up at someone needing to get by. Picking up the book and tucking it under her arm, she found her Nana at one of two tables in front. Flora was combing through a hardbound edition of *The Life of Mozart.* She wanted to talk to Nana. Her great great-grandma glanced up at her and the girl wanted to talk. But there were a few others present and the room, however threadbare, constituted a library. They whispered in hushed tones.

"I'm getting hungry Nana."

"We'll get some lunch here. There's good sandwiches. Did you find anything?"

"I got a couple of books."

Melinda tapped the Mozart book. "We can check that out."

"Nooo," Nana stretched the word out and made a face, her voice barely audible, "I'm just glancing it over."

"You like classical music."

"I don't know much about it. It just sounds nice."

"I like to read while I'm listening to it."

"Me too, 'cept you're only sort of half listening, aren't you?"

"Yeah."

They signed the books out and went for lunch. Nana had a meeting today with the events coordinator about her birthday party. The South Club was of inadequate capacity for the amount of guests expected at the party. Between out of town family and her friends within the gates at Sunny Glen Palms, the larger ballroom and concert hall at the North Club would be a more appropriate venue. The South Club was constructed to serve the developments that began in the early nineties and continued today. Yes, the South Club had sufficient amenities to serve this community of newer properties– including a twenty-five meter indoor lap pool, a good-sized outdoor pool, courts, a fitness center, public computers, a small bar and restaurant, and a modest auditorium. But the North Club outsized it and included such additional amenities as a concert hall, a woodworking shop, an arts and crafts facility, a billiards room, a larger computer center, a lapidary, a radio club and a station with low transmission power, and a model train club with an impressive model railroad setup of one hundred and fifty square feet.

Nana had her meeting with the events coordinator at two o'clock and that gave them an hour to enjoy the jazz trio which had set up around the grand piano at the front of the lobby while they brought their sandwiches over to one of many tables nearby.

There were some phone calls last night and Flora was readying herself for the sight of people she hadn't seen in quite some time—in many cases not for a good number of years. Sharon had called, and Melinda had spoken to her mother only upon being summoned and then only briefly, her end of the conversation mainly monosyllabic.

"Nana."

"Yes."

"When is my mother coming?"

"She'll be here next Thursday."

"How long is she staying with us?"

"She's spending the week. Why?"

"Oh," Melinda tapped her foot and studied the musicians nearby, "I don't know."

"*I don't know*," mimicked Flora, "never heard those three words uttered as much as I have this past week."

"Sorry," said Melinda.

"Stop apologizing. "

"You going to tell her about the meds? My quitting them."

Flora sighed, "I don't think so."

"Nana, I wish nobody was coming. I wish it could just be the two of us. To celebrate. I-I mean I want you to have a big party and everything, cause you deserve it and all but, but…"

Flora held her sandwich in front of her and considered her great great-granddaughter.

"Spit it out child."

"Oh Nana, I just, I don't know."

Flora shook her head and took a bite of her sandwich. "Well," she said with her mouth full, "you certainly do a good job of keeping yourself in the dark."

They finished their lunch, Flora tipped the trio, and then they went to look through the glass at the model trains. Melinda signed onto a computer at the lab across the hall. It was now time for Flora's appointment with the events coordinator, whose name was Ellen Everitt. Her office was behind the ticket office, not far away from the lobby and the music. She was a well-endowed woman of medium build and spiky hair, and looked to be in her forties. Mrs. Everitt indicated a chair in front of her desk.

"How do you do Mrs. Wheeler," she smiled brightly. "May I call you Flora? I like to be on a first name basis."

Flora leaned her cane against the large mahogany desk in front of her and slowly settled into her seat. "You most certainly may young lady."

"And I'd be very happy if you called me Ellen." She smiled broadly at Flora, then picked up a sleek pair of designer glasses and replaced them to her nose.

"Now Flora, I've got a list of all the, the many wonderful components of what we are *all* looking forward to be one of the most important events in our history here at Sunny Glen Palms."

"Oh," Flora sighed, "I'm just a little old lady with another big birthday."

"Tush tush," said Mrs. Everitt. "You're amazing."

The pleasant young woman staring back at her from the other side of a rather imposing desk shared only the most very recent part of Sunny Glen Palms history, but even she had to know this event was a first. No one had up until now turned one hundred and Flora wondered secretly if her name wouldn't turn up in one of Windmere Properties sales brochures, the poster child for adding years onto your life with all of the great amenities on offer.

"Shoo Flora," Ellen chuckled. "Your day is a big one, and we want it to be something you'll remember for the…"

She hesitated.

"The rest of your life."

Ellen leaned over and handed Flora a sheet of paper. It was a list of all the provisions for the party– from the rental of the facility, to the catering and open bar to the audio equipment for speeches and the slide show presentation to a live bluegrass band.

"Make sure everything's there, just how you want it."

Flora eyed it through her bifocals, tracing a finger along the itemized list. After a brief silence Ellen spoke. "Now, just a minor detail about the business end of this wonderful party. I've contacted the Business Office and they–"

Flora glanced up sharply. "My great-grandson, that'd be Nathan Wheeler, should be taking care of payment."

"Yes," said Ellen, "we've taken care of the deposit. Now as to the, um, matter of the balance…"

It was obvious this was not an easy part of her job.

Flora smiled. "He's footing the bill. You need only contact him. At the phone number on record."

"Well, er, yes… We, I mean the Business Office has tried. Apparently without success."

Flora drummed her fingers on the arm of the chair. But that's impossible. Perhaps there's some, some mistake with the telephone.

"A mere formality," said Ellen, "and I didn't want to trouble you with it. But the Business Office felt it necessary to bring it to your attention."

There was a pause in which Mrs. Everitt shuffled some papers around. At last she spoke. "Flora, let's keep our eye on the ball. We'll get the finances straightened out. I apologize, it's just that with only about a week to go—"

Flora was sure she was going to mention the Business Office again and cut it off at the pass. "I'll get to the bottom of this. Have you got Nathan's phone number?"

"I believe I do." Ellen wet a finger and leafed through a few pages. In the margins of one lay his name and number. She dialed it and passed the cordless phone over to Flora.

"Thank you." Flora held the phone up to her ear and after a few rings came a recorded message.

You've reached the voice mail of Nathan Wheeler. I'm sorry I missed your call. Please leave a message.

She said it was Nana and please call me at home. Then she passed the phone back to Ellen, frowning. "I'll get to the bottom of this."

"Not to worry," said Ellen.

"How much is due," asked Flora.

"Let's see," Ellen once again leafed through the stack of papers, "the balance is nine thousand nine hundred and seventy three dollars."

"That's a pretty good sum."

"Yes."

"I will make some calls. May I phone you tomorrow?"

"Of course."

Flora shook hands with Ellen, retrieved her hickory cane that leaned against the desk and went in search of Melinda.

*

When they'd at last reached Mimi's driveway after a good number of turns beyond the front gate, Steve had pulled up behind them considering one last ditch effort to circumvent their hospitality at the house he stood to inherit. He'd only been to the house once when his kids were little. He knew that stepping beyond the threshold of that house meant a time obligation not only to entertain, but be entertained. He had a lot of work to do in that briefcase. The day was getting away fast and his mother's internet connection was finicky. But this encounter with his relatives would only become more awkward with each objection.

So Steve followed them inside resignedly, gripping the briefcase in one hand with the laptop slung over the opposite shoulder. He returned to the car for a modest carry-on. Since his aunt and niece had already set up camp in the guest room, which had two single beds, he wheeled the suitcase into his mother's room and set it on the bed. It felt strange to consider sleeping here. Steve removed his tie, opened the blinds and stared intently at two golfers in the distance on the course that bordered what he guessed could be considered his mother's backyard.

Upon arriving the women had put tea on. They spoke to one another in their native tongue while from the small laundry room that sat between the kitchen and the door entrance to the garage they could hear Steve attempting to connect the high-speed internet to his laptop without success. His frustration grew not only with the failure at hand, but the fact he was compelled to restrain himself from exhibiting any anger in the presence of his hosts whose insistence had brought about the unfortunate situation. It was uncomfortable– there was only a kitchen stool to sit on and his legs didn't clear the marble top table upon which he'd set the laptop. His mother wasn't exactly a computer person but really, the arrangement lacked any sense. This setup was ergonomically problematic. He at last gave up and cussing under his breath returned his laptop to the case, replaced the wall plug to the behemoth host computer, his mother's tedious machine of far less computing power. One hour in and the best he could do was send an email to his superior stating that his mother was in grave condition and he'd be out of circuit for a day. He cc'd his immediate inferiors and sent it off.

He'd entered the kitchen to find his relatives in the living room curled up on the sofa reading, and with some sense of culpability had no doubt his muffled ranting had served to disrupt their own concentration.

"Darned technology," he said by way of apology, as if the entire blame for all the fussing about could be attributed to a machine and peripherals. His brief smile came with some effort. "We're slaves to it."

The ladies looked up from their books at him, Marion somewhat uncomprehendingly, Elise with the detachment one might have in watching an actor on the cinema screen.

"I'd like to treat you both to dinner," Steve said.

But Elise said she had something under way in the oven already, and he'd indeed heard her shuffling about behind him while he hassled at the computer. So they'd eat at home. While the roast cooked and the ladies began dicing vegetables, Steve changed into jeans and a golf shirt, and returned to the rental car to fetch a decent bottle of wine.

The dinner was excellent, the Pinot Noir did the trick. But the conversation was a bit stilted, and Marion did most of the talking in her eager if broken English. Her features bore a striking resemblance to that of his mother. The sharp nose that lay as if placed on broad and full cheeks, the brown eyes, the mouth that seemed to return to a pout in the gaps between speaking, the dimpled chin. Steve searched in vain for a hint of resemblance between himself and his cousin. Elise was a little detached and ruminative, poking about her plate abstractedly and glancing up every so often at Steve and her intent bright green eyes put him on edge a bit.

Marion spoke and Elise translated, about his mother as a young girl, something for which he seemed to know next to nothing about. His own narrative was an outline at best, and began where his father entered the story. There was a war over there and his father had nobly rescued her and brought her back and they worked hard, bought a house and raised children.

Marion engaged Elise again to describe her schooling to be an educator and subsequent years teaching the sciences at a private school.

At last Steve leaned back and sighed, swirled his wine glass and regarded Elise.

"And what do you do?"

"I'm an editor at a magazine called Viva La Vida."

"What sort of magazine is that," he wanted to know.

"Oh…" she leaned back, puffed her cheeks and blew a sigh, "a how do you say, amalga… amalgamation of things. Politics, entertainment, popular culture, philosophy, economics, fashion."

Elise spoke briefly about her own career in the publishing world in Paris as her mother looked on proudly, having witnessed her daughter's struggle to rise in the ranks. A brief sketch of one woman's reliance on her intuition and skills to ultimately assume the position of senior editor with one of the most prestigious magazines, published in six languages, with the largest circulation on the continent. The mention of this noteworthy achievement elicited a grunt of acknowledgement from Steve as he speared a piece of roast pork. Her husband, Elise said, was a pediatrician.

Their own divulgences seemed to elicit no questions in response, no invitation to elaborate. So they asked about his business– his actions upon arrival suggested it to be a concern of paramount importance– but in answer he vaguely alluded to a conglomerate of many diverse organizations that dealt in a vast array of commodities in the financial services sector. Elise cocked her head sideways at him, straining at comprehension. He may as well have been talking baseball to Marion.

The sharp ring tone of his cell phone served to curtail a somewhat obfuscatory dialogue that didn't seem to be going anywhere. Steve started towards his mother's room to retrieve it and they heard him just beyond the door speaking in neutral tones. At last he returned to the table bearing the news that Tom, Mimi's other son, would be flying in the day after tomorrow.

Elise raised the Pinot to divvy the remainder among the three of them but Steve laid two fingers over his glass and shook his head.

"Thank you," he said, "I'm okay."

She drained the bottle between her and Marion's glass. They talked a little while longer and Steve excused himself to his mother's room. They could hear the shower running as they cleared the table and Elise washed and her mother dried the dishes. They spoke in low tones in French. They both felt strange and Marion was glad beyond glad that she had Elise for company now. She didn't see it back in Saint Etienne d'Orthe, she didn't see it on the flight over, it began to dawn on her when they sat with Mimi and now it hit her full force, and she was overcome with emotion.

When they'd finished the washing up she clutched her daughter in an embrace and very silently shook against her.

"What's the matter, mama?" But no sooner had Elise asked the question she knew the answer– it was a multi-headed monster that her mother faced. It had caught up with her, everything that brought them here, far away from home and its comfortable predictability and clutter, and friends, and family. Everything was catching up with her mother.

"I'm going outside for a cigarette," Marion said, "I don't feel comfortable smoking here. Inside the house I mean."

Elise nodded and held her mother's elbows in her hands. "Can I get you anything mama," she said with an urgent squeeze.

Marion shook her head slowly and said thank you. "Thank you for coming here with me. Why don't you call Etienne and check on things."

Elise laughed. "Go and wake him up in the middle of the night? I'll phone tomorrow." She let go her mother and Marion fished a pack of Dunhills from her purse, undid the bolt on the side door and let herself out. There was a lawn chair outside the door with plants on either side of it and they needed watering. She spied a hose attached to the side of the house. She unraveled it, turned on the spigot and trained it on the plants briefly. Then she sat in the chair and lit a cigarette. She was afforded a view of the street and presently a man walked by and glanced first at the house and then at her. She waved but he'd already returned his gaze back in front of him and continued along the sidewalk. A few moments later he came back from the opposite direction and began to approach her.

The man was Frank Alsatian. He had been doing some walking he wouldn't ordinarily have done that evening. He'd left the house and headed in the direction of Mimi Brooks' house for no other reason than the chance to pass it two times. Earlier he'd passed by and seen the strange car in the driveway. He proceeded to the South Club. On the walk back an emergency paramedic vehicle passed him, siren off. He detoured and walked along Pioneer Greens and it was hard to imagine his day had begun there twelve hours ago in the blazing sun with a mammoth hangover. Now he'd passed and he knew it was her sitting there and he'd retraced his steps and then crossed the street to the orange glow of her cigarette, a beacon that now guided him towards her.

"Hello," he said, "it's me. Frank Alsatian. We met last night at the South Club."

His nerves were all keyed up– he spoke rapidly, and then purposefully slowed himself. "We met. Last night."

"And danced," said Marion.

"Yes." He was markedly calmed by this acknowledgement. He said, "I just wanted to see how you are getting along."

"That's verree kind. Thank you."

"How is Mimi?"

"She is well. Thank you. She comes home to us. Verree soon. I'm sorry for my bad English. I read nice, but my speaking is terrible."

"No problem," said Frank, fists shoved into his pockets and shuffling his feet.

She stubbed her cigarette out with a heel on the walkway. "Monsieur Al, al–"

"Satian. Alsatian."

"Yes Monsieur Alsatian, would you like... come in a little?" She pointed at the door. "For a cup of tea, or, or... I'm sorry we done bottle of wine."

Frank nodded and followed her into the house.

Elise was perched feet up on the sofa and had her book in her hands. She looked up with some dismay at the guest her mother returned to the house with.

"Hello," said Frank. "Don't get up. I just wanted to look in and see if– see if you needed anything."

"That's very kind of you, Mr.–"

"Alsatian," he finished. "Frank."

She indicated a chair across from her. "Please sit."

Frank gripped his knees and sat on the edge of the chair in the uneasy manner of one who might have to spring up at a moment's notice. Elise related the news about Mimi to him and he nodded gravely, his bloodshot eyes very intent.

"Are you very confident with the doctor," he asked.

"Oh yes, Mr. Alsatian. Very much."

"Please call me Frank," he leaned forward and tapped the table twice. "You know, it's so important to be confident in your treating physician. People often forget doctors are not machines, they are human and they make mistakes. Have you considered a second opinion?"

"I don't feel that's necessary. Not yet. But I understand what you mean."

He nodded and glanced briefly at Marion and just like that the three of them were quiet. "Look," Frank spoke at the floor, "I... had a few drinks in me last night and I guess we got off on the wrong foot."

"Wrong foot?" Elise's brow furrowed. "Oh I see. Yes. No, don't worry Mr. Als—"

"Frank."

"Frank, yes. It's quite alright, Frank. No bad feelings."

Behind the door to Mimi's bedroom the sound of a man's voice and the escalating conversation only served to ruffle Steve, who was sitting up against the headboard with papers spread out in front of him on the bed. It was after nine o'clock— who could possibly occasion to drop in for an impromptu visit at this hour in a placid retirement community? Now he stood at the closed door with an ear pressed to it. When the voices wouldn't stop he swiped his jeans from the floor and stepped back into them with no small measure of agitation, resolved to seek out the source of the disruption.

Everyone started at the sound of the bedroom door cracking open. Steve stood barefoot in the jeans and a white tee shirt and looked from the women to the intruder. "Hello," he said. "I'm Mrs. Brooks' son."

Frank remained seated and regarded the man in the doorway. "Frank Alsatian. Pleased to meet you."

Steve Brooks gave neither his name nor any indication he was stepping any further than the bedroom doorway.

"Well," said Frank clamping his hands to his knees, "I'd better be going."

But Marion had already poured a glass of filtered water and placed it on the glass top table between he and Elise.

"Surely you're welcome to stay a little while longer Frank," said Elise, unfolding her legs to return to a sitting position.

"It was nice meeting you," said Steve and closed the door behind him.

Frank looked at Elise imploringly. "I don't want to intrude."

She nodded and said it's okay.

"Well," he said, "Bet you're glad she's able to come home."

"Yes. Very much. My mother wants to cook for her and, how do you say, pamper? Yes and pamper her back to health."

"That," said Frank Alsatian, "is very admirable."

"And you," said Elise, "have you any family here?"

"Yes," said Frank, staring at the floor. "It's just my wife and myself. Here I mean."

"Oh. And how do you call her?"

"Elizabeth. Libby, for short."

"And how is she," asked Elise, and there was a long pause. "I'm sorry I'm maybe nosy."

"No," said Frank, "it's just that she. She has certain ah... health complications that are beginning to need more and more... attention, I guess."

Marion stood behind Elise and asked if he was hungry. There were leftovers.

"No, really, he put a palm up, that's okay. I just wanted to make sure you were okay. My house is just up the street."

He was about to give the house number, then thought of the prospect of a guest with Libby alone there at the house. "I'll give you my phone number," he said. Marion rummaged through drawers in the kitchen and returned with pad and pen.

He scribbled it down in very neat cursive handwriting and placed it on the table in front of him, then got up to leave.

"Thank you for checking on us Frank," Elise got up and he clasped her hand in his, nodded and then took Marion's hand in the same manner and said call on me should you need anything. When Marion had closed the door behind him, she glanced at Mimi's bedroom door and saw that the light was turned out. She turned to her daughter and sighed. It was a long sigh and seemed to speak for the both of them.

3

Meet the Gastons. Not exactly what you'd call morning people, at least not in the Florida portion of their migratory cycle. They made the long trip to the Sunshine State from their main home outside of Toronto usually in October, sometimes as late as November. They typically stayed until April, sometimes as late as May. They stored their game in a deep freezer in the garage and that was what Sugar now pored over while Joey, one of their two hunting dogs, looked on. She was as unclothed as the dog and when she'd fetched all she wanted she closed the door on the deep freezer and the cold fog within. She quit the garage and stepped into a tidy house bathed in sunlight. The Gastons had recently moved from an older section of Sunny Glen Palms, and were now on the high end of the housing market. Their new home was part of the very latest development and it had two stories, although the upstairs was not enclosed, it was more like a loft, and the high ceilings gave the house a distinctive style and grace which the other houses clearly lacked. These homes had proper front doors. On the Gastons' walls– a sparse collection of abstract modern art, mostly geometric and sleek, austerely framed works that didn't clutter the walls. The kitchen was the first thing you ran into off the garage, beyond that a spacious living room furnished efficiently with little garnishment. The furniture was also modern, angular and sleek– lending it an austerity much in harmony with the minimalist nature of the artwork surrounding it. There were folding chairs in the garage that would be fetched as needed for tonight's dinner party.

Philip had prepared a breakfast of oatmeal bran garnished with fresh strawberries, pineapple, and cantaloupe. The Gastons had a strict diet regimen that complemented an exercise routine for which they availed themselves of the South Club amenities. But despite all the strict attention to body maintenance, they'd not foregone the pleasure of less amenable agents like cigarettes, drugs and alcohol.

They took their plates to the screened porch out at the side of the house, the rays of the sun pleasant on their bare-naked bodies. When they'd finished, Sugar answered a whistling teapot, pouring them out green tea and honey as Philip fetched a lighter beside the gas grill, sparking a rather large joint and poring over a magazine. "Hey babe," he said half to the magazine, "how about that Flora. My God the old gal's still running on all cylinders. Doesn't she look just great."

Sugar slumped down into a chair, setting her teacup in front of her delicately. "I think she'll outlive us all," she said while studying her fingernails.

They sat each to their own thoughts a while, Sugar staring into space, Philip dropping the magazine into his lap and shutting his eyes. Then Sugar spoke. "Honey."

"Yes sugarbaby," said Philip, his eyes still closed.

"Let's go to the beach."

"Uh-huh."

"I wanna hit the beach bars."

"Okaaaay."

"And get drunk on margaritas."

"Today?" He shielded his eyes and looked over at his wife.

"No," she said. "Tomorrow, silly goose. We're entertaining tonight."

"Right."

"The Shutmeyers said they want to take their daughter to the beach while she's here. They said why don't we come with them."

"Sure. We'll all go."

They finished their teas and Sugar went about sweeping and tidying up the living room for tonight's party. Among their works of art, at the foot of the stairs that led to the loft, was a strange montage— a painting equally disturbing and beautiful, an odd splash of colors on canvas that at a certain viewing distance served to form the profile of a woman. But upon further analysis the painting held a more profound meaning that both of them recognized, independent of one another, after they'd acquired it. The mutual discovery became an amusing abstraction for them. When they encountered someone for whom they thought they might care to step past the sparse territory of acquaintance and into the deeper forest of friendship, they'd single out the painting for attention and ask the viewer to gaze upon it a while. They told them not to look too hard. They wanted to see if their new friend could see what it was they saw.

*

Flora slept in. When the sun's rays had finally overtaken the blinds and pierced the darkness of her room, she started up on one elbow, wincing in pain. The aches were all over the place today. She laid back down and stared at the ceiling.

Last night as Melinda immersed herself in her latest book, Flora took the cordless phone to the screened in porch, shut the sliding glass doors under the pretext of not wishing to disturb the girl, and with her tiny decorative address book for bait she quietly went about fishing for information.

She didn't get a bite until she got her great-granddaughter Susan, Nathan's sister, from Philadelphia. After they'd exchanged a few laughs and reminiscences and Susan gave Flora a rundown of her and her husband's itinerary for their trip to her birthday party the coming weekend, Flora at last steered the conversation. How that went—

'And how about Nathan?'

'Oh Nana. Oh God, I'm sorry to tell you this.'

'Tell me what.'

'It's not good news. Bad news. Oh damn… I mean darn.'

'What happened honey. Just spill it.'

'Trouble in Boston.'

'Yes?'

'Nathan.'

'Yes.'

'Well, it seems he's sort of, sort of gone off the deep end.'

'What on earth happened?'

'Oh Nana, everything! First he got laid off from his job. I mean not due to any fault of his own or anything, just something beyond his control. I mean Nathan survived a bunch of layoffs at that place over the years. He worked so hard.'

'I knew that.'

'Then his marriage suffered.'

'Oh God.'

'Yeah. He and Anne started having issues and their kids, you know, are in college. Or were, anyway. His investments tanked, he lost his shirt in the stock market, oh God, that's why Roger and I never fool with any of that nonsense, it's no different than Vegas, you know? Well anyway, Nathan was really going through the ringer and about a week ago? He goes and tries to, oh Nana, he tried to end it all. He tried to end it all and, and I had to fly up there

65

and it was a mess and Anne was all to pieces and said she was done with him, all of it and it's a mess and I'm so sorry to be the one to have to tell you this, oh God I had no clue he was so, so… depressed and, and oh…'

Here she broke off and Flora could hear her sniffling on the other end of the line.

'There there,' she said to the telephone.

Susan regained her composure. 'I'm sorry to be the one to have to tell you this.'

'Does Sharon know about all this?'

'Some, I guess. Nathan and her had a sort of falling out. Right after Sharon's divorce.'

'Well.'

'Yeah, happens in the best of families I guess. But Sharon reached out to him after all this.'

'Where is he now?'

'That's just the thing. Nobody knows.'

After Flora had replaced the phone she sat a good while and thought. Then she got up and closed the sliding door behind her. She told Melinda goodnight and to be sure and give her eyes a rest, taking a glass of milk to her bedroom only to lay down with a busy mind, and that's how she found herself waking up now, still on the bed and bearing the news.

She glanced at the digital clock— it read three minutes after nine. Rolling over to one side and then pushing herself up, Flora reached out for the cane. *Soon*, she thought, *it'll be a walker.* She was a little upset and her hip ached and she was convinced it was a bad day she faced outside her bedroom door. She began to dress in a listless and methodical manner then pulled the door open. The girl had breakfast on— eggs going, bacon already set aside and bread in the toaster. She said it was one of the few things she knew how to do in the kitchen. They sat and ate and had coffee. Melinda never fooled with coffee before but sipping it while chattering away with Nana made her feel grown up, and she imagined it might perhaps make her able to live to a hundred.

Afterwards Melinda went to the den and picked up her book. But she couldn't concentrate and set it aside and turned on the TV. Flora's living room was well furnished but under-utilized and everything seemed to happen in the den. She took the remote and started changing channels. There seemed to be no paucity of weight-loss devices and programs. There was an anti-aging cream on QVC she thought would make a great gag gift for Nana's birthday. There was also quite an abundance of preachers. She began to shop around. The first one she tried had boyish features with pearly white teeth, he was well-groomed and impeccably dressed in a sharp-cut suit. She imagined he wore an expensive cologne rife with the marked scent of prestige. She thought he had tremendous charm and charisma and from the looks of things he had the audience spellbound. The camera panned the crowd from time to time and nobody was asleep, like she sometimes noticed on those few occasions she went to church with her father. There was a toll free number for his ministry. His words were calm and convincing and seemed to suggest that the Lord wanted them to prosper. It seemed it was just fine with the Lord to go out and make a ton of money. She wondered how this squared with the parable about it's easier for a camel to pass through the eye of a needle than a rich man to get through the gates to heaven. She changed the channel. Perhaps she'd figure it out when she was older. She landed on a close shot of another guy in a suit with a pock-marked face and hair going to gray. Now this fellow was a whole different ball of wax.

—with dancing and shouting in the temple… look what the Lord… has done unto thee-ah… the Bible said-ah… that four came and began to pray-ah… that four of em' came… and they said what must we do to be saved-ah… there were five thousand more… all the spirit of God is blooming… Philip who was one of the deacons… he took four of his daughters-ah… down to the city of Sumaria… and the Bible said-ah… that these four girls went to phrophesayin… and the Holy Ghost fell in Sumaria… and great joy came to the city-ah… now it's spreading all over… it's multiplied hundreds and thousands-ah… they're receiving this power from on high-ah… the Bible said now the Lord… is that spirit-ah… and where the spirit of the Lord is… there is liberty-ah… the Holy Ghost-ah… was come to convince the world-ah… of sin, of righteousness and of judgment-ah…

She switched the TV off and picked up a dog-eared paperback of *The Bell Jar*, thumbed the pages, considering it, then called to the kitchen.

"Hey Nana!"

"Yes, child. You don't have to shout."

It amazed her that her grandmother, two generations younger than Nana, had already lost half her hearing. She lowered her voice.

"I-I was thinking… I don't know, um…"

"Spit it out."

"I'm just going to the pool. Could I take the golf cart? Just to the pool."

"What's wrong with your legs?"

Melinda considered this. "I just thought it'd be good to keep the battery charged."

Flora stepped into the doorway. "I was going to ask you to take me shopping. Later. You can drive it all the way to the store out on Coral Beach Boulevard."

"Really?"

"Really."

Flora stepped over and sat on the sofa behind Melinda. She gathered the girl's fine hair with her brittle fingers that were only beginning to cede to arthritis at the knuckles.

"Now if this pretty hair isn't the very same stuff I had in my youth. It's as if I'm looking at my own self as a girl." She tapped the crown of the girl's head, lightly. "Quite an inheritance," she said.

Melinda didn't let anyone touch her hair, but it felt like a massage when Flora arranged it and began to braid it into pigtails. Nobody said anything for a long while and Melinda was glad she had turned off the television. Flora kissed her great great-granddaughter lightly on the crown and tapped it, signaling she was finished. "Go on and take the cart to the pool. I reckon you could use the practice."

Melinda gathered her swimsuit, suntan lotion and *The Bell Jar* and she felt as if she were as weightless as air and didn't have a care in the world. She tried to talk herself out of it but couldn't. It was strange, but she decided not to worry, there really wasn't anything much to worry about here right now except what book to read next and then she remembered her mother would enter their world in a few days. She dismissed the thought and on the way out the door, after a stream of assurances to her great great-grandmother she said over her shoulder, Nana you're the coolest.

"I'm just an old lady gone a little soft in the head. Don't be too long. We've got some shopping to do."

Melinda packed her things in the cart's basket at the back, climbed behind the wheel and felt all at once like a grown up. She decided to detour a bit and have herself a good old time, make a tour of the south side of Sunny Glen Palms. She was grown up, tooling around public streets with stop signs and cars in a motor vehicle– a diminutive one yes– but a motor vehicle no less. She came to a complete stop, turned onto Matterhorn Drive, keeping to the right, and then she pressed the pedal to the floor and went straight, looking at everyone's lawns and waving to those outside like a grown up would. Like the golf cart her thoughts went this way and that. She thought about the golden boy preacher with the big smile in the nice suit and the nicely gelled hair and she puzzled over this once again. At the end of Matterhorn she spied the beginning of a paved path– beckoning her to the more exotic locations of the golf course and its cut grass, high grass, ponds and cypresses. She turned onto it, puzzling at the dilemma that the ebullient words of the handsome preacher had presented her. About the money and all.

Melinda's mom wasn't religious, but her dad often took her to a non-denominational church, and she picked up the Bible and plunged into it at the very beginning and made it through to the end. Her dad made less money than her mom and she knew from the tender age of eight it was the source of much of their bickering. Her dad used to dwell a lot on that parable about how Jesus said it is easier for a camel to go through the eye of a needle than for a rich man to enter the kingdom of God, and now she pondered over this. She wondered because the handsome fellow with boyish optimism and charm was telling everyone that the Lord wanted them to succeed and be affluent. She thought of the long-haired guy with sandals wandering around the countryside like a raving lunatic and convincing his apostles to just give up everything and follow him around upsetting the status quo. She didn't recall him saying anything about money except to be good stewards and render unto Caesar what was his due. She didn't remember him instructing anyone to go out and amass a fortune.

"Hey there," a commanding voice startled her out of her reverie. A man in khaki shorts and an expensively knit golf shirt, white with blue and gold stitching, approached her.

"Are you golfing," he wanted to know.

"No," she replied.

"Then get that cart out of here. This pathway is for Club members only."

"Okay."

69

"And don't do it again."

She stuck the gearshift into reverse and backed onto the grass. She just turned around and got herself right out of there. A little ways down the path she calmed a little, with a tinge of regret at being so utterly compliant. She glanced over her shoulder. The man was already trudging back up the hill, returning to the other golfers. She stopped the cart and gave him the finger anyway.

*

Early that morning when Marion woke up she could hear Elise and Steve speaking in the low reverent tones of church in the kitchen just outside her door. By the time Marion got up, fussed with her hair at the tiny wall mirror, and put a robe over her pajamas he was gone.

Elise said, "He was packing his car when I got up. There was a letter. He was going to just leave a letter. I don't know, he seemed jumpy. From the start."

"Perhaps we scared him off. With our cooking."

Elise couldn't tell if her mother was serious or joking.

"Maybe it's just his way of dealing with it Mama."

"Oh," said Marion. "Taking off? Running away?"

"He got a flight at noon. He's going to visit her first and then fly back."

Marion shrugged her shoulders and nothing more was said on the matter.

Elise thought it would be a good idea for them to go for a swim before spending the day with Mimi. They changed into their swimsuits, packed some things into one of Mimi's straw beach bags and walked the short distance to the Club. Along the way they talked about home. Etienne and the children were getting along fine so far. *Stay as long as Mama needs you*, he'd said, and she knew he meant it. Elise checked her email on the public computers when they got to the Club and the magazine had only cc'd her on a few relevant emails. No major publication deadline, no big fires to put out, nothing to intrude on her holiday leave. She was covered. The pool beckoned. They walked back out of the room into the brightly lit lobby of the South Club and from there when they'd figured their way out of the building, they pushed the double doors open onto the brilliant sunshine and the pool area was densely populated, it was early yet and so they had their pick of chairs. They decided on two chaise lounges by the poolside. Elise set the bag down and they removed flimsy white caftans to reveal modest but stylish one-piece bathing suits and then they applied sun lotion. The water was cool and Marion bobbed and weaved as Elise took some laps and the exercise did their spirits a world of good. When they got out they sprawled on the lounges and let the sun and the breeze slowly dry them.

Not too long after they'd shut their eyes and lay on their stomachs listening to the soft din of distant conversations around the pool– a close-up voice, very present, distinct and strangely familiar. "Oh ladies, it warned, ya gotta be careful in this sun. Florida sun is strong. Use some of this."

The voice belonged to Shirley Hagoden and she stood looming above Elise, blocking the sun and waving a plastic blue bottle around as if it were a magic potion.

"Oh, thank you," Elise said. "We already did."

By now Marion had propped herself up on her elbows.

"What number is it you got," Shirley wanted to know.

"Number… number…" Elise fumbled around in her bag, while Shirley set about spreading her towel across the back of the chaise lounge next to Marion's. "Want some company?" she asked, although she'd already settled herself comfortably onto the lounge.

"Of course," Elise replied, she'd by now fetched the dark brown bottle and read number eight to Shirley Hagoden.

"No no," said Shirley, "that's not strong enough for this sun. Here ya go, use mine. Number eighty," she wiggled it at Marion. "Just to be on the safe side."

Marion took it and dabbed some sparingly here and there while Shirley removed her sandals and got herself good and cozy. She wore a one-piece white bathing suit and a simple hat with a band and a green cellophane visor.

They listened attentively, their brief nap interrupted while Shirley droned on about her kids and grandkids back in Michigan. *They're coming next week and I've just got to get that house in order. My son's driving me nuts.*

Marion relaxed again, closing her eyes with the hope that perhaps their new friend's voice would blend in with the chorus of voices surrounding them. But Shirley Hagoden's voice didn't work like that– it was all sandpapery with only a hint of soft edges. She had the voice of one who'd smoked cigarettes a good while and it didn't sing, it jostled along like a train on its last legs and then it would get up a head of steam and charge the hill.

It was rambling along and then suddenly it made a sharp turn into more urgent tone. "*Quick*," said Shirley, "get up and go into the building like it's nobody's business. The guard's going around checking badges."

"*Qu'est-ce qui se passe?*" Marion began to stir, shielding her eyes and looking from Mrs. Hagoden to Elise. "What?"

"The *guard*," Mrs. Hagoden spat out in a whisper, "it's the guard and he's checking for badges. We'll have to get you both guest badges. Until then we gotta hide you!"

Elise was now clear on the matter at hand. Marion, still puzzled and somewhat disoriented, followed her daughter and they walked across the pool deck and back into the building under the auspices of having to fetch something. Mrs. Hagoden had assured them she would take care of Bobby the guard should he raise any suspicions.

After the guard made his rounds and sufficient time had elapsed, Mrs. Hagoden walked to the parking lot to fetch her faux coconut cups from the golf cart and ordered three coconut rum kahluas from the South Club bar. Alcohol was prohibited in the pool area, but she was game to break more rules and calculated at least another hour before the guard made his rounds. She went in search of her fugitives and found them eying the yoga class through the door window in much the same manner as her husband Gerry had the day before.

"It's okay," she said, "the coast is clear."

The colloquialism was lost on both of them, but they got the point nonetheless. They followed her to the lounge to collect their drinks, Shirley winking conspiratorially at the girl behind the bar. When they returned to the pool with their drinks there was a new occupant on Elise's lounge chair. She wore denim cutoffs and a striped white tee shirt that covered her bikini top, her dark brown hair with red streaks braided into pigtails. The girl had straightened the seat and sat with her back against it, her knees pulled up and a book propped between them. She did not look up– her eyes were glued to Sylvia Plath's *The Bell Jar*. Elise thought her a little young to be reading such a book. For a second they didn't know what to do about the chairs but at last the girl took notice of them.

"Oh, did I take your seat?"

"That's okay," said Shirley, "there's plenty to go around. Who are you, young lady?"

"My name is Melinda Jane Rutherford," she said.

"Oh," Shirley mouthed the name Melinda to herself, and her face lit up. "Are you Flora Wheeler's great, great, great…"

"Great great-granddaughter."

"Yes!" Shirley poked a finger at the air as if she'd hit upon a major scientific breakthrough. "Aren't you a cute little peach! You must meet our new neighbors, Missy Melinda. They're visiting us from France and their names are Marion and Elise."

The French ladies beamed and Melinda started to get up, but Elise waved dismissively and pulled a deck chair towards the burgeoning group. Marion nodded at the paperback placed at Melinda's feet on the lounge, having by now spied the author's name and translated the title. "You like this," she asked, "you like it very much?"

Melinda, enamored of their accents, brightened. "Oh," she said, "I love books. I just love to read."

She was fussing at her braids and seesawing her ankles on the lounge. Mrs. Hagoden wanted to put in her own two cents, but before she'd a chance to expound on the virtues of Reader's Digest, Elise stood up and said, "Melinda, I'm going for a swim. Would you like to swim?"

"Oh," said Melinda, "I would really really like that."

They left Marion and Mrs. Hagoden to each other and for a while the two just sat sipping their drinks and watching the pool dwellers basking in the sun. At last Mrs. Hagoden said to Marion, "How is she? Your sister?"

"Oh," said Marion, "she's get better. Each day, the doctor say. Improves."

"That's fantastic," Shirley said. "I am so happy to hear good news. Really. So happy."

"We will go today. For visiting."

Shirley said great, and there was an awkward silence while she tried to figure out what she might say next to the dear woman whom she believed only half-comprehended her words.

"Mrs. Brooks," she said. "Mademoiselle Brooks. I would like it very much if you and your daughter accepted my invitation to play Bridge tonight. Over there at the North Club at seven o'clock."

Bridge. The universal language of playing cards. It seemed to Shirley that Marion understood. "Oh," Marion said, "maybe we see how we feel. Later."

"Nonsense," said Shirley, "we can all go in my car. You will love it. You will absolutely gobsmacking love it."

"We will love your car?"

This gave Shirley a great big belly laugh. "No, no, I mean the Club. The layout. The card game."

"*Oh-ho!*" exclaimed Marion, bringing the back of her hand to her mouth and bursting into laughter, I see, and she and Mrs. Hagoden got right into it then, a fit of the giggles that neither of them seemed able to shake. Marion regained her composure for a moment and then lost it just as fast, Shirley giggling along saying, "I'm not laughing *at* you I'm laughing *with* you." Marion nodded and they laughed a little more.

The Gastons had begun to settle in now, across the pool and near the hot tub. Not long after them came the Shutmeyers. Elise and Melinda were wading in the pool up to their necks and talking. Marion watched them as Mrs. Hagoden droned on about Bridge strategies a while and then fetched a paperback from her straw beach bag. It was a brand new book, a spy thriller, and she wiggled her drink while scrutinizing the book jacket.

Elise climbed out of the pool and lowered herself into the hot tub and a conversation with the Gastons and the Shutmeyers. Melinda returned to her chaise lounge and rubbed a towel at her hair, draped it onto the back of the chair and picked up her book.

"Well," Shirley glanced up from her book. "Are you enjoying yourself Missy Melinda?"

The girl didn't care too much for this newly ascribed nomenclature, she shrugged and kept her eyes on her own book. "I guess so."

"Maybe you'll get a chance to meet my grandkids. They're coming down next week. Will you still be around?"

"Mm hm."

Melinda let Shirley talk awhile, feeling all the more grown up at not having her mother or Nana around to correct her manners, *answer the lady when she's talking to you*. She had tuned Shirley Hagoden out altogether and merely nodded at the pages of *The Bell*

Jar like a grown up until at last Mrs. Hagoden petered out and brought the spy thriller from her lap back under her eyes, calm was restored and Melinda could pick up the story again.

Soon Elise returned, speaking animatedly in French and bearing the news that she and Marion were now expected at the Gastons' for dinner at six. They began to gather their things for the walk back. Mrs. Hagoden raised her head and cupped a palm over her visor.

"Leaving us already."

"We go to visit Mimi now," said Marion.

"Of course," said Shirley. "Tell her I said hello. And we can't wait to have her back."

"Thank you Mademoiselle Hah-go-den."

"And don't forget about Bridge tonight."

"Oh," said Marion, "sorry. My daughter tells me we go to a dinner party later."

"Oh?" Shirley placed her book in her lap, "I suppose we can try Bridge another night."

"Yes," said Marion and explained to her daughter in French.

"Oh certainly, Shirley, my mama would very much like to go with you and play. I- I don't know Bridge myself, but mama... she will go with you next time."

"Sure," said Shirley, "we can go another time."

She drew her book up under her nose, reading words and sentences that didn't register. Her mind was elsewhere.

*

Later that afternoon. Flora Wheeler replaced the cordless phone to its base and sat and stared a good while at the calendar posted on the kitchen wall, a Sierra Club issued 2004. January. A winter scene suggesting a quiet serenity, snow-covered cedars in the Grand Tetons, Wyoming. Saturday. One week to go. Mrs. Everitt was not pleased with the bad news, but she was extremely gracious and thought perhaps something could be worked out and said she'd get back to Flora on the matter after discussing it with the Business Office. Frank Alsatian was putting the finishing touches on the large-scale German Messerschmitt model airplane, standing back from it with a small brush and studying it in the manner a painter might regard a canvas. His garage door was open to vent the enamel fumes of paint and glue. He lowered the volume on the radio and the squawking of the talk show host, walked to the door at the back of the garage, cracked it open and said c'mere Libby, I want you to see this. Gerry Hagoden was out walking aimlessly somewhere in the vicinity of Meadowbrook, or Greenwood, or perhaps Newbridge Greens. Gerry was admiring the landscape and letting his thoughts go wherever they may. He was letting his hair down today because it was Saturday and Shirley had run out of chores to assign him. Shirley Hagoden was home from the pool and she was having another temper tantrum that would play itself out the way they usually did. She was upset at her son Jimmy because he kept switching the date and time of their arriving flight and it was seriously screwing with her social calendar and everybody was changing plans and what was a woman to do? Mimi Brooks was playing rummy with her sister on the food service table in Room 327, and Marion could tell her sister's moves were slow and deliberate and often lacking any sense. Marion played on and hoped her sister would get her game back, a little at a time. The Gastons were preparing to while away an afternoon making love on the screened-in porch where anyone might happen upon them. Melinda Jane Rutherford was in the Lapidary at the North Club, marveling at the many sculpted wire and gemstone creations. The one that caught her eye was a model of a tree done in gold wire with petrified wood and emerald and jade stones. The girl studied it. Around this exquisite tree, faeries danced in colorful frozen motion. She picked it up and held it in her hands and thought if she had enough money she'd buy one for her Nana, for her one-hundredth birthday, because it was clearly a creation of tangible and exquisite beauty and after all, how often did anyone turn one hundred?

*

Sugar was still in front of the vanity mirror in the master bedroom poking at her hair and making faces when the doorbell rang the first time. The big front door was open but at the screen door Ron Shutmeyer observed protocol, a hand over his eyes pressed against the screen while talking to his wife.

"C'mon in you silly goose," said Philip, uncorking a bottle of Cabernet Sauvignon in the kitchen. "Silly *gooses*," he said when

Vanessa appeared behind Ron. Ron had a twelve pack of Corona and maneuvered it into a crowded refrigerator. He removed his sunglasses and stuck them into his shirt pocket. Philip hugged Vanessa and clapped Ron behind the shoulder a few times.

"Can we do anything," asked Vanessa, although if the past were any indication the Gastons would have every little thing impeccably arranged.

"No, just relax and enjoy yourselves. We've got venison and Canadian sausages marinating. I'm gonna go grill em' sooner or later. Meanwhile," he swept his arm broadly at the living room, "let's relax."

Philip poured Vanessa a glass of wine and Ron fetched a beer from the fridge and said let's start drinking.

"We're ahead of you there, pal." Philip raised his glass. "To youth. To youth and old age."

"To youth," said Vanessa, and they sat down together on sleek-designed furniture around a cut glass table bordered with lightly stained glass.

"My wife and I are going on a cruise in a little over a week."

"Oh wow," said Vanessa, "I'd be packing already."

"Not much to pack on *this* one," Philip smirked, lighting a cigarette. "At least not in the way of clothes."

He exhaled and batted a hand at the smoke.

"Ah *hah*," Ron nodded slowly.

"Where is this one going?" Vanessa settled herself in on the sofa next to Ron, propping a foot underneath her thigh.

"Jamaica. We'll dock there for three days."

"Sounds wonderful," said Vanessa.

"It's gonna be fun," Philip nodded.

"Well hel*lo* there." Sugar appeared behind the sofa and the Shutmeyers. "Don't get up." She had a pitcher of margaritas in the fridge and poured one for herself. She wore khakis and a tank top and skittered around the hardwood floor in her slippers.

"How are you two?" She greeted the Shutmeyers in a shared hug. She'd not sat down a minute when a knock knock and hello issued from the front door. And from there the guests arrived in a steady stream until there were about a dozen assembled in the living room listening to Rod Stewart croon the golden oldies on their modest CD player that sat on a bookshelf at the far end of the large living room. The guests included Tommy and Debbie

D'Antonio, Marion and Elise. Sugar was fetching extra folding chairs from the garage when Philip hollered *fetch two more* to her. His surprise guests had arrived.

Flora Wheeler held her great great-granddaughter's arm, raising the old hickory cane to step carefully over the threshold. Her eyes lit up upon viewing the interior of one of these newer homes. "My word," she said to Philip while scanning the room, "haven't we come up in the world."

"We'll try and not let it go to our heads," he said, relieving Melinda of a loaf of fresh-baked bread. "This is your first time to our new digs. Welcome. And how are you, young lady?"

"I'm good," said Melinda.

"Not you silly goose," he cupped a hand to the back of Melinda's head, winked and then nodded at Flora, "I meant this young lady."

"Oh Philip Gaston," Flora winced, "who are you kidding?"

"What are you drinking Flora?"

"Water."

"There's Cabernet Sauvignon or..."

"I'll have a glass of that as well."

They followed him into the kitchen and he poured Flora a glass of water, then wine, and handed a tall glass of lemonade to Melinda.

"Delicious," she said after a sip, "is this natural?"

"Fresh squeezed. Only way to go."

"Wow. I never drink anything but the sugary supermarket stuff."

"Well, then the worm has definitely turned for you. Sorry there isn't anyone more your age around. Just us old fogeys."

"Oh," said Flora, "she's practically all growed up. Acts like it anyway."

She gave a playful pull at one of the girl's pigtails. "She'll fit right in, don't you worry."

"After you," Philip indicated the living room. "I'll introduce you to the masses. Tell me your name again honey," he took the girl's elbow.

"Melinda."

While Melinda wrung her hands, Philip said *okay listen up everybody*, and motioned his wife to turn down the music.

"Here on one arm I have our dear old Sunny Glen Palms friend, my wife and I's oldest friend who is about a week shy of a hundred years of age. And when I can get her to tell me where the hell the Fountain of Youth is located at Sunny Glen Palms, I get first dibs, eh?"

Everyone laughed and he said, "I hear it's somewhere near the hot tub at the South Club. Or maybe the hot tub itself."

Philip raised his glass at the others and they laughed again and raised theirs. Then he continued his toast. "On the other end of the spectrum, and in keeping with our wide variety of guests is her great great great—"

"One to many," said Flora and everyone laughed again.

"I'm sorry. Great great-granddaughter Melinda." Everyone beamed at them and now Melinda really felt grown up, standing there next to her Nana, a full inch taller. She wondered if people shrank, if her Nana hadn't shrunk over the years. She blushed a little and looked down at her lemonade, rocking on her feet and willing the spotlight were away from her and her Nana. Philip continued on.

"Five generations." he said, raising his glass again, "May you live to see a few more, Flora."

After a robust round of ays, everyone again raised a glass to Flora. "Easy on the toasts," she beamed at Philip, "you just might get an old lady drunk." With that she lifted her cane and stepped forward and Ron Shutmeyer indicated his seat on the sofa next to his wife. The Shutmeyers hadn't occasioned to meet a person of such advanced years, and they now clearly delighted in their good fortune. Vanessa had drained her second glass of wine and her husband was off to fetch her a third. She was a quilting enthusiast and had entered a few competitions in Michigan. Flora had done more than her share of quilting over her life and this was enough common ground for Vanessa to start the ball rolling. From there, Vanessa wanted to know the particulars of life in rural America, just after the turn of the century. Vanessa wanted to know what life was like before a developed electrical grid, before organized water distribution and modern plumbing, before telephone and the introduction of party lines, before radio and television, before the advent of fast food and supermarkets, before the breadth and predominance of publicly-held corporations and the growth of the insurance industries and other such modern-day albatrosses that pretty much served to suck the joy out of life. She wanted to know. Two and a half glasses of wine in and Vanessa wanted to know, and Flora loved the telling.

Meanwhile, opposite them— Melinda Jane Rutherford found herself comfortably wedged between Marion and Elise and was glad to avail herself of another opportunity to hear the lovely exotic accents. It almost didn't matter what was being said, the mere sound of her new friends' voices dancing on her ears was enough of a tonic and she periodically closed and re-opened her eyes. It turned out both of these women loved books, Elise had in fact studied literature in college and Melinda wanted to know about that. She was feeling very sophisticated at this gathering of grownups, and she wished it could go in interminably, that she'd somehow be able to avoid returning to face that dreaded school and the undesirables that inhabited it. She was Melinda Jane Rutherford, and she was discussing literature with two French ladies and little Mel would just have to wait. She replaced her lemonade to the coaster and saw Nana talking while at the same time observing her from across the table. Marion was saying she was struggling through books in English and had almost finished the Gore Vidal, which she enjoyed but wished she didn't have to employ the translation dictionary so much. She asked about how Melinda happened upon *The Bell Jar*.

"Did you know," said Melinda, "there's a library here. Right here in Sunny Glen Palms."

"Really," Elise brightened at this news, she knew there was much to explore here and thought once they had her auntie back home she might do some exploring. "I think," she said, "I would like to go with you next time you go."

"Okay," said Melinda, "but I'll warn you. I get distracted and I can be in there for hours."

"That's alright. I can sit and read. That's what a library is for anyway, isn't it."

"Do you have children?"

"I have two."

"How old are they."

"My daughter is seventeen and my son is fourteen."

"I'm fourteen. Do they read?"

"Yes," said Elise, "they read. They do sports. My daughter does gymnastics and my son football."

"Wow," said Melinda, finding it hard to imagine her refined and cultured friend's son participating in such a savage activity. "That's a dangerous sport. Don't you worry?"

"She means soccer," said Tommy D'Antonio, leaning into their conversation. "That's football to them."

"Oh yes," said Elise, "of course. I mean soccer, to you."

"Melinda you're right," said Tommy. "My wife here was an ER nurse and we strictly forbade our kids to play any football. American football, that is. They played soccer and we went to every match, one or the other of us. Every match."

Debbie nodded in affirmation and Marion was relieved to see that the conversations in the room didn't appear to be of a political or ideological nature tonight. Tommy picked up their empty glasses. "What are you drinking," he asked.

"Thank you, whatever red wine is there," said Elise.

He returned from the kitchen with two glasses of Merlot. Melinda didn't think he looked like much of a bookworm, and in fact he wasn't. Tommy D'Antonio hadn't picked up a book in a good while. But he told them he enjoyed Tolstoy, and at college had read *Anna Karenina* and *A Tale of Two Cities* both twice and Melinda thought that was no small feat.

Sugar perambulated around the room with a tray of hors d'oeuvres, laughing and chatting up the guests, the consummate hostess. Philip was walking a plate of raw meat to the grille and Vanessa reminded him about an upcoming Super Bowl party and wondered which team he was going to root for. His voice rang through the large room.

"Who cares? Who pays attention anyway? We're so drunk by halftime, it may as well be Jeopardy on the television."

He chuckled, and Ron chuckled with him and took a swig of beer from the can.

"I do like the halftime show Philip," said Sugar.

"Well," he was at the sliding glass doors about to go outside to the grille, "the Super Bowl is just a good excuse for a party."

Sugar had a little halftime show of her own last year at the Nolans. Alcohol could have a profound effect on a woman who was otherwise pretty demure and reserved by nature. It had done the job by halftime and she danced and was coerced little by little onto the platform of the dining room table, she was barefoot by now after all, and then she commenced to lift her shirt. This was something she picked up at Mardi Gras. New Orleans and Mardi Gras were becoming an annual tradition for the Gastons, but last year Philip had unwittingly booked a nude cruise for the same week that was both non-refundable and eagerly anticipated. So it had to be here— the shirt lifting ritual— in the Nolans' house in Sunny Glen Palms, and she wasn't wearing a bra and everybody saw. Nobody minded and she flashed a few more times and then let her husband take her hand and guide her off the table back onto the shag carpet, back down to earth.

Philip grilled and it wasn't long before he returned with a sizable plate of cooked cuisine and placed it on the island counter in the kitchen, where the guests could line up for the feast and serve themselves buffet style. And oh what a feast it was. There was cooked venison and Canadian sausages, Flora's homemade bread, potato salad, regular salad and dressings, Debbie's green bean casserole, dessert items of cheesecake, strawberry shortcake and coffeecake. The bountiful spread was not wasted on a single person in that house, not a one.

*

Dinner at the Hagodens was pretty dull by comparison. Swanson frozen chicken pot pie. Gerry and Shirley sat in muted silence and he could tell something was bugging her, but he couldn't seem to draw her out.

"I wonder how Mimi's girls are doing," he said.

"They're just fine, honey. She gets released tomorrow. In the meantime they rated an invite to the Gastons. For dinner."

"Tonight?"

"Um hm."

They each played with their food. For a while there was only the tick-tocking of the grandfather clock in the living room, a remnant from Michigan.

"Well," Gerry said at last.

"Well what?"

"Oh nothing."

"Gerry Hagoden you are a strange bird sometimes. What are you going to do with yourself tonight?"

"I-I don't know. Hadn't given it much thought."

Shirley had to hustle it for Bridge and the time had gotten away from her and it was already pushing seven o'clock and she just wanted to take her golf cart and whizz on over to the North Club. Gerry cleaned up what little dishes there were. The phone rang and he listened while Shirley talked to their granddaughter then their son Jimmy. Her initial bouncy and upbeat tone took on a somber shade and she hung up before he could ask to speak to his son.

"Now he's saying it might not be until the weekend before they come. Something going on at work. Dammit, why can't they just make a plan and stick with it! Why can't anybody just stick with it, just stay true to their goddamned word!"

She paused to catch her breath. "Now I'm late for Bridge! Dammit!"

She flung the calendar book hard at the floor, and Gerry just knew what was coming.

"I'm not going!"

"Well," he said, "maybe you should call Edna Norton and—"

"Oh, she's not going anyway!"

Shirley sat on the ottoman, shrugged her shoulders and rubbed her hands against her temples, her short hair flopping.

"Nobody, nobody can make… commitments these days!"

Gerry said, "I'm going for a little walk."

"Oh, go ahead! Just go!"

And go he did, previously he had it in mind to look in on Marion. And her daughter. Now there was no plan, but that was nothing unusual. Temperatures had cooled and the air had a little chill to it. A few blocks away, he had a notion to return for his lined windbreaker then decided against it. The usual calm that accompanied him on these walks was not along with him tonight. He was uneasy, he kept to the sidewalk and there seemed to be more cars on the streets than usual and he hoped nobody thought he was up to no good. Tonight he couldn't seem to keep his mind on the landscape and it didn't roam, as it often did, to the clever scenarios he'd conjure up from his imagination about those who inhabited the houses he stepped past. Gerry felt a little like a runaway.

His feet took him to the corner of Burgundy and Sunset Boulevard, and from there it wasn't very far to The Timberlands, where those fancy new houses lay, where he hadn't dared venture before, as his presence might be more conspicuous there among the larger lots and homes with more space between them. He paused at the corner, there by the big green wooden sign with white lettering that marked The Timberlands. From there he could hear them, just the faintest din of voices, and he stood silent. His feet led him down the blacktop, and then a left turn and it was just a few houses down and there they were, the one house that was fully lit up. The voices came from around back and he did a walk-by and tried to keep his head forward while he glanced surreptitiously at the house. A few of them were on the screened-in porch to the side and their voices betrayed a lively conversation. It seemed a few of them had glanced at him and he was unsure just where to go from there. If he cut through the yards it would take him back to the creek the Gastons' backyard bordered on, and then to Pioneer Greens. Or he could just turn around and go back. He was beginning to feel a little ill-at-ease, incapable of making this simple decision. After he'd paused there at the dead end, he decided against cutting through the stranger's yard, which might result in an embarrassing situation that would only serve to tarnish his reputation.

So it was back the way he came. He kept his eyes in front of him and he'd just got past the Gastons' house when a familiar voice boomed from the screened in porch at the side.

"Gerry? Gerry Hagoden, that you?"

It was Ron Shutmeyer calling out. He continued walking, then turned around resignedly to acknowledge this recognition. He stood still and waited.

"Hey Gerry," said Ron. "C'mon in and have a beer."

His better judgment told him he should just wave to Ron and walk on, hoping his name didn't spread around that party as a snoop, his better judgment told him he wasn't invited in the first place and it was bad manners to crash a party, it showed a clear lack of social decorum, but his feet nonetheless took him reluctantly across the lawn and to the screen door of the porch.

Ron Shutmeyer swung the screen door open and Gerry approached tentatively on the walkway with his hands in his pockets, *yeah yeah I was just out for a stroll and well waddya know, fancy meeting you here* and all that. He would just banter a little with Shutmeyer and be on his way. Then he heard her voice, and saw her just beyond the doorway at the table, facing him. The French woman. Taking a drag from her cigarette and glancing over with a look of recognition.

Shutmeyer was saying, "Well by God, c'mon in and have a beer Gerry, I'll get you one from the fridge."

"Well," said Gerry, "no harm in that."

He stepped over the threshold and felt like an awkward teenager at a dance or a party with an ambiguous guest list. His heart raced as he stepped inside the screened-in porch. Tommy D'Antonio was seated next to Marion, and he hollered, hey there Hagoden! He approached them hastily with the idea of squashing the attention they were quickly drawing to him, but this only had the opposite effect. They were all saying hello and Gerry dug his hands in his pockets. Marion smiled and he nodded to her while engaging D'Antonio on the subject of golf. Shutmeyer had gotten waylaid by the host and hollered to him again. *Hey Gerry c'mon in and say hello to the Gastons!*

"Hi Gerry, welcome to our humble abode." Philip Gaston, an unlit cigarette in his mouth that slurred his speech somewhat, had remembered his name, despite their brief and merely ankle-deep interactions. He pumped Gaston's hand and to Gerry the man's grip was loose beyond loose. Next thing he knew the three of them were walking their beers out towards the back patio. He scanned the room and Elise smiled and waved to him. Gerry was surprised to find Flora Wheeler sat next to her on the sofa, and he stooped to say hello. She was seldom seen around lately, and now here she was hanging around people mostly half her age at a party on a Saturday night. Flora took his hand and asked if he and his wife were coming to her party next week.

"Oh," he said, "we thought that was just for family."

"Nonsense. It's at five o'clock at the North Club. I expect to see you and…"

"Shirley."

"Is it Geraldine or Shirley?"

"Both," he said. "It's kind of confusing."

"Well," she said, "hope we'll see you there."

When he stepped down through the doorway and onto the patio, he found Shutmeyer, Gaston, and another man he didn't recognize. They were sat in near darkness around a round glass-top table, their faces dimly lit by citronella candles, and Gaston shoved a chair with his foot in invitation. "If you're hungry," he said, "there's still a ton of food on the counter."

Gerry shook his head. "Oh, I've had dinner already," he said, drumming his fingers. "I was just taking a walk and saw Ron here and thought I'd stop by a minute. Thanks for the beer."

The beer tasted good, it was cold and somehow the night seemed warmer out there on the patio, the men sat and didn't say anything for a good while and then Ron Shutmeyer said, "Great dinner Philip."

"Did you get enough?"

"Oh. I'm stuffed."

"Well, I'm not waiting on *this* any longer."

Philip Gaston reached across the table and grabbed a lighter and a small marble pipe. He lit the pipe and the pungent odor hit Gerry Hagoden right in the face, he was downwind and knew instantly what it was. Gaston passed it to the stranger, who drew heavily with a concentration amplified by the orange glow. He went to hand it over to Gerry who shook his head and passed it on to Shutmeyer, who took it and finished the job. Gaston leaned back in his chair and exhaled.

"*Beautiful night*," he said, glancing up at the sky. And when Gerry looked up he saw it clearly was. A moonless night and the stars were dotting it up pretty good. He took a swig of beer and reclined a little.

"So," said Gaston to Shutmeyer, "my wife tells me we're going to the beach tomorrow."

"Man this is good smoke," the stranger on the other side of Gaston said. "Where'd you get it?"

"My son," said Gaston. "Kid gets the best shit."

He tamped fresh marijuana into his pipe in a careful and studied manner and said to Shutmeyer, "We can fit five in the jeep." Shutmeyer thumbed up and said, cool.

The marble pipe made the rounds again and landed on Gerry, and he considered it between thumb and forefinger. At last he brought it to his mouth and drew lightly. It'd been years. Decades. When the kids were really little, they'd gone on vacation to the Grand Tetons, rented a Winnebago and drove it out there through the Badlands and parked it for a week at the State Park. They had hippies for neighbors and Gerry liked to walk around that park, even back then how he loved to walk. One night he walked right into a campsite and there was a gathering and there were a lot of funny cigarettes being passed and he took each and every one in turn. When he walked back at daybreak he was giddy and lighthearted, there was a song in his step and in his head. But Shirley was anxious and upset– one of the kids got sick, for two days straight it rained and he got the silent treatment.

Now not long after mildly inhaling, he felt the blood rush to his head and he drummed his feet on the concrete to assure himself he was still there, firmly planted, although he wasn't. He shivered. He couldn't figure out what to say to Shutmeyer, or Gaston, or the third man. He looked at the beer and swigged it to relax, perhaps slow a mind that was already beginning to race. Gaston was talking about hunting back home up north. "My son and I," he was saying, "will just sit up there in the tree for hours. In total silence, eh? Not a word between us. And I swear to God it's the most meaningful time we get to spend together."

"That's so cool," said the third man. "That's really cool."

Shutmeyer left to get another round, and Gerry said not me, I better be going soon, but then he thought he'd better stay put a while and let the effect of the drug wear off a little. At least he didn't have to worry about driving. Shutmeyer returned and placed a Corona in front of each man. Gerry didn't push it away, he'd drained one and now this one tasted good, it was early yet and it wasn't going to rain and there was no sick kid. Maybe this was what retirement was all about. Maybe he should drink more. Maybe he should let his hair down.

Ron Shutmeyer asked if he was alright.

"I'm fine," he said without hesitation. "Nice evening."

"Yeah man." Ron Shutmeyer tipped his bottle at Gerry and Gerry tipped his back.

"Gerry, how long've you been retired?" Gaston asked.

"Oh a little over two years I guess. We've been here almost two years."

"Where from."

"Michigan."

"Excellent move. Those damn winters'll take years off of your life."

"You betcha."

Gerry couldn't think of anywhere to go from there, so he just leaned back and said, wonderful night. Everyone sat silent a while listening to the crickets, and then the third man muttered something Gerry didn't catch but which triggered a fit of laughter from the men that made Gerry a little uneasy at whatever shared secret they might have between them. Shutmeyer nudged him and then suddenly it was contagious and he got caught up in the laughing fit. It took him by surprise and when it had abated after a few minutes, Vanessa Shutmeyer appeared in the doorway.

"Hey girl," said Gaston.

"What are you silly boys up to."

"Nuttin," said Shutmeyer, holding his head in his hands and still shaking with laughter.

Gerry took a swig of the beer and thought about standing up to get going, realizing with a dull panic that he had a room full of people to get through. He hoped the D'Antonios might have moved on, did they know what he was up to out here? He left his beer just shy of empty and stood himself up to shake hands all around, thanking Gaston, who again had a fish for a handshake.

"Hey Gerry," said Vanessa, "didn't know you were here."

"Me neither. I-I mean…"

This brought a peal of laughter from the table and Gerry shuffled his feet and got real shifty-eyed. Glancing over Vanessa's shoulder he spied Marion, now standing between Elise and Sugar Gaston in the living room. Things were already awkward and he hadn't even said anything to *them* yet. He joined, disingenuously, in the laughter– what else was there to do.

"It was nice to see everybody," he said, still shaking his head. "When you going to join us on the course?" he asked Shutmeyer.

"Soon's my daughter brings my clubs down here from up north. Next month."

Gerry drew his chair for Vanessa to sit and said, "Great, see ya'll soon."

"Bye Gerry," called Gaston. "Thanks so much for stopping by. Anytime, eh?"

He waved and turned to enter the living room. The three ladies were looking long and hard at a painting hanging just by the staircase. Marion turned and Gerry froze for a moment, captivated by her soft brown eyes. It was as if he hadn't till then let his glance linger long enough to fully appreciate them.

"Good evening, Monsieur Hah-go-den."

"Hello Mademoiselle Brooks."

This drew a soft laugh. "No," she said, "is Mademoiselle *Legrand*. Brooks is Mimi."

So now every time he opened his mouth, it seemed only foolish and empty-headed things came out of it. "Sorry," he said.

"Oh is easy mistake, don't worry. How is Shirley?"

"She's okay. I was just out for a walk…"

He paused, here he was explaining himself once again, it seemed to be his imperative since he walked in the door.

"Oh,"– Marion took his elbow– "would you like… to go home… join us? We leave veree soon."

"Oh that's alright, thank you. I could use the exercise."

Gerry started to say goodbye to the other ladies, but they seemed engrossed in the painting and he didn't hang around to find out why. The painting disturbed him for some reason and he couldn't put his finger on it. It didn't portray a monster, or a demon– it wasn't heavily laden with dark colors, or anything like that. He looked at it and he didn't understand it, and he began to think that perhaps this painting might not understand *him*, the mystery that was Gerry Hagoden, and then he was sure beyond a doubt he was very high on that stuff and needed to get out, move around and get some fresh air pronto. He gently shook Marion's warm delicate hand. He shot a sideways glance at the screened-in porch where he came in earlier. Tommy D'Antonio was still there and he sounded pretty well drunk. He was joined by not only his wife, but Flora Wheeler and her great great-granddaughter. He turned and left by the front door to avoid another faux pas.

Once outside he took a deep gulp of the cool crisp air and suddenly a feeling of calm enveloped him. Things were going to be alright, there was nothing anyone could hold against him, complete darkness descended. There were less streetlights here in The Timberlands. He'd let his feet guide him home.

*

Flora Wheeler had put money matters out of her head, was light of heart and had by now added the D'Antonios to her guest list. This Tommy fellow was really something else. Are you sure you're not Irish, she kept chiding him, because his eyes had a certain sparkle you just don't very often see, not even in a hundred years. His wife Debbie met his mirth with a lightness of her own–

these people were good spirits, Flora knew, and they said unequivocally that they would be there at five sharp so as not to miss any of the festivities. Things on the patio were wrapping up and once again Vanessa Shutmeyer found herself wishing that her husband didn't drink so much. Sometimes it just went too far, really. Had for years. By the staircase– Sugar, Marion, Elise. That painting. Marion snapped her fingers and whispered something into Sugar's ear and then Sugar's eyes lit up and she nodded and grasped Marion by the shoulders, hugging at her. Elise studied it, still puzzling at whatever sublime meaning was lost on her.

*

By nine o'clock the streets had become pretty well dead. The only thing Gerry met on Sunset Boulevard was an emergency paramedic vehicle, just before he turned off of that main artery. Its sirens were off, but the yellow flashing lights were on– they were taking somebody to the ER, or perhaps to the morgue. He felt his heart begin to race, thinking about his own mortality. The Hagodens were observant Catholics, but Shirley was clearly the more genuinely devoted. Gerry sometimes felt like he just went along for the ride, like he still hadn't quite made up his mind after sixty-seven years. He wasn't sure why. Gerry, she said, questioned too much and needed to go more on faith. There were a lot of thoughts about his mortality lately and he weighed those thoughts after the EMT vehicle passed him, it was as if the flashing lights had somehow triggered them. He was terribly afraid of death and always had been. With each passing year the fear only intensified.

A security jeep slowed up beside him and he shielded his eyes from the beam of a flashlight.

"Everything okay, sir?"

"Everything's just great," said Gerry. "Just walking home."

The jeep rolled along lazily and Gerry, shaking his head after it, continued along the sidewalk. The whole episode seemed to happen in slow motion. The analogous nature of the rows of houses, the predictability of the landscape design had begun to gnaw at him a little bit while his thoughts continued to wander. He started at Sunny Glen Palms and then worked his way back through the years. To General Motors and his climb to middle-management. Further back to the plant and his locker and his employee number, and all those numbers he'd had to memorize over the years. To St. Bart High School and its antiseptically clean hallways, frigid nuns and the priests, the rigid rules and standards he'd been obliged to live by. Back to grammar school and lockers and numbers. Every time he'd come up for air it seemed like something pulled him back down under that sea of responsibility, with the rest of those who remained anchored under it. Now here he was at 1168 Tammany Drive, just another house among many identical ones. Here he was walking in the freedom of retirement years and his days were numbered. Here he was in a cleverly developed community designed ultimately for profit.

There was beauty in the simplest things– like the velvety green grass all around that began to glisten in the moonlight as the sprinkler systems turned on and hissed and whipped water around. There were those tall palms, there was climbing ivy and bougainvillea, there were neatly groomed bushes and flourishing flowerbeds that held nature's liveliest colors. He glanced all around him as he strode past each indistinguishable house, as if he might miss something important. He heard the soft whine of a golf cart and the beam of its headlights played on the street. The cart came to a stop beside him, the girl eyeing him with a vague curiosity and then Flora Wheeler's voice, diminished but no less sharp. "Want a ride the rest of the way?"

"No thanks," he said. "Nearly there."

They were practically whispering.

"Okay then."

"I like the walk," Gerry said. "It's such a nice night."

"Lovely evening. Walking does a body good. I had a few less years on me," Flora said, "I'd be right there alongside ya."

Gerry nodded and the girl seemed impatient to get going. He waved them on and said he'd see them soon. He hoped he hadn't said anything obtuse, or in a kooky manner.

When he reached 1168 Tammany Drive he stood in front of it at the base of the driveway. He gazed upon the left side of the building and then the adjoining right, 1170. It was ultimately Shirley's guiding light, via her sister Alma and brother-in-law Mike, to sign the papers and assume ownership of this modest home. It was mainly by Shirley's guiding light they'd be attending mass tomorrow. With Alma and Mike.

All at once he was caught in the headlight beams of an approaching car. It was Mimi Brooks' ladies and Gerry watched them turn into her driveway and then the whirr of the automatic garage door opener and the car disappeared into the house. He regarded a sudden and unexpected impulse to knock on their door as drug-induced and frivolous. Instead he returned his attention to the stucco building in front of him, one side of which he owned outright.

A mansion sometimes appeared in his daydreams— a white antebellum house with a sizeable horseshoe driveway, tall Roman columns lining a grand porch that covered the whole front and sides of the house. There were sturdy canvas awnings of the old-fashioned style at every window. There were two chimneys, because there were two ornately tiled fireplaces. There was fine china and silver for frequent guests. There was a long wooden bannister along a winding staircase with hand-carved end caps at the base of the stairs. There were floor to ceiling length windows from which hung heavy velvet and lace curtains. There were three stories and a basement with a wine cellar. There was a long stretch of yard at the back with a hammock strung between elm trees by a little creek and nearby weeping willows. But this was the retirement home of wealthy industrialists, doctors and lawyers and the like. Houses as detached as their owners from the world of payment plans, pyramid structure get-rich-quick marketing schemes, school loans, union dues, hospital bills, attorney fees, credit card interest, and mounting debt that followed one to the grave. Why waste his time even thinking about that house forever bound to an address in his imagination.

4

A cold front swept across the Midwest and then on down into the Gulf Coast and Hillsborough County, where it ran smack into a menacing tropical storm system off the Atlantic. Palm trees yielded to a tempestuous wind and a heavy rain fell down without intermission. For three days the sky remained dark and ominous. Activities were cancelled at both the North and the South Club. The pool at the South Club had the derelict look of abandonment –bereft of suntanners, shuffleboarders, swimmers, volleyballers, bocciballers, paddleballers, gossipers and ordinary loiterers. The streets were as free of golf carts as the golf greens.

By Wednesday morning the storm had exhausted its fury. The sun rose at 7:22 EST, illuminating streets, volleyball courts, tennis courts, paddleball courts, and the pool deck– all of them puddle-riddled. The air held the scent of blacktop– the grass and the shrubs, the flowers and the foliage all dewy and glistening in a soft new glow of sunlight.

When Frank Alsatian opened his eyes from a deep sleep, he immediately noticed the empty twin bed across from his own. *Libby is missing* was his first panicked thought. The digital clock read 8:27 and he rolled over onto his side. Sunlight crept through the blinds and the room had an eerie calm and stillness absent heavy rain lashing at the windows. With an ache of despondence he imagined Pioneer Greens soggy with rain, leaving a round of golf out of the question for days to come.

It was getting tiresome being confined to the house with Libby. She was getting up earlier than Frank and yesterday he had woken up in a similar panic, only to find her in the utility room in front of the washing machine stooping to gather up the laundry. Frank peered over Libby's shoulder and saw at once that she was folding damp and soggy clothes. 'Don't you think you ought to run those in the dryer first' he said, and Libby turned to face him. 'What for? They'll only get wet again.'

Her measured tone had given him pause for thought, she spoke so matter-of-factly that for a moment her words appeared to convey perfect sense.

'Well,' he'd sighed, 'we can at least dry them and wear them first.' He reached around her and began gathering some of the tidy wet pile to plunge them into the dryer. Libby stood still and then she spoke very softly. 'Oh dear. God. Frank, do I fail you? As a housewife.'

'Huh? What on earth?'

'Because I know I forget things.'

Frank continued gathering the soggy clothes mutely.

'I make an awful mess of things.'

'That's alright.' Frank regarded his wife in the manner an archeologist might view a curious artifact. Her hair was unkempt. Her eyes were damp and a little swollen and she wiped at them with the back of her hand. She said, 'I think I'm finally becoming human. I'm taking on human form.'

Frank threw the last of the damp clothes into the dryer, puzzling at his wife's words and not wishing to encourage any further expansion of her haphazard and disconcerting thoughts. Instead he pushed the button on the dryer and the clothes began to tumble dry.

Now, one day after– on this morning– the telephone started ringing, with no evidence of scuttling feet to retrieve it as it rang unanswered into the voicemail. He lay on his back and heaved a sigh at the ceiling. Libby was missing. He willed himself to an upright position and planted his feet on the floor. He couldn't spend the rest of his life chasing after his wife. Libby's bed was unmade, the rumpled sheets suggesting a violent sleep, her pajamas strewn across it. Frank passed the closed bedroom door, making for the master bathroom and switching on the light. He stuck his tongue out at the vanity mirror and thrust a Dixie cup of tap water at his cottonmouth. On his sallow face the whiskers had the sparseness of a comic book character, his beard's rate of growth had slowed to where he needn't shave but every other day. His bladder was overfull and he commenced an interminable piss, a piss of a duration greatly at odds with his growing panic at the evidence of his wife's absence. He finished his business urgently, and then stood stretching and scratching at the seat of his pajamas, hesitating in front of the bedroom door. He placed a tentative hand on the doorknob and pressed his ear to the door. Nothing. When he nudged it open the television was dead and there were no other signs of life. He went into the kitchen. The light on the coffee pot

94

glowed and the pot was half empty. He went into the utility room. No activity, no Libby. Opened the door to the garage. Car. No Libby. He went back through the house and stepped down into the sun porch, scanning the rear of the property and the pond. Nothing. Finding himself oddly devoid of the panic he'd felt just a few days ago on actually locating her there, he poured himself a cup of coffee and brought the television to life. On the Fox News channel a glamorous news anchor ran down the day's top stories. No breaking news, but at the bottom of the screen the terror alert showed code orange and Frank wondered what steps he might take to stay on guard, there had to be some protocol, perhaps a number to report any suspicious activity? He'd heard of something like that. He wondered if there wasn't a number in the Sunny Glen Palms directory to report a missing person, or perhaps someone may have already phoned in concerning his wife's suspicious activity. The world was out of control and steps needed to be taken. He badly wished to hear Libby in the kitchen behind him fixing his breakfast, would that he could rest assured she hadn't wandered away from the premises. There would have to be protocol now regarding his wife and he knew it. He began making a mental checklist as he stared at the television. The car keys would have to be hidden. Was there a gadget to keep one's doors locked from within? He'd have to inquire about that at the hardware store. What hardware store? There was only Walmart. He could ask Gus at the Hobby Lobby if by any chance there remained a single independently owned and operated mom and pop hardware store in the vicinity. He had to start getting a handle on this awful situation. Such thoughts now began to invade his consciousness morning, noon and night.

*

Tom arrived with the bad weather. He rang his mother's number repeatedly, sometimes leaving a message, sometimes not. With each message a marked increase in agitation, a mounting sense of urgency. His appeals were in vain– they ended up with other messages in an auditory dead letter office, like stowaways on a ship without captain or crew. The blinking light on the tiny plastic answering machine went untended. At last with a sense of resignation he rang his brother Steve. He had booked a flight out of a very meager pocket. He'd only ever been to visit Mimi on two occasions and then only briefly. He wouldn't know the first thing to do on touching down in Tampa and he wasn't very good at these things. He drummed his fingers on the Formica table in a dreary one-room efficiency in Cleveland while once again the ring tone droned on and on. He got his brother's recorded voice as he'd come to expect, and despite his best efforts to quell the anxiety in his tone, knew his brother would cop to it even over the phone. Not ten minutes later Steve rang back, sounding even more formal and detached than usual. He'd taken down Elise's cell number, but had somehow misplaced it. He measured his words but didn't mask his annoyance. *Damn it*, he thought, why couldn't his wayward soul of a brother just do the normal thing and get a cab? The tension over the line escalated and it was all they could do to avoid a seething invective between one another.

At the same time, it was with great enthusiasm even a heavy rainfall couldn't dampen that Marion and Elise set about facilitating Mimi's change of venue to the far more agreeable comforts of home. When they pulled the car out of the rain and into the garage, bore her over the threshold and eased her into the recliner, Mimi's eyes sparkled as they took in her familiar surroundings. Not long after they'd settled themselves, the phone began ringing and Elise picked it up and then paced the floor in the kitchen, responding in English to a voice that issued very loudly through the phone. It was so loud that if Marion had more command of the English language, she would have been able to discern the words on the other side of the conversation from where she sat. The voice railed on at a pace that left Elise ruffled and confused by what it said. Enter Tom.

He arrived at the house late that dreary afternoon, tired and bedraggled after a long wait for the shuttle. What appeared before them was a man bearing a likeness to his mother, more so than his brother Steve. His hair was longer than his clean-cut brother's and it hung almost to his shoulders in strands with the straightness of a mop head. He wore thick-lensed glasses that he pushed up at intervals. Behind these an unremarkable set of grey-blue eyes that darted this way and that. An unbuttoned rumpled windbreaker and a button collar shirt couldn't conceal the onset of middle-age paunch. Mimi had told Marion and Elise that her son had recently gone through an extremely tumultuous marriage that had culminated in divorce. It seemed that regular personal hygiene was lost on him– there was dirt under the fingernails, his long hair lay unwashed and uncombed. He was tall and awkward and it was evident his mind was a good ways from peace. He was twenty dollars and a tip shy of settling up with the driver, in a high state of agitation, and the airport shuttle van lingered in the driveway. Mimi fished through her handbag, ferreted out her purse and crushed a twenty into his hand. There were no other bills for the fetching and at last Marion drew a ten-dollar note from her purse and handed it to Tom. He muttered his thanks and then dashed off to the waiting van, whose driver had become a little vexed at the inconvenience and begun laying on the horn. The three ladies remained standing and no one said a word. Tom returned with a single leather bag over his shoulder and Mimi directed him to the only available accommodation, the collapsible futon bed in the den.

And so Tom stepped over the threshold and into their lives with a marked awkwardness. There are those people who move about with a casual grace and an understated presence. Tom Brooks was not one of these. He stood before them and fidgeted, flexing his fingers and shifting his weight from one foot to the other. Mimi and Marion held hands next to each other at the kitchen table. Elise did her best to inform him of his mother's condition while Mimi looked at him, shaking her head and following up each detail with a dismissive comment so as not to worry him. This went on a few minutes. At last Mimi rose and helped him out of his jacket and embraced him, the first gesture of greeting since his arrival. He proffered a hand to his cousin and then his aunt at the kitchen table. He'd been in the house for a full fifteen minutes without so much as a polite word and this smile on introduction appeared closer to a grimace. He shook hands and excused himself to the den to settle his things. Within hours the floor became all but impassable– riddled with socks here, a dog-eared paperback there, all manner of personal effects strewn about the carpet and serving to transform a tidy and comfortable den into an uninviting mess. This was how Tom showed up.

*

Shirley Hagoden loved a good storm. For her, it served to break up the monotony of sunshine. She woke up later than usual, she puttered around the house, buried her nose in mystery paperbacks, straightened out her sock drawer. Gerry, by contrast, grew restless. By day two he'd begun pacing the rooms like a caged lion, much to his wife's chagrin.

"Waddaya got ants in your pants," she said, sipping at her tea and peering over the rim of a Robert Ludlum paperback.

Gerry merely heaved a sigh, shrugged his shoulders and parked himself in front of their personal computer in their quasi office. His hand returned to the mouse and he scrolled down a webpage of boats, recreational motorboats. Boats glorious boats! His current object of desire also served as a bone of contention, a disruption to the relative peace between he and his wife. A few weeks back the boats had hatched an enthusiasm that snowballed into an outright obsession and he spent an inordinate amount of time reading up on them. He was beginning to price them. He began to contact marinas concerning docking arrangements and rates. He decided he simply must have a boat. He was preparing to wrench a significant portion of their retirement savings toward that end. To this his wife Shirley stood in vehement opposition. Gerry gave his sales pitch more than once. The vessel would provide hours of enjoyment, they could show it off and share it with friends– imagine extended cocktail hours, imagine chilling the Chardonnay and watching the sunset out on the water, imagine some extended trips to the Keys and wherever else they might take a notion to go, what a way to get there, at the very least it was an investment that could be sold when they were no longer able to enjoy it, and so on and so forth. At last he'd run out of breath and met the dead silence of his wife. He'd ask her *what's wrong*, and the speed with which she replied *nothing* was inversely proportional to the size and severity of the coming storm. After three days he'd failed to win her over.

The last hard sell was yesterday afternoon and it left him standing by the side door watching the heavy rainfall and wanting let out. Their tempers cooled amidst paltry verbal exchanges. He knew better than to initiate any further discussion on the topic. Now, perched in front of the computer, Gerry hit upon a topic that might smooth out the marital harmony that had been lost in the tempestuous sea of boats.

"Hey, sweetie pie," he said, "I forgot to tell you. We're–"

"*What?* Come in here Gerry. I can't hear a single word you're saying. Honestly," she dropped her paperback and sighed, "nothing like trying to have a conversation shouting from one room to the next."

Gerry jumped up and stood in the doorway to the kitchen area. "*I was saying,*" his voice rang out a tad over conversational level, "we are invited to a party. This Saturday."

"Whose party?"

"Flora Wheeler. She's turning one hundred. Years old."

Shirley dropped the paperback to her lap. "I knew that. I didn't know we were invited."

"Well doll face," he shrugged, "we most certainly are."

"But we haven't got any formal notice."

"Better than that," said Gerry, "the lady asked me herself. In person."

"Where?"

Gerry hesitated, drummed his fingers on the doorframe. He hadn't told her about the party. About the Gastons.

"Well?"

"She ah, she passed by. On the street. On the golf cart. With her granddaughter."

"You mean her great great—"

"Whatever."

For a moment they silently regarded one another in the easy manner which years of mutual existence allows.

The doorbell chimed. They both turned their attention to the open door. Gerry gaped. In the doorway a lady appeared, a lovely portrait with a background of yet dewy grass aglow in the bright new sunlight, her visage ornately framed by the neighbor's bountiful wall of bougainvillea. She wore a floral print dress of the brightest colors with a gold and turquoise shawl draped over thin shoulders, and a headscarf just below which hung matching tiny turquoise earrings on dainty ears. It was Marion Legrand.

"Well," Shirley said, "are you going to let her in or what?"

Gerry sighed, pushed the door open and Marion entered the room with measured steps, there was something careful and uneasy in her manner. Shirley motioned at the sofa opposite her and said, "Come, sit down, please."

"Oh thank you. I don't want bother you."

"Bother? Not at all."

"Mrs. Ha-go-den, I'm sorry, it's we…we."

She was all a flutter, kneading the back of one hand with the other.

"Come," Shirley repeated, leaning forward and tapping the seat of the sofa, "sit down a minute."

"C'mon," said Gerry, "Sit down," smiling broadly as to put her at ease, but she remained standing in front of the sofa.

"My daughter, she cooks today and. We have- no no we *need*. It's *blanc…* white. It's for cooking a *dindon?*" Marion made a broad sweeping gesture then flapped her arms. She said, "This bird we cook, and it flies, it's, it's a—"

"*Turkey!*" –Shirley's voice was loud enough to cause Gerry to grimace– "and it's *flour* you need."

"Oh yes yes, but we are also forgetting"– Marion made a squeezing gesture with her hand.

"The *baster*," Shirley jabbed a finger at the air, mouth agape and nodding wide-eyed as if this were a game of charades. "We've got one. And enough flour to feed an army. Gerry. Third drawer bottom left. Flour in the pantry."

There was clearly something wrong besides the flour and the baster and they could tell. Marion wished she'd had sufficient command of the language to convey it, she was struggling to light upon the words, and Shirley felt obliged to help her locate them and bring them to daylight. She got to her feet and gave Marion's shoulders a brief squeeze, once again patting the sofa cushion. "Now," she said, "how about Mimi? How's she doing?"

Mimi had taken a turn for the worse. Shirley read it immediately in Marion's face, sitting there directly opposite her, fumbling with her hands.

"Is there anything I can do?"

"She– we try our best. She's very… slow, yes? Slow and so quiet."

"Oh God," said Shirley, "I just know she'll come around, maybe it'll just take some time. How's her son?"

"Not so quiet." Marion rolled her eyes, with a telling glance at the floor.

"Oh he's the one got divorced," Shirley directed her words more to Gerry than to Marion– lighting a cigarette and batting a hand at the smoke– "bad run of luck with his job, investments, that sort of thing. He's a piece of work, from the sound of it. If there's anything we can do,"– she reached across and patted Marion on the knee– "will you please not hesitate to ask? There is no order too tall for the Hagodens, right Gerry?"

And then she deemed it best to change the subject for a while. She began to recount their vacation to Europe a few years back and Gerry prayed fervently that she wouldn't send him to fetch photograph albums.

So Marion accepted along with the flour and the baster the invitation to linger, and linger she would. Gerry turned the sound down on the TV and the Today Show. He'd a notion to sit beside Marion on the sofa, then dispelled it and ended up on the chair adjacent his wife and opposite their guest. He drummed his fingers and with a twinge of guilt wished his wife weren't present. Why couldn't she have left for the pool by the time fate brought Marion Legrand to their door? Now what brought *this* on, why could he not curb these odd impulses that demanded a certain containment as the conversational efforts spun like wheels in the mud– he wondered just how much of his wife's words Marion understood, assuaging and laden with comfort as they may have been. In fact about only half of his wife's words reached that woolgathering noggin of his. His thoughts had gone from recreational boats to something more perplexing, this flower basket of emotions he felt at the sight of Marion Legrand. He watched Marion, Marion watched Shirley– when Shirley glanced surreptitiously at her husband he met her glance and then soon returned it to the colorful and exotic guest who graciously bowed her head and made affected smiles at Shirley. Gerry hoped like hell she wouldn't mention the Gastons' party.

Shirley prattled on, a recounting of a very brief and hectic encounter with the city of Paris, and her impression of the city.

"Oh Shirley," said Marion, "we would love it if you come to visit. You stay with us? Paris is– No, no." She couldn't find her words.

"What you mean to say," Shirley said, "is that there's more to France than Paris."

Marion looked perplexed. Indeed without her daughter to translate, the conversation did have the feel of grinding gears. Elise would have been the better candidate for the errand from a practical standpoint but Marion had beaten her to the door and it wasn't merely a matter of enthusiasm for the task or cabin fever or unease at her sister's noticeably slower firing synapses or the chance for a stroll in the sun. First and foremost it was two days of Tom.

"You know," Shirley sighed, tilting her head at her husband, "if it were up to good old money belts here, we'd have a *yacht* to entertain you out on, take your mind off things. He's got it in his head we just have to own one. Course he'll have to get a job first. Waddya think honey? Maybe all that walking around could be put to good use at the Home Depot. You could walk around and help people find things."

Gerry rolled his eyes and frowned at his wife, unfazed to the extent Marion couldn't understand her sarcastic spiel. At the same time he wasn't exactly thrilled at her bringing the issue up in the safety of the compulsory civility that company begs, it seemed gratuitous. It was a cheap shot.

"In the meantime," said Shirley, "we would offer our guest room if it weren't for the fact that, my son, his family? They are visiting us. This week."

"Oh no, thank you. Tom. He leaves today."

"So soon," Shirley said and the room went quiet.

"How long will you stay," asked Gerry at last, fidgeting a little. "Here, I mean."

"Oh," Marion shrugged, "my daughter... she's return, must go back... next week. But I change my... plane. It's more easy I stay than her. More easy I stay, yes. I stay."

Gerry sure hoped his wife saw no trace of that quiver, the way he started ever so slightly at their guest's clumsy words.

*

When Flora had fully awoken, managed to struggle up and go about the house drawing the blinds the girl hadn't yet got up. She hesitated by the guest room door, then turned the knob slowly, cracking the door open just enough to afford a reassuring glance at the girl sound asleep under the blankets.

There were two blinks on the answering machine. The first message was from the Business Office. Could she ring them at her earliest convenience? The second was from the girl's mother.

Nana. Sharon here. Listen, I have a chance to get an earlier flight. Gets into Tampa at seven o'clock tonight. I wanted to see how that sits with you. You can call my cell anytime. Love you, bye bye.

She picked up the cordless and took it to the porch at the back of the house dialing her great-granddaughter Sharon.

"Hello Nana."

"Hi there."

"How's it going?"

"Oh, just getting my coffee going."

"How's Melinda?"

"She's fine. Still asleep at the moment."

"Oh that sounds like my beloved teenager. Always sleeping in late."

"She's sometimes up before me putting the breakfast on."

"Get out. Really?"

"God as my witness."

"How's the weather down there?"

"Well, truth is, been a bunch of rain here lately."

"I saw you got that storm on the news."

"Well, it's bright and sunny now. So you're coming to us tonight."

"Well, I was thinking about it. Waddya think?"

"Well, it's much the same as when you came down last. Just moved to the other side of the tracks so to speak. One of them fancy new homes. I remember you sleeping on the floor at the old place like it was yesterday. Y'was probably around Melinda's age, huh?"

"Oh a little younger."

"That's right, I don't recall you being too mischievous. Least not yet."

She could hear Sharon laugh at the other end. "And how's my little girl behaving?"

"I'd say she's behaving like a lady. A nice young lady."

"Well I'm happy to hear that."

The line got quiet, and Flora heard a marked sigh.

"Nana, does she miss me? I- I mean… does she ever mention me."

"Not particularly."

This met with silence on the other end.

"Now Sharon, don't get your feelings hurt. I only mean she's busy enjoying herself. You know how they are when they're passing from child to grownup. Their nature just isn't very sentimental yet."

"I know. She's having a good time though?"

"I'd have to say yes. She is, honey."

"I just hope I don't intrude on it."

"Well goodness sakes, three'll just be a nice crowd. We can certainly lay the table for one more and deal three hand rummy."

"She's playing cards with you?"

"Oh every now and again. After supper."

"God."

"She's pestering me to play bocci ball. I told her I can't be stoopin over pickin up those balls."

Sharon laughed. "Nana, now don't go throwing your back out. You have to dance at the big party."

"Might throw it out doing that."

"How's the planning going? Maybe I can help you with it."

"Oh," said Flora, "*they* take care of all that. Just don't forget to pack your swimsuit. And sun tan lotion. I don't keep it and I sure keep forgetting to buy it. Memory's not what it used to be. Melinda keeps having to bum it off everybody."

"Nana, I just stepped out of a meeting. I'll see you tonight, I am so happy, so happy."

"Do we need to come and fetch you from the airport?"

"I'm getting the same shuttle we got for Melinda. I'll call you as soon as I land. Are you sure it's not too late. I'm not putting you out?"

"Nonsense. Call us when you land."

She hung up the phone and went to fetch a cup of coffee. She'd have to tell Melinda when she got up. Imparting the news was a disconcerting prospect as the girl was clearly enjoying time and space absent her mother. Flora shook her head and glanced at the kitchen table, now bereft of prescription meds. The girl was contented, seemed to conduct herself much the same as any other teenaged girl. She kept to herself more, but there was no harm in that. Plenty of introverts in the world and she was just another of them. Flora heard sounds of stirring behind the door as she dropped bread into the toaster and began to set butter and jam on the table.

Melinda walked into the kitchen stretching her arms and yawning, saying that the thunderstorm woke her up in the middle of the night. They sat down to breakfast. A good book kept her up long past midnight and for a little while she imparted some of the story to Flora. What did Flora like to read, she asked. Flora replied that for many years the Bible had comprised most of her reading. She liked a good murder mystery, she read biographies of people she found interesting.

"I think you're way interesting, Nana."

"In what way."

"You're so mellow. Nothing gets to you."

"Bah. I'm just tired. And *re*tired. There's nothing left to get me but old age. And I'm already pretty well past that one. Now it's just a matter of waiting to die."

"Do you think you'll go to heaven?"

"I don't know. I don't trouble over it much."

"Well. Just don't die before Saturday. That'd pretty much put the kibosh on the party."

Flora slapped at the girl's hand. "Silly."

Melinda fidgeted with the tablecloth. "Do you believe in an afterlife?"

"Well all I know is if I'm gonna go to a higher place, I sure hope I get a new body to carry myself around in," Flora sighed. "All new parts."

"Doesn't it matter to you?"

"Matter to me. Maybe when I was young."

"How about *now*?"

There was a marked urgency in the girl's tone.

"I don't know. It's kind of a wait and see, isn't it?"

Melinda nodded ruefully and said, "Sometimes I want to end it all. Right now."

"Oh hush. Don't talk such nonsense."

"I mean, when I see the lives my mom and dad lead, how wretched. All they ever do is work like crazy and they still worry about money. It's all they ever talk about. They steer every topic of conversation to money."

"Well. Your life might just turn out different. If it bothers you so much I don't see why it wouldn't. But money does matter sweetheart, trust me. Money matters."

"But then," Melinda continued, "I see some of the beauty in the world. I see the people who set about trying to capture it, see inside it, live in it. And then I don't want to die."

"Pshaw. Such talk. Put them dyin thoughts out of your worrisome little head young lady. They'll only stop you livin."

Melinda thought about this for a while. She drummed her fingers on the table. "I haven't even fallen in love yet."

"There you see?" Flora nodded resolutely, pushing herself upright to begin clearing the table. "Now that's somethin' to look forward to I guess.. Oh by the way," she called over her shoulder as she shuffled toward the sink, "your mom's comin' a day early."

"As in when?"

"Tonight."

"What?"

Flora heard the scuffle of the chair and in an instant the girl was hugging at her, arms around her bony shoulders and head pressed to her back. "Please say it isn't so."

"Now pull yourself together. Surely it's not as bad's all that."

"But I like it how it is Nana. Now."

"Well. Your mother and I have a whole lot of catching up to do. You can go off meantime and do your little things."

"You won't tell her about the meds, will you? I mean my not taking them and all."

"I don't see as why I shouldn't."

"No. Please, Nana. Not right now. She'll have a cow. I-I'll tell her when I get back."

When she gets back, thought Flora. She hadn't given a lot of thought lately to the relatively brief duration of the girl's visit. *When I get back.* The words made a painful stab at her spirits. She was beginning to get used to having someone around. There was an unspeakable void that she somehow hadn't noticed, a vague emptiness in her day-to-day existence before Melinda arrived and the girl's presence had simultaneously drawn attention to it and filled it.

"Well, how d'you expect to keep it from her?"

"I'll just palm them. We can even leave the bottles on the dresser. She doesn't *watch* me take them."

"Well. That sounds logical enough. We'll make the best of things."

"Now I've got anxiety. Big time."

"Well don't get yourself all worked up young lady. These things usually turn out better than you expect. Look at the bright side. Now you've got a bocci ball partner."

"Nana. You want to read Outer Dark. I think you'd like it. It's all about the Depression and Appalachia, you know, and this girl gets pregnant and has to run away and then she finds out her brother–"

"Well now don't go spoiling the story."

"Okay."

"Leave it on my dresser. I only ever read in bed."

After Melinda had packed her things into a beach bag and stepped out the door into the bright sunshine, Flora ruminated over that second phone call. The Business Office.

*

When Frank saw Gerry Hagoden on the other side of the street he shrank away but it was too late to avoid the inevitable encounter. He felt a little conspicuous– Frank never went for walks and now here he was trundling along the sidewalk.

"Hey there," Hagoden lumbered across the street, failing to look both ways. "Nice weather's back."

"No golf yet," was all Frank Alsatian could manage to grunt in response, and when Gerry was beside him he glanced around furtively and muttered, "Libby's gone. I can't find my wife."

Frank looked beyond Gerry's shoulder as if attempting to discern something in the distance. Gerry wanted to tell him about the boats, he just had to tell somebody all about the boats. He'd shelve it for now.

"Uh oh. Where did you see her last?"

"At the *house*," whispered Frank with some irritation.

"Well," said Gerry, "when?"

"This morning. Or, or last night. I don't know. I got up and she was gone."

"Maybe she just got restless."

"She's always restless."

"Maybe it's the weather."

"Yeah right. The weather. Look, I better get on the job."

"Did you call the office or anything? I mean like the guard gate, security?"

"No, not yet. Thought I'd look around a little first."

"Well, let me help you."

Gerry put a hand on Frank's shoulder and Frank recoiled a little.

"That's okay."

Gerry threw his hands in his pockets and began to rock back and forth on his heels. "No, really. I mean it Frank. Let me help you find Libby."

"Well. What do you suggest?"

"We divide into teams—"

"Teams. Teams of one."

"Whatever. Best to stay on foot, you cover more ground, you hit more nooks and crannies. How bout you take the South Club and vicinity and I'll head for the North Club and vicinity."

"I was gonna head back and get the golf cart."

"That'll work."

Frank dug his hands in his pockets and grunted. He was sleepy, his wife was unaccounted for, and now here he was taking orders from this palooka. He bit his lip. "Okay Gerry. Thanks."

Gerry waved dismissively and headed back to his garage. He hollered into the house, "Honey! Sugarplum! Are you going to the pool? Need the golf cart?" Shirley hollered back yes she would and he saw the bicycle tires needed air. He took the old hand pump from where it hung on the wall and, huffing and puffing, set about inflating both tires. When at last he met up with Frank back in the street Gerry said, "You got my cell number right? You got your cell phone?"

"Yeah. Right here." Frank was getting a little uncomfortable with Hagoden running the show. It was Frank's wife not Gerry's, after all, who'd gone missing.

"Okay," said Gerry, "let's go. I'll let you know at the first sight of her."

Frank shook his head and brought his finger to his lips.

"*Right*," Gerry lowered his voice to a hushed conspiratorial tone, "*gotcha*."

He cycled for the North Club, his head turning one way and then the other, eyes scanning the landscape. He was a man on a mission, he was up to the task, and he aspired to be the one to recover the missing party. He very much wished to ring Frank Alsatian and report the sighting of his wife. He tooled around the neighborhoods near the North Club first. These older sections were the genesis of Sunny Glen Palms over twenty years ago and the modest homes appeared as shanties next to the sleeker more modern structures that comprised his neighborhood. Yet these weatherworn bungalows, with their rusting cast iron rails and plain cushioned chairs that bedecked the simple front porches had more of a tropical look to them. And they had front doors. Still, when he gazed upon them he saw less insulation. He saw paint peeling inside and out. He saw plumbing problems. They were more difficult to sell on the open market.

At last he completed his tour of that end of town and pedaled over to the bike rack just outside the North Club. He dismounted his bicycle and the warm sunshine felt good on his face. He was out wandering again and it felt good to be up to his old tricks. A mission was thrown into the mix, and the gravity of the matter was not lost on him. Frank's wife had disappeared and it was their exclusively shared secret. Except of course, potentially the management of Sunny Glen Palms. He wondered if there might be any compelling reason for property management to expend much energy on the task at hand. Was there anything at stake regarding Windmere Properties in these matters, might there not be any liability implications should she get hurt? He thought probably not. He'd just passed the Lapidary when he glanced a familiar face coming out of the computer center. It was Sugar Gaston. He averted his eyes and turned left. He doubted she would remember him much from the party, considering her level of inebriation. He was on a mission and besides, there was a certain risk at being associated with such people. She called out *hey there* and he turned around expectantly, but she'd addressed someone else entirely. He went about his business.

At the same time, Frank Alsatian was having no luck at running down his wife. He had never seen the South Club pool so overcrowded, and he covered his eyes and scanned the crowd over and over. Just when he thought he was ready to turn from the fence and police the building, another pang of hope would hit him— surely with this many people to draw from, one just had to be Libby Alsatian. He avoided walking the pool deck, fearing he would be too obviously looking for something. At last he trudged back along the garden path and into the South Club. He thought of saying something to the receptionist at the front desk— she'd been employed by Sunny Glen Palms a long time and would remember Libby– it was only a few months back when her regular pool visits ceased. He headed for the desk and the woman was indeed on duty. Frank couldn't recall the name, but he caught the name badge on the pocket of her blouse.

"Hello Doris."

"Well hello there," she greeted him familiarly. "How are you getting along?"

"I'm okay," he said, feigning affability. "Doing fine. Glad the nice weather's back."

"It sure is. Anything I can do for ya?" She was chewing gum and it always appeared as if she enjoyed her job.

"Well, he said, it's… it's my wife."

"Uh-huh."

"Seems she's gone missing."

"What's her name, she leaned forward confidentially."

"It's Elizabeth Alsatian. Libby. I'm Frank."

"Right, Mr. Alsatian. Have you alerted security?"

"No, no. Much too early for that."

"Well, if you don't see her by the end of the day, you for sure should let them know. I'll keep an eye out for ya."

"That's very kind of you. Thank you. Thank you Doris."

"No problem. I'm sure you're worried. But she'll turn up. Believe me, they always do."

"I appreciate that." Frank lingered, drumming his fingers on the reception desk, and then started away.

"Oh, let's make sure we have all of your contact numbers Mr. Alsatian," Doris called to him.

"Oh, sure."

Doris checked his home phone against the directory and wrote down his cell number. He waved, leaving her to chew gum and smile, and turned to commence a complete building search. Frank wondered at Doris and all of the working staff for that matter. They were not people of much means and they would not be venturing to far off exotic places to ride out their golden years. They grew up here and would stay here, Frank mused, in modest homes of wood-paneling and the scent of nicotine, buying cheap beer on subsistence incomes amidst their families and their family troubles, ever vigilant for the next job loss, jail time, or whatever other shady stuff people of that sort of class got up to. He combed the entire premises from the computer lab on the second floor to the auditorium, the indoor pool, the weight room, the yoga room, the auxiliary rooms, with each perusal that pang of hope tweaked and then deflated just as fast. He looked under every nook and cranny and still there was no trace of Libby.

*

They were getting ready to take Tom to the airport when it happened. Elise heard a thump from the bedroom and knocked rapid fire on the door. When there was no answer, she tried the handle and the door opened and there was Mimi half dressed and sprawled out on the floor. Elise rushed to crouch at her side. She patted and stroked Mimi's arms and her back, trying to coax her to consciousness. She called to her mother get me a towel, run it underwater. "Get me a cold and wet towel, quick!"

She felt Mimi's wrist and it had a pulse and she sat on the floor and raised Mimi's head to her lap and took the towel from Marion as Tom stood in the doorway and said what's wrong what happened oh God is she alright? Mimi's eyes fluttered awake and she tried to raise herself, but Elise held her back and said *attendre, attendre wait, wait.* Marion returned with a glass of water. Elise said maybe get something sweet and Tom produced a crumpled candy bar from his pack. "Is she alright, are you okay mom?"

Mimi smiled and said, "I-I don't know what happened, the blood rushed to my head, and I just–"

"Ssshh." Marion knelt on the floor, placing a glass of water to Mimi's lips while Elise cupped her auntie's head in her hands.

Marion addressed her daughter in their native tongue. "Do you suppose it's the medication? Perhaps the newness of it."

"I don't know, mama, I don't know. But surely we should call the doctor. The doctors."

There was now in addition to the heart specialist, a doctor of internal medicine treating the pneumonia.

"I knew it was a bad idea for her to go to the airport."

"She wanted to so badly mama. We just couldn't refuse."

"I just hated her having been cooped up. For so long."

"Well. What do we do?"

Marion heaved a sigh and gave Mimi another sip of water. "Take him to the airport. I'll stay with her and call the doctors."

"No. You won't understand them completely. I have their numbers in my phone. I'll call them on the way to the airport."

"I'll start the turkey going as soon as I can."

"You'll be alright?"

"Yes. Of course."

"How about the Hagodens? You want me to call them?"

"You just make sure you get him to the airport. I'm okay."

Elise cast her a doubtful glance.

"Really," said Marion. "Just help me get her changed and back into bed."

Tom kept pacing about the room while the ladies went about situating Mimi in the bed, Mimi propped up on pillows and reassuring them that she was alright, the bed had served to break her fall, no her hip didn't hurt, she was alright, she didn't know what happened but maybe she just needed to put her feet up. As Elise was about to pull out of the garage, she glimpsed someone in the driveway. Elise got out of the car and approached a hardy old lady dressed rather warmly, considering the temperature, in a wool sweater and wool knit hat. She had a large bag slung over her shoulder. She said, "I'm Louise Boardman from next door. Sorry I wasn't here to let you in last week."

Elise could sense that Tom was getting anxious about the time, and she quickly directed Louise to the house and got back behind the wheel so as not to cause Tom to miss his flight. She certainly didn't want that– she'd simply had enough, they'd all had enough of Tom.

Louise called out after she'd opened the door and Marion peeked in the living room and beckoned her into the bedroom. Louise had baked a pie and so first she leaned against the kitchen counter, withdrew it from her bag and plunked it down. Marion immediately liked Louise. Louise arrived literally on the heels of Tom and couldn't have been more diametrically opposed to him in character. Her walk and manner was brusque and efficient and she removed her coat, draped it across one of the kitchen chairs and said, "Well, let's see the little lady."

Mimi brightened at Louise's presence, and Louise told her don't get up, don't get up dear, and gave her a hug. Patted her on the shoulder and pecked her on the cheek, chucked her under the chin and said, "I bet you're glad to be home." Louise didn't stay long, but said she'd be back later. Marion implored her to have turkey dinner with them but she said she had leftovers to finish and would come by after supper. She left with the same haste as she'd arrived, leaving Marion and Mimi in each other's exclusive company for the first time since they were little girls who shared a bedroom. No husbands, children, or anyone else present. Marion was worried and Mimi could tell.

"I'm so glad you're here," Mimi said to Marion in French. "I wasn't sure you would make it in time."

"Sssh, don't be silly. In time?"

"Don't say anything to Elise. Please. Don't say anything to anybody. I feel like my days are numbered."

"No no. Don't say that."

"I wouldn't. If I didn't feel it so strongly. I would not have asked you to come."

"We will make you think different. We'll help restore you to health."

But Mimi shook her head determinedly, gazing intently into Marion's eyes. "Sister. I feel it. I know it."

"But–"

"I believe the doctor knows it too. But when she saw you had come… she would not have released me back home if you weren't here."

"What is it. What's wrong?"

"It's my heart. I've been on blood pressure medication for years. But lately it doesn't seem to help at all. And I keep having dreams."

"What kind of dreams?"

"About death. About dying."

"Oh sister," Marion stroked Mimi's hair, "I remember you having dreams, nightmares. Waking up in the middle of the night, in a sweat, panting, all out of breath. Do you remember?"

"I remember I'd wake you up. You'd climb into the bed and stay with me until I got myself back to sleep."

"That's right. And I'll do it again all the same," Marion took Mimi's hand in her own. "As many times as I must."

"Sweet sister, how those years went so fast. They went too fast."

"You're not going to die."

But Mimi shook her head.

"You're not going to die," Marion repeated, "that's not how it's supposed to happen. That's not how it goes, little sister. It's me first."

"Well," whispered Mimi, squeezing her sister's arm, "you better get a jump on me then."

Marion cried.

Mimi, with delicate fingers, swabbed at her elder sister's tears, said, "Don't leave me. You're the only family I've got."

*

Frank ran into Shirley Hagoden in the parking lot of the South Club. She was climbing out of the golf cart, negotiating her beach bag and her giant multi-colored pool noodles with some difficulty. "You haven't seen that husband of mine anywhere, have you?"

Frank shook his head. "Uh uh."

"Well, how's Libby getting along?"

"Oh she's okay," said Frank. "She's resting."

"Seems to do a lot of that these days. Everything okay?"

"Sure," said Frank, "sure. Everything's just fine."

Everything's *just fine*, he repeated acerbically when Shirley was out of earshot. He hopped into his golf cart and then clicked Gerry Hagoden's name in the cell while he steered the cart out of the South Club lot.

"Hello."

"You got anything?"

"Nothing," Gerry sighed. "No leads."

"Shit. Shit shit shit."

"Yeah, I know."

"Your wife's looking for you."

"My wife's always looking for me."

The line was quiet and then Gerry spoke. "Did you tell her anything?"

"No. I played dumb."

"Okay. Tell you what. I'm gonna do a once over and then we can convene at fifteen hundred hours back at base camp."

Frank cringed at all this military jargon from a man who hadn't served. "That won't be necessary. I'm going to look around a little more and then head for home."

"What are you going to do?"

"I don't know."

"Waddya mean you don't know?"

"I mean I don't know."

Frank tooled around haphazardly along the grid of roads on the south side, turning his head and looking in every direction. At last he pulled the golf cart into his driveway, got out, stood for a moment in front of his house. He prayed that when he entered she would be there. She would be there and he wouldn't yell, he wouldn't holler one bit, he'd act as if nothing had happened, just crack a beer and sit down, they'd carry on like nothing happened.

But the house was as deserted as he'd left it that morning. The coffee pot was still on and he poured himself a cup. Nothing had been moved, nothing altered in any of the rooms. There was nobody at the back of the house by the pond. Why didn't he just let her sit there, maybe that's all it would have taken, just let her sit by the man-made pond underneath the palm trees. Maybe that was the furthest she'd go, maybe that would have been enough room for Libby.

He flopped into the recliner and he didn't even bother to turn on the television. The coffee had gone stale. It was very still, very quiet, very calm in that room. Then he flung the coffee cup hard at the wall, just to the right of the entertainment center that housed the TV. A full cup, and the tiny brown rivulets began to stream down the wall. Frank gazed at their progress to the floor. Then he cupped his face in his hands and he howled. Once he started he couldn't stop himself. *"Pull yourself together,"* he shouted at himself, *"pull yourself together Alsatian!"*

When at last he'd exhausted himself, he kicked the foot-rest open and reclined fully so as to be able to stare at the ceiling. All he could think was how could she do this to me, I worked hard all my life, I served my country in Korea, I raised a family, supported my wife and kids, and all I wanted was a little rest on the way out of this life and now this, I'm playing the parent again. I can't even golf without it nagging at the back of my mind, I'm going to have to do something.

Frank never thought he'd make it through boot camp. It wasn't so much physical as psychological. Up until that point he'd thought the hazing inflicted upon him by his fraternity brothers at University of Maryland was the worst trauma he'd ever be subjected to. Boot camp beat that by more than a hair. How he hated boot camp. He thought of escaping, quitting, finding a way to get a discharge, honorable or dishonorable. But at last he'd left boot camp in California and gone to Korea a Marine. It was late in the conflict and he saw one firefight. It was dark and he was moving through the bush and the bullets whizzed by his head and one nicked him in the arm. The combat lasted almost a full hour. It was the scariest hour he'd endured in his entire life and the closest he'd come to dying. He saw his short life pass in front of him. None of the corporate nightmares that would plague him through his subsequent working life could beat that one single hour for its singular intensity of fear. And there were a lot of corporate nightmares, a lot of sickening power plays, he'd had his share of boardroom tension, survived more than a few rounds of layoffs towards the end of a long career as a project manager for Westinghouse Electric Defense Division. He'd suffered many a long day and night straining like hell to meet a deadline, he'd suffered the wrath of his superiors, he'd suffered the cockiness of younger up-and-comers gunning for his job. He'd suffered from colitis, had ulcer after ulcer, and started at anxiety meds when they came into vogue. In short, he'd suffered. And now here he was once again. Suffering.

*

Elise couldn't drive fast enough. Her urgency had Tom a little on edge and there was an economy of words between them on their way to the airport. Some awkward silences between his phoning in messages to the doctors' call center with her cell. Elise preferred this sort of tensity to the other option, which would be suffering yet another of Tom's extended and too-often pointless monologues. Her ears had suffered enough. His stories were unabridged, and he had a nagging tendency when he was prattling on about something and came to a point where he'd forgotten a name or a place to pause, snap his fingers, tap his forehead and then agonize over a detail that was entirely inconsequential to the story. It was a good thing he hadn't tried journalism, she thought, an editor would certainly have their work cut out for them.

Two long days of long-winded Tom. His own drought in money and wealth made him no less preoccupied with the matter. Over two days of darkness and rumbling thunder they received a full account of how his mutual funds took a nosedive in October of '97, how all it took was a few bad investments to plague him the way pain rides the arthritic, how his marriage suffered as a consequence, how his wife had sought various methods for balancing and peace as she called it. Meditation, yoga, new age gurus, Native American spirituality, sweat lodges. These little stabs at happiness only served to draw her away from him, her soul-searching cast her adrift from Tom's world. To Elise it seemed improbable he could ever have been married, from all appearances a wife would have been consigned a handful of eccentricities. She got the sense he'd placed great stock in things of tangible value which held nonetheless only the most banal essence, he'd somehow got lost in the most superficial objects of desire, and when his house of cards fell, he had nothing much to fall back on. He had no interests to speak of. He hadn't even the most inane hobby. After two days Elise was unable to contain herself from that which she least abided in others, that which she herself was very unaccustomed to– the casting of judgment on another's person. But Tom was a teddy bear who'd lost his way in the nursery and none of his troubles and his own soul-searching could drive away the loving and tender assuages, the worry, the encouragement of his mother. Elise looked on incredulously as Mimi wrote him a check, stuffed it in an envelope and carefully planted it in his bag this morning when he wasn't looking.

Elise pulled up at Departures and dropped Tom off at the curbside. He said thanks and she knew the gratitude was meant exclusively for the ride. He was nearsighted in all matters beyond the immediate. He was moody and overbearing. He talked too much, and not enough about his mother's health issues, and yet a troubled conscience shared her relief to be rid of him. However, half the way back to the house on Highway 75, she found herself purged of every last trace of her pointless guilt.

*

Shirley was tooling around on the golf cart, on her way back from the pool. The Hagodens' golf cart was a cute little piece of work, customized in true Motor City fashion. It had a glittery finish, shark fin taillights in the back, a mini faux Cadillac hood in front. It had a combination AM/FM radio and CD player built in to the faux wood dashboard panel. Gerry used it exclusively for the golf course. Otherwise Shirley took it at every opportunity for which the car was unnecessary, to her mind the use of the car was becoming redundant. She even chose the tricked-out cart for long jaunts down Sunset Boulevard to the Winn Dixie, and to the fresh catch fish stand near the very end of Coral Beach Boulevard. She called it her little fun machine. She washed it, she waxed it. She repeatedly charged the battery. It was Shirley's little fun machine.

Mimi's garage door was open and the car was gone and Shirley thought she'd just go and have a look, because the dark cloud over Marion's face that morning came back to her and she wanted to see if it might have lifted to allow things to brighten up a little.

She parked the golf cart in the driveway, went around the side of the house and rapped on the door. She was chewing gum because she was trying to cut back on the cigarettes. The heavy door behind the storm door gave way and there stood Marion, a smile forming at the sight of Shirley Hagoden.

"Hey Marion," said Shirley, stepping over the threshold and walking past her and into the kitchen. Marion put a finger to her lips and beckoned Shirley to take a seat at the table.

"She rests. Mimi."

"Oh," said Shirley, "maybe I'll come back another time."

"No no," Marion implored and there was a wayward look to her red-rimmed eyes.

Shirley flopped down into a chair. "Is everything alright?"

"Oh Shirley. This morning Mimi, she, she fall. Fall down. In there." Marion pointed at the closed master bedroom door.

"My God. Is she okay? Have you called the doctors?"

"Doctors."

"Her doctors. Have you talked to them."

"Oh, Elise, she does that."

"She taking Mimi's son back to the airport?"

"Yes. Now."

Shirley leaned back and sighed, said oh my God.

Marion fished a Dunhill from the pack and proffered one to Shirley. Shirley immediately removed the gum from her mouth and fidgeted to dispense it.

"Let's we go and… sitting outside," Marion said, "we smoke there."

"Sure thing, it's a lovely day."

Marion went first to check on the turkey in the oven. The sun had already fatigued Shirley, her eyes were getting heavy and she felt a nap coming on. Marion came out with two glasses of iced tea and set one down beside Shirley.

"We don't need, give plants water," she said.

"Everything's blooming real nice," Shirley said, as Marion stooped to light her cigarette. The two sat quietly for a moment while Shirley tried to regain her train of thought. She could think of nothing else to say except call us if you need anything.

Marion nodded and Shirley said, "I mean it. Anything."

They heard the sound of a car approaching and looked up to see it was Elise turning into the driveway. She pulled into the garage, got out of the car and came around the side of the house to them. She smiled and said hello to Shirley, said excuse me and addressed her mother in their native tongue.

"Did the doctors call?"

"No."

"I left messages with both my number and Mimi's."

"Good."

"How is she?"

"She's okay. She's resting."

Elise said sorry Shirley, but Shirley merely exhaled smoke and said it was like music to her ears. Elise translated this to Marion, causing her to laugh a little. Then Elise asked Shirley would the Hagodens like to join them for dinner tonight.

"That'd be wonderful, if I can only find my husband."

"Oh."

"He always seems to go missing."

Elise translated and Marion laughed again while Shirley heaved a sigh, stubbed out her cigarette and shook her head. "The turkey will be done in about an hour," Marion said to Elise, who passed the news on to Shirley.

"What can I bring? Oh, I know. We've got a cherry pie in the fridge. I swear I haven't so much as laid a finger on it."

"Well," said Elise, "don't feel you have to."

Marion said, "Louise... next door... she come tonight."

"Oh wow," said Shirley. "For dinner?"

Marion shook her head.

"She say she had...how to say... left overs? To finish."

"Oh," Shirley waved her hand, "she always says that." She thumped her chest with a thumb, "*I'll* get her over here."

Marion got up to stretch and Shirley thanked her for the cigarette and said, "Are you sure Mimi's up to all this company?"

Marion understood and said, "I think it's the best thing Mademoiselle Hah-go-den."

Shirley loved the ring of that name to her ears and looked at her watch. "Five thirty then?"

And five thirty it was. Gerry had returned just after five, appearing somewhat despondent. "What's wrong with *you*," Shirley had asked him when he walked in the door.

He wanted to keep it a secret, he felt it somehow to be a solemn duty and he knew how guarded Frank had become about Libby– but he looked at his wife getting dressed, his stout little wife, with her flabby waistline as she pulled on a shirt he'd gotten her for Christmas and it seemed they were going out somewhere and he said, "So where are we off to?"

"We've been invited over to Mimi's house for dinner. Ya got twenty minutes, make it snappy."

She regarded him while she fixed a bracelet on her wrist. "What's wrong, what is it Gerry?"

"Shirl," he said, "Libby's disappeared."

"Where to?"

He sighed and sat on the bed. "If I knew that, we wouldn't still be looking."

"We?"

"Me and Frank. And don't tell him I told you."

Shirley sat down next to him on the bed. "Well," she said, "I just knew something was up. Has he called… I don't know, the authorities. The, the police or anything?"

Gerry sighed and shook his head. "No, he wants to give it a little more time. We've been searching all day."

"And?"

"Nothing. We've been combing all of Sunny Glen Palms. All day, honey."

Shirley rubbed at his back and said, "Well that's awful good of my Gerry to kick in and help."

She sighed, mussed Gerry's hair a little. "Waddya suppose he'll do, Ger? When he finds her? I mean, he might have to put her in a, a home or something."

Gerry shrugged, then his face clouded over. "Have we got anything to bring? To dinner? Wine, or..."

"I've got two bottles, a Chardonnay and a Zinfandel. Bring your beer if you want honey."

Mimi's house still had the Christmas decorations out, a mini tree, servers and seasonal trinkets spread about the furniture. Their festive potential had remained dormant, lost on the house's steady stream of inhabitants, until this moment. They sat down to a very sumptuous dinner of turkey and all the trimmings, Shirley Hagoden said the grace and the French ladies did their best to push this morning's episode to the back of their minds. Both of the doctors had returned their calls— the pneumonia doctor said he felt it had nothing to do with the medications and to leave the dosage unaltered, the heart specialist said it was probably just too- much-too-soon and to keep her posted, Mimi should back off the dosage if the dizzy spells continued. Louise was there, from next door, she'd caved under Shirley's coercion and she was glad of it. Gerry passed her the gravy and the mashed potatoes and the cranberry sauce and finally held the plate of turkey and asked did she like white meat or dark? He laid down the tray at last, looked at his plate and asked his wife why don't we do this more, why ought turkey only be for one day of the year?

Shirley merely shrugged, it was a rare occasion his wife didn't have an answer. Elise asked till what time is the library is open, and Shirley said nine o'clock, the whole North Club is open until nine. Ours closes at seven, unless it's Pub night. Gerry sure hoped Elise wouldn't mention the Gastons' party.

"I think I might go and fetch a book later," she said to her mother in French, and just as fast she apologized to the group and Shirley said, "I told ya go on, it's like music to my ears." Gerry Hagoden couldn't agree more with his wife.

*

Flora had lost both an interest and capability for cooking somewhere in her mid-to-late eighties. It was Swanson frozen entrees that sat in front of her and Melinda now. The girl played about with the food in the black plastic tray in front of her. Nana had helped her put her hair up and a few stray wisps hung loosely around her ears— she assumed not just the look of sophistication

121

but the *feel* of sophistication and she'd determined it would be with this look that she'd greet her mother.

"Your momma'll be here by eight o'clock at the latest."

The girl said nothing, stabbing her fork absently at the frozen vegetables.

"You sure are awful quiet tonight."

Melinda nodded solemnly. She said, "I don't know."

"I don't know," Flora echoed and tugged at the girl's elbow.

After she'd helped Flora with the dishes, Melinda said she thought she'd feel better if she could sit in the library for a while. "Well," said Nana, "don't be too long now. And for the love of Pete, drive careful."

It was already pushing seven o'clock. Melinda changed into a long-sleeved shirt and pulled a windbreaker over her head. The temperatures were falling. Darkness was not far away. It was dinnertime and the streets were already quiet. Her enthusiasm was tempered by the thought of her mother's visit. She hoped her mother wouldn't bring her work down with her. She hoped her mother wouldn't try and be too bossy.

Melinda detoured and took Hammermill Drive, and when she came to the Coco Palm Circle cul-de-sac to the right of her, Shirley Hagoden and the French ladies came into view. They sat on lawn chairs smoking cigarettes and chattering. She slowed the cart.

"Hello," Elise called and waved. Melinda drew a wheel up on the grass and stopped the cart.

"Where are you off to little lady," said Shirley.

"The library."

Elise stubbed her cigarette at the ground and wanted to know did Melinda want some company.

"Sure," Melinda patted the seat next to her. "Hop in."

While the two ladies spoke together in French, Shirley said she thought there were age restrictions on golf carts.

"Oh," Melinda said, "I'm seventeen."

Shirley shot her a skeptical glance and said just watch you don't hit any of us old people. Melinda tossed a feigned smile at this and then Elise clambered aboard and they were off. Melinda sat up straight and drove with one hand on the wheel, feeling like a grownup, with her hair pulled up and doing grownup things with her exotic new friend sitting beside her. Melinda didn't wish to speak about her mother and Elise thought it better not to talk about her aunt and so instead they talked about books they'd read and movies they'd seen.

"When I grow up I really want to be a famous actress," said Melinda, "but not a glamorous one. I want to be a serious actress. A serious one." When her friend didn't respond she cast a sidelong glance and repeated for emphasis, "A *real* serious one."

"Well," Elise smiled, gripping the roof and drumming her fingers on it, "I wait to see your first picture. Then I can say I knew you when."

They both laughed a little, the night was clear and bright and suddenly Melinda's head was full of ideas. It would not be very long before she could drive a car and drive as far away from Manayunk and Philadelphia as she wished. She would drive the car across the country and she would have a boyfriend, and he'd never talk back to her and they'd go to the Grand Canyon and watch the sunset arm in arm without a word between them. Then they'd head off blissfully for the state of California and the world would be her oyster, and she'd keep a cool professional distance from her mother but send her money regularly to take the heat off. Her mother wouldn't have to work and would be forever indebted to her famous daughter. It would be Melinda who'd wield the power but she wouldn't let it go to her head, wouldn't let it get the better part of her good nature. She'd invite Amanda Peters to visit her once she got settled, because Amanda was the only girl at school whom she could trust not to try and take advantage of her newly found wealth. Amanda was the only one she cared to be around, outside of her secret crushes on a few of the boys, crushes which never lasted because they were all immature and sooner or later they'd do something silly to lay bare their foolishness, their impishness. She'd be a serious actress and take on only serious film roles.

She turned onto Sunset Boulevard with a new air of confidence and stayed to the right while a few cars passed her on their way out of Sunny Glen Palms. An emergency paramedic vehicle whizzed past, its siren unsounded. When they got to the library they found no one else there, and Melinda gave her friend a very grownup tour of a modest collection Elise reckoned was inherited from those residents who'd expired.

"The books of the dead," she said and this elicited a puzzled look from Melinda. "You mean Tibetan Book of the Dead?"

"No. I mean all these books. They must be donated when people… pass on."

"I never thought of that. Maybe you're right. Well, last but not least," said Melinda, "feast your eyes on a magnificent collection of reference books behind the glass doors of these cabinets, look, a whole collection of Encyclopedia Britannica."

"But they're locked."

Melinda raised a concurring finger. "Right," she said. "You have to come here during the day when there's a librarian on duty to get your hands on those."

"Librarian?"

"Sure, volunteers of course. If I lived here for good, I'd definitely volunteer. I'd volunteer six days a week, maybe seven."

Elise laughed at this. "You'd feel– cooped up, no? Cooped up after just a few days."

"Yeah," said Melinda distractedly, "maybe so."

"Oh look," exclaimed Elise, and pointed to a set of Molier's works. She reached for a volume and began thumbing through the pages, said maybe this is boring for you. Melinda, glancing over Elise's shoulder as she fanned the pages, thought the French playwright would probably fail to hold her interest but didn't let on to Elise. They roamed quietly about the stacks of books for a while. Melinda was enjoying this time with her friend, at the same time dreading the thought of returning to a house with anyone besides her Nana there. Melinda wanted terribly to linger in that roomful of books as long as possible, anything to postpone the inevitable and unavoidable encounter with her mother. She still hadn't mentioned anything of it to her new friend.

Elise heaved a sigh, glancing up at the wall clock behind the librarian's desk in front of the room and yawning.

"Maybe it gets late."

"Just a sec," Melinda called from behind the bookshelves, replacing a pulp fiction paperback she was sure would only serve to disappoint. She retraced her steps and pulled a few volumes from the Moliere collection.

On the way back, on the golf cart, Elise said that she and her mother had planned on visiting the Salvador Dali Museum in St. Pete on the way back from the airport today but something came up and they weren't able to go after all. Would Melinda like to go tomorrow, they would treat her to lunch and then go see the museum exhibits.

Melinda brightened at this, turning to face Elise. "Would I ever!"

"Let me see if it's possible my mother can join us or not. But we go for sure. I want to see it before I go back."

It was mixed feelings that hit Melinda then. There was joy in their special plans and a matching sadness at the mention of her inevitable departure. It was beginning to dawn on Melinda that perhaps people came and went and sometimes you never saw them again. Elise went on about how famous the museum was worldwide and how she admired Dali's work since she was about Melinda's age. Had Melinda heard of the Spanish surrealist?

"A little bit. But I want you to show me. And explain stuff."

"Oh. Well. You will see you don't need so much– so much explanation. It's really something you see through *your* eyes, maybe it has different meanings to different people. It happens like this all the time with my children and me."

Melinda had lost sight of the fact that her new friend had her own children, around *her* age, and Elise's words made her think about her mother. She had left that Philadelphia airport under a certain strain, her mother not sure whether or not she was doing the right thing with *her little girl*. Well, she left there as Mel, but now she had her hair pulled up like a grownup, she was making grownup plans with her grownup friends and she was Melinda Jane Rutherford, and soon she'd have return address labels of her very own, with her very own address.

They started back and Melinda trolled along on the cart once she'd quit Sunset Boulevard, her foot depressing the pedal to half-speed. Darkness had fallen– it had rained yet again while they were in the library and the air had become thick and moist, the streets eerily laden with mist and fog.

"Spooky," said Melinda. "I'll bet the golf courses would feel like the moors in the English countryside."

"Like Wuthering Heights," Elise said.

"Only there's alligators out there you know," said Melinda, her eyes fixed on the road in front of her.

"*Alligators?*"

"Sure. My mom said there were a whole bunch of em here when she was my age. I saw one the first day I got here, sunning itself. Behind Nana's house. Right by the golf course."

"*Really?*"

"Sure. They must've built this place right on their natural habitat."

Melinda was glad of the fact that knowledge was for once being imparted in the opposite direction. She had piqued her new friend's interest. Casting a sideways glance she said, "I hear they attack only if provoked. Or if they're very hungry."

Elise laughed, glancing anxiously at the swampland not too far beyond the houses they passed. "Well, is this why everyone here seems to hide at dinner time?"

Melinda was a left turn away from Mimi Brooks' house, to the left was an entrance to the golf cart pathway for Pioneer Greens. She stopped the cart dead in the middle of the street and turned to Elise.

"You want to take a spin around the golf course?"

"What for?"

"Oh I dunno, just somethin to do. Maybe see an alligator or something."

"You might run into one with all the fog," Elise sighed and said, "I must help my mama do the cleaning up. I get off here."

"Okay."

"Tomorrow we call you when we have plans. Would your Nana like to come with us?"

"Oh no," Melinda said immediately. "I don't think she'd be up to it. I don't think that sort of thing would interest her much, anyway."

Melinda pulled the cart into the driveway. Elise took a golf score pencil and scrawled Melinda's cell number on the flap of a book jacket.

"You can tell me all about the alligators you meet. In the morning."

Melinda brought the cart to a halt at the entrance of the forbidden path into the golf course and sat there, hesitating, watching the mist drift along the wide landscape the path opened on to. She thought– *to go or not to go, that is the question.*

Her foot answered the question and the golf cart trolled along the pathway, with a seeming hesitance of its own, into the thickening fog. Soon Melinda was enveloped in the heavy mist surrounding her on all sides. The beam from the cart's headlamps could not pierce very far into the thickness but could pick up the path. Melinda trundled along into the wisps and swirls of smoky mist with a mounting anxiety. Fear was a strange thing, and it seemed to her that she was testing herself, how far she might go before it immobilized her, until it got to the point where she sat frozen in fear and unable to move a muscle. Was there such a point of paralysis, she wondered. What was it propelled her along into nowhere, did she hope to disappear never to be seen again, come out the other end of Pioneer Greens from an alternate reality, older and wiser and perhaps more beautiful, a woman of independent means? There was a break in the mist and she could barely discern the shape of a footbridge up ahead in the distance and she drove on towards it. A wispy gauze of condensation blanketed the bridge, the soft ripple of the creek waters an eerie intrusion upon the silence. She hesitated there in front of the bridge that loomed before her, tiny and insignificant in the light of day but an imposing and mysterious landmark in the dead of night. It took a long time for her to gather her wits.

She forged ahead, wondering if the golf cart could outrun a hungry alligator. Twenty-five miles per hour top speed. She'd heard alligators could hit thirty miles per hour on the run, could that possibly be true? She wondered about this and decided it was best to turn back as soon as an opportunity presented itself.

Then she saw it– a figure appearing out of the ominous mist on the path in front of her. It seemed to stumble and stagger along with erratic movements. She stopped the cart. Then the girl jammed the gearshift into reverse and the cart began to lurch haphazardly, she turned the wheel this way and that and next thing she was off of the path with the rear wheels spinning in the wet grass, she was afraid she'd ditched it and she got out to run as fast as her skinny little legs would carry her, but the apparition was right up near her now and she saw it was a lady. The lady had black hair peppered with gray, it was as mussed and disheveled as the rest of her, she was mumbling and staring at Melinda with a nonchalance that did nothing to curtail the girl's mounting panic, nothing to stop her *freaking out*. Melinda thought to run, but it was just like one of those bad dreams with your legs unresponsive, the nervous system somehow temporarily disabled.

Melinda screamed.

That got no reaction from the woman– she spoke calmly and evenly. She said, "I'm lost."

Melinda hesitated. She looked from the golf cart back to the stranger.

"Lost?"

"Yes."

"Waddya mean. How?"

"I-I don't know. I went for a walk. Out here. A long time ago I think."

"Are- are you a ghost?"

The woman looked at the ground and laughed lightly as if at some private joke. "It's beautiful," she said. "Out here. I've been here all day."

"All day? Doing what?"

"Just admiring. Everything."

Melinda regarded this strange creature in front of her. *Admiring. Everything.*

"Well," she gulped, "it sure is creepy here at night. Tonight, anyway."

"I feel as if I'm taking on human form."

"You an alien or something?"

"Oh *no*..." The woman seemed to be taxing herself to ferret out a thought from some profound and arcane awareness, that's what it looked like to Melinda, as if this new-found creature had some inner dialogue going on as she regarded the outside world through wary eyes.

"No," she continued, "let's just say a... a spectator? All my life, a spectator, an onlooker an–"

"Look here," said Melinda, forcing a bravado as a means to curtail some of the mounting fear at the encounter of this strange woman and her odd words, "what's got you wandering around a golf course? I mean it's like, the middle of the night. Where do you belong?"

To this the woman laughed delicately and for a moment Melinda glimpsed a woman of refinement and grace– her visage suggested Jackie Kennedy to the girl. Then that calm serenity left the woman's face, once again she became serious and absorbed, chasing after thoughts. She cast furtive glances in every direction, sighed, and whispered, "I belong here. I guess I belong here."

"My name is Melinda Jane Rutherford. What's yours?"

"My name," said the woman, "is Mary Elizabeth Warren Alsatian. For some reason they call me Libby."

5

Breakfast at Flora Wheeler's turned out to be a pretty solemn affair. Flora glanced from Melinda to Sharon and said, Well I guess the cat's got everybody's tongue. When they did get around to talking, it was only to bicker about whether the girl was allowed to go off for the day to the Dali Museum with strangers after what had happened last night. 'Stop treating me like a child,' Melinda hollered. 'You are in my care and supervision until you reach the age of consent. Eighteen. Got that young lady,' Sharon hollered back. Flora camped out in her bedroom, hesitant to move until the storm showed signs of abating. It wasn't as if she hadn't witnessed such scenes in her day, it had just been a while and they never did get to sounding any better. She listened to Sharon berate Melinda on the other side of the door. 'You scared the bejesus out of your Nana, and she doesn't need this kind of excitement at her age.'

Because how it turned out last night was like this. Melinda had ended up tooling around on the golf cart with the woman from the mist way longer than she'd anticipated. The woman was uncertain about her address. One sedate street after another, the golf cart hummed through the neighborhood until at last her eyes lit up at the sight of Tammany Drive, but they were all the way at the other end of it and the woman kept giving false alarms, *here it is! No, no that's not it.* Each house was as indistinguishable as the next. Melinda had an inkling the circumstances might beg some adult intervention, so they ended up at the Coco Palm Circle cul-de-sac. She pulled up half on the grass half on the street, told her confused passenger to stay put and went up to ring Mimi Brooks' doorbell. Elise appeared in the doorway and Melinda pointed at the golf cart and said we got a missing person on our hands. Elise fetched her coat and followed Melinda to interview the stranger, who remained bolt upright and shivering in the cart. When Libby announced her name, Elise looked at Melinda. 'I know where this woman belongs, she said. I know where she goes.'

It was well after nine o'clock by the time they'd brought her to the house with the lawn plaque bearing the names Frank and Elizabeth Alsatian. Melinda thought, oh my God how did I miss that. When Elise walked back from the Alsatian house to the cart she said it looked as if Libby's husband had been crying because his eyes were a little red, a little puffy. 'Poor guy,' said Melinda. It seemed to her a precarious domestic situation and she shivered a little after she'd dropped Elise off at Mimi's for the second time that evening. But it would pale in comparison to the scene that lay in store for her at Nana's house.

'Where on earth have you been,' came her mother's only greeting words no sooner than she climbed out of the golf cart. 'You had both of us half scared to death. Your poor old Nana, she's beside herself.'

Melinda trudged into the house solemnly, her head down. All at once she felt like a little girl– just like a little girl– all over again. When she got in the house she camped in the bathroom. For a long time she stared in the mirror at her own reflection. Even with her hair pulled up all rigid and ladylike, all she could see was a little girl with freckles. She sat on the edge of the tub a good while with her head in her hands. When she finally emerged from the bathroom, her mother had already turned in and she fumbled around in the darkness of the guest room. She lay awake most of the night and she could hear her mother on the twin bed across from hers in a sound sleep. She couldn't turn on the light to read away her insomnia, like she'd grown accustomed to do. Instead she kicked her leg against the mattress and willed herself to be anywhere else.

*

When the French woman brought Libby back, Frank had just hung up the phone with the Hillsborough County Sheriff's department. He'd asked Elise to hold on there, just a sec, while he phoned the police and said disregard, wife just turned up. 'I can't thank you enough, can't thank you enough,' he said to Elise, gathering his shivering wife in his arms. Libby let him pull her to him, her head in her hands, saying 'I'm sorry, I'm sorry honey.'

Neither he nor Elise knew of anything else to say, Elise just nodded her head and neither stepped beyond the threshold nor lingered around. Once again thanking her profusely, he shut the door. He'd taken his wife's hand and led her towards the bedroom. He sat her on the bed, and for a moment he wanted to strangle her. He got up and fetched a blanket, wrapped it around her shoulders, and kissed her lightly on the top of her head. He undressed his wife and then dressed her in her warmest flannel pajamas. She was very compliant throughout, she kept mumbling apologies, repeating *I've been bad* over and over like a mantra. He kissed her lightly on the forehead and said, honey you had me worried to death.

He'd slept with one eye open all night. He'd locked the bedroom door knowing full well she could unlock it just as easily. In the middle of the night he'd gotten up to go to the bathroom and afterwards stood watching his wife in a deep sleep. In the morning, when the sun shone through the blinds, he woke from a half-sleep riddled with waking dreams to see she hadn't beaten him out of bed this morning. After they'd both gotten up and dressed and had coffee and breakfast, Frank told Libby they had some shopping to do and would she come with him? He didn't want to waste a minute getting those doorknobs, the ones Gerry Hagoden told him about. The ones that could lock a door from both sides.

*

Mimi Brooks had turned in early the previous night, right after Elise got back, the first time, and they'd done the washing up. Both Elise and Marion were early risers, and this morning the sunshine was a welcome sight. They'd had their coffee quietly on the sun porch, closing the sliding glass doors so as not to disturb Mimi. Marion endured an ongoing battle to interpret the Tampa Tribune, rising every now and again to press an ear to the door of Mimi's bedroom. It was nearly ten o'clock and she still hadn't turned out. Marion told Elise she thought her sister had looked a little pale last night. Marion had an eye for these things. Elise could sense her mother's mounting anxiety.

"Something's wrong," Marion said. "I think I will knock on the door."

Elise followed her mother and to their great relief a feeble voice answered Marion's knock. Elise returned to the back porch and not long after her aunt was up and shifting about, languidly approaching the glass doors, with Marion just behind her. As Elise folded her book and started to get up, Mimi cracked the door and said *bonjour*.

"How did you sleep, Mimi?"

"I thought I slept well. But I don't feel like it."

Elise rose to put an arm around Mimi. Mimi touched her niece's pajamas, running her fingers along the silk. She said, "now that's fine material."

Marion and Elise each took her by an elbow and settled her into one of the wicker chairs, and then Marion started toward the kitchen. "I'll get your coffee."

Elise said, "The doctor called this morning. She is changing your prescription. She wants you to take it easy."

"I am taking it easy. Look how late I sleep."

After they'd had breakfast in the kitchen and put another pot of coffee on, they cleared the table while Mimi rummaged around in her closet, she had something to show them. Elise got up to lend a hand and she returned to the kitchen bearing a few voluminous photograph albums in her arms, Mimi following close behind. She set them down on the kitchen table in front of Mimi's chair. "Let me get my reading glasses," Mimi said, and went to fish them out from among the cluttered drawers Steve had been cursing in the laundry room just a few days before. As Mimi sat down, they hovered over her shoulders. "Come," Mimi patted the chair next to her. "This is going to take a while."

Mimi pushed aside a few of the volumes while the ladies pulled their chairs to either side of her. A frail but agile hand, bony and veiny, turned the cover of one of the black leather bound volumes with gold embossed bordering. It opened upon a series of black and white photographs preserved by a protective plastic covering. Marion had not seen the old photographs for almost seventy years, so they were almost as fresh to her eyes as to those of her daughter. There were many photographs their father had taken with a camera she recalled had fascinated him to distraction. He owned a second, just to take apart and piece back together. This enabled him to glimpse the attributes of the mechanism by which this miracle machine served to capture a moment in time. There were baby pictures of the pig-tailed young girls posing with their older brother in front of a livestock barn, cows behind them bicuspid-chewing on straw. They had only a little over a year between them, Marion the elder, but you couldn't see it. In another one they stood in front of the hearth in crushed velvet dresses, beaming and wide-eyed on Christmas. Then standing beside their aproned mother, helping to clean out the chicken coop. In bathing suits and helmet-like bathing caps, perched in the sandy dunes of the beaches of Biarritz. The array of photos continued through their teenaged years and ended with Mimi's wedding day at the modest church where her family had been part of the congregation throughout countless generations. Elise turned a photograph over and the names were scrawled on the back in cursive. *Marion. Miriam.*

When Mimi left Saint Etienne d'Orthe for America, a war bride, she had barely turned seventeen years old, leaving a family which had hardly stepped foot beyond Bordeaux country. To her parents her leave taking was tantamount to waking the dead– for all they knew they might never see her again. Her mother had solemnly turned over the albums to Mimi so that she might take the family with her in the only imaginable manner, so as never to forget the ones she was leaving behind. It was Mimi who was vouchsafed care and custody of the photographic record of their family, their youth.

Elise kept glancing from the photos to her mother and aunt– she'd never seen such an expression on her mother's face in all her years. It was as if she beheld another woman entirely, as if her mother had by some arcane magic conjured up a ghost-self from the distant past. When at last they'd exhausted two volumes, Mimi fetched the third and last– a very tattered red leather-bound volume, this one replete with letters written in Marion's hand, the paper gone brittle with age.

Among these letters were photographs that Marion had enclosed inside of them. Elise recognized her school pictures, but there were others she hadn't seen before. In one of these she lay cradled in her mother's arms, Marion leaning against the trunk of a fig tree. It was a perfectly framed shot on a clear and sunny day, springtime flowers blooming all around them. It was an image that drew their attention immediately and Marion peeled back the plastic and took it out to examine it up close. Mimi looked from one to the other at their interest. "Take it," she said.

"We can scan it mama," Elise said.

"No. Take all of them. They're yours now," said Mimi. She merely shook her head at their protestations. "I've had my whole life to enjoy the pictures, those letters. It's time you both had the same chance."

"We can scan them when I get back," said Elise, massaging her mother's shoulders. Nobody said anything for a good while. Marion had removed her reading glasses, and Elise could see her mother's soft brown eyes were glistening. Marion brought the back of her hand to one eye and then the other.

"Mimi," said Marion at last, "how do you feel about a swim? It has been so long since we took to the water. Together."

"I think," said Mimi, "it would be really something to go to the beach."

"We'll wait a little for that dear sister."

"Well," Elise said, "how about we take Mimi on Sunday? To the beach. If she feels up to it."

They looked at one another and nodded.

For the moment, Marion had her heart set on taking her sister Mimi to the indoor pool for some mild exercise, perhaps sit by the outdoor pool and in the hot tub for a while. Elise, still set on the Dali museum, went to the phone to call the girl and begin to ready herself for their outing.

When the girl answered her phone she was crying. She composed herself, explaining she'd gotten into trouble for their adventures last night.

"Trouble?"

"My mom was angry. She said I made her and my Nana worry. Being late like that."

"You didn't say your mother was here."

"She got here last night."

"Oh but you shouldn't stay angry with her."

"She shouldn't stay mad at me."

It was quiet on the line and then the girl said she thought she wouldn't be able to go to the museum after all. This started a fit of tears on the other end of the line– Elise had no idea what to say. "I'll call you back," the girl said and then the line went dead.

Over at the Wheeler residence, Flora and Sharon sat on the sun porch, the glass doors shut, huddled in a sort of private conference. Flora was doing her level best to assure Sharon that Melinda's companions the evening before were decent enough people, hardly inclined to abscond with her daughter and never return. Sharon had calmed herself down enough to listen to her great-grandmother's take on the matter.

"Honey," Flora was saying, "it'll do the girl a world of good. She's a sensitive creature and I s'pose it'll be like church to her. Go and give her a hug and tell her you're grateful to be here with her, that nothing bad happened last night, which is true after all. She showed up in one piece and she really wasn't that late. Now go in there this instant and do as I say."

To Flora's mild amusement, Sharon looked imploringly at her with a pure innocence not much different from Melinda's. It was, after all, a rare soul that'd take exception or talk back to a little old lady on the brink of her hundredth birthday. She had a certain power in seniority and she was shrewd enough to wield it now. Sharon stood up and Flora harrumphed to herself and said, goodness sakes.

In a little while the house turned quiet. Flora shuffled into the kitchen, she could see Melinda already making preparations in the guest room while Sharon sat at the kitchen table poring over the Tampa Tribune. Flora leaned over her shoulder and inquired in a voice barely above a whisper. "Well, how did it go?"

"As well as can be expected," muttered Sharon, turning a page distractedly.

The girl came out, her pocketbook over her shoulder and kissed her Nana and then very hastily her mother, goodbye.

*

Frank didn't have too much trouble finding doorknobs that could lock on both sides. He had some things to fetch at the Hobby Lobby for the next model airplane project and Gus was there today. Frank kept an eye on Libby in the car he'd parked as close to the storefront as possible while Gus directed him to a neat little hardware store up the highway and over the bridge in Gulfport that just might stock such a fixture.

Frank drove their Ford Explorer right on past the Home Depot. The logistics weren't good for minding Libby and besides they might run into someone they knew there. It was a nice day for a drive over the Bay Bridge and he was in a driving mood. They found Hess Hardware, tucked away on a side street just outside of downtown Gulfport. The man behind the counter had a ruddy face bearing a gray grizzled beard and a pudgy nose riddled with tiny veins. He wore suspenders over a rumpled white dress shirt and a substantial paunch.

"Sure," he said, "we got em. They're called double cylinder doorknobs. Now, they're a bit unusual as they represent a safety hazard in the event of a fire since you'll need a key to exit. Might want to check with your homeowners association or whatever to see whether you're allowed to replace the standard one you got."

"Right," said Frank, "I sure will." He knew full well it was a snowball's chance in hell he'd be running over to Windmere Properties to make sure he wasn't in violation of any building regulations. He bought knobs for the front and side doors and one for the door in the rear, in the sun porch.

Up to this point, Libby hadn't bothered herself about what it was they were actually up to. She brimmed with curiosity as Frank set the bag in the backseat. "What you got there?"

"Oh," Frank measured his words, "some new doorknobs is all. Betty Molnar, you know, Betty Molnar?" he said and waited for Libby's acknowledging glance. "Betty Molnar got these security doorknobs for herself after Joe passed away, you know? She got a little nervous being alone and all. Can't be too careful. Thought we'd get some ourselves."

He knew Libby was considering his words carefully. He was anxious to change the subject and lend some pretext for his having driven all the way over the Bay Bridge to Gulfport. "Hey," he said, "I thought we'd go to the beach today. It's been a while."

"B-but we don't have our suits." Libby furrowed her brow.

"I know. It's too cold to swim anyway honey. Thought we'd just walk around a little. And then I'll take you to lunch."

Libby brightened at this and the matter of the doorknobs, the little errand for which they'd gone so far out of their way was as long forgotten as last week's stock market closing numbers. Frank could count on one hand the number of times they'd availed themselves of the white sands of the Gulf beaches since their retirement had brought them from the Baltimore suburbs to sunny Florida. He wasn't sure exactly why that was. He drove west along an unfamiliar county road he hoped would run him straight to the beaches. Libby sat silently, and that suited him just fine. There had always been long silences in the course of their marriage, and they were comfortable silences; there were many times where there simply wasn't much to say to one another, and neither of them cared to talk just to hear themselves talking. Lately, though, Libby had jumbled that easy silence; she would talk and talk and talk to herself and he was all too often unsure of what she meant. He dismissed a lot of it, holding out hope that he could still present his wife socially without embarrassment, without having to interrupt and talk over her when the eyes of their conversational companions started to glaze over. His hope was misplaced though, and he always knew it once her thoughts got clouded over, when her mind got befuddled, when she simply failed to make one iota of sense. He'd finally begun to believe it was just a phase she'd get beyond.

"We never go to the beach," said Libby, and it was clear to Frank his wife had slid into a lucidity that propelled him into the painful hope which, despite himself, he clung onto with every fiber of his being. His eyes scanned that county road for signs pointing to one of the St. Pete beaches.

"You know, I was just thinking that myself Libby. You're right."

"We should move here."

"We are here."

"No, I mean here. Near the beach. Our own house."

"Well," Frank drummed his fingers on the steering wheel, imagining the challenges of reigning in someone in the early or maybe not-so-early stage of Alzheimer's in an urban environment without strict boundaries. He glanced across the seat at Libby.

"You know," he said, "it's great having all those amenities at Sunny Glen Palms. Don't have to go far to do anything."

"Except get to the beach."

They came to a stoplight at a busy intersection, nondescript strip malls lay in every direction. "Well," he said, "what are you in the mood for? For lunch I mean."

"I don't care."

"Well then how about some seafood. You know. When in Rome."

Libby brightened at this and Frank glanced at his wife and for just a moment he thought he could discern the old Libby, back again– the sharp-witted, demure and thoughtful woman he'd spent the greater portion of his life struggling beside. He felt his shoulders go a little slack. Suddenly he wasn't suffering, in that moment he was granted a reprieve from his anxieties and thought once again *maybe it's just a phase, a damned phase, we can get some medication, I've got to get on this, pronto.* They were at a stoplight in a humdrum neighborhood on a very ordinary day and he reached over the gearshift for Libby's hand, took it and said, I love you honey. He hadn't said this quite so directly and sincerely in several years and it caught the both of them by surprise. By the time he'd caught his breath and choked back tears the light had gone green and the car behind them was honking, the moment lost to them. He let go of Libby's hand and he made a chastising gesture at the rear view mirror to display his annoyance to the car behind them at being rushed, prodded. She said I love you back to Frank but it was too late, the moment was gone. He hoped it wasn't too long before they could park the truck, get something to eat, and then remove their shoes and go for a long long walk hand-in-hand along the vast stretches of white sand, gaze out upon the ocean waters, maybe even get their feet wet.

*

Marion swam a few laps while Mimi swirled her frail arms and legs in graceful motions at the end of the indoor pool, which was roped off into lanes. When she'd finished her laps, Marion joined her sister and they kneaded the water with their forearms, adjusting their bathing caps and speaking to one another. Their exotic language echoed in the large room enclosed in glass walls that afforded a view of the outside, resplendent with colorful landscaping and a man-made pond. There was a smaller pool of warmer water and Marion climbed into it and guided her sister down the ladder and so they waded there a while, the warm water soothing to their bones.

They got out, toweled off and gathered their things. The outdoor pool had filled up– there were many relatives still visiting for the holidays and empty chairs were becoming scarce. Marion saw Shirley Hagoden waving her paperback at them from under the shade of an umbrella at a table near the poolside. "Gotta stake your ground early around here this time of year," she said when they reached her. She had company with her around the table, which was covered in playing cards.

"Well hello there Mimi," Shirley beamed. "How's our girl?"

Mimi nodded and said she was enjoying the swimming.

139

"Well," Shirley said as she riffled the cards, "don't you go and overdo it now."

"Welcome back Mimi," said Edna Norton. Mimi recognized the other two women, and as Shirley introduced them to Marion, they said they were just thinking of heading to the Club for lunch and they offered their chairs to Marion and Mimi. They thanked them and sat down under the shade of the umbrella while Shirley gathered up the cards and shuffled them distractedly. Edna looked up at the sky and said, beautiful day.

Everyone nodded and then Shirley took it from there. "You know," she said, "all these snow birds, down for a break from the cold. Have you got sun block? My son Jimmy's arriving Saturday. He's my oldest. My grandkids can't wait. They were chirping like crazy this morning on the phone."

"What does your son Jimmy do," Mimi asked.

"Oh, he's a big shot. At 3M. Regional Vice President, my Jimmy. In Minneapolis. Doesn't let it go to his head though."

"Will he stay long?"

"They do a week every year," Shirley tapped at the deck of cards on the table. "My daughter-in-law," said Shirley with an air of solemn conviction, "is a peach. A real *peach*. I mean,"– she lit a cigarette and batted a hand at the smoke– "I'll tell you what, that kid'll do *anything*, anything she can do to help. She was a godsend helping us when we packed off for this place a couple years ago. She's *wonder*ful. So's my grandkids. Now, my *son*,"– Shirley pulled from her cigarette– "he's another story. He can be a piece of work, he's wound pretty tight. Not like his father. Here, you need sun block? He'll get away from the office,"– she wagged her finger– "but not without the work. Oh no, he'll be on the laptop, on the cell phone, checking on things, you know. Always checking on things." Shirley shrugged and said, "but what are you gonna tell 'im?"

Mimi smiled at Shirley, and behind the sunglasses, behind her soft brown eyes her mind raced at the thought of Steve, Tom, their wives. The distance between her sons and their spouses, the distance between them and herself. She scanned the pool and saw families talking, laughing, relaxing. Tom'd appeared more despondent than usual to her and she worried, she'd been up a good part of the night worrying about Tom.

"Hey look," Shirley was pointing a finger and then waving and smiling and the ladies turned to see just what had caught her attention. "That's Flora Wheeler," she said. "Woman's turning one hundred years old this Saturday and Gerry and I are invited to the big shebang. Gonna be dancing and everything. That must be one of her relations come down already. Gonna be a lot more of em to follow."

They all waved, the four of them, to Flora and then Flora mouthed a *hello*, winked, shot a thumbs-up at Mimi. Her relation– a dark-haired woman in a plain blue one-piece bathing suit that didn't hide her chunky thighs and belly. Her hair crowded her face in natural curls and she had a freckled face with perfect teeth and one of those smiles that seemed the picture of cheerful; it engaged every part of her face, from dimpled chin to twinkling eyes and the creases in her forehead, it all seemed a combination for good cheer.

It was true– the sunshine cheered Sharon Rutherford. It was true that the change of scenery gave her heart a new thrill. It was true that she was glad to drop her dreadful work and leave it back in Manayunk Pennsylvannia on the dining room table of her townhouse, just leave it strewn about there. It was true she was utterly and totally engrossed in the easy company of her oldest living relative. It was true she felt like a kid all over again when she and Nana dawdled around Sunny Glen Palms in the golf cart and ended up at the pool. All of these occasions for cheer were distilled into that smile, broadcast to the four ladies under the umbrella at the other side of the pool. What they didn't see, what Nana herself could only guess at, was that melancholic thread running through this Florida tapestry as she wondered just exactly where it was her daughter Melinda fit. What they couldn't see was the dejection she felt at being excluded from her daughter's plans for the entire day.

*

They decided they'd have lunch first. Melinda followed Elise, her new D&G pocketbook slung over her shoulder to complement a certain grownup swagger that she hoped exuded sophistication. The pocketbook was her big Christmas present from her mom, and her dad had not hesitated to express his opinion that it was outlandish and impractical. They stepped into Cha Cha Coconuts on the St. Pete Pier, and they were seated outside in the warm and brilliant sunshine. Melinda hung the pocketbook over the back of her seat and they studied the menu. They ordered seafood platters, Elise ordered a glass of wine and Melinda inquired as to whether the lemonade was fresh squeezed, which it wasn't. She frowned disapprovingly and passed the menu back over to a waitress who was almost twice her age. Elise gave a contented sigh, shielding her eyes and scanning the Gulf waters. At last she gazed upon the girl. Elise wondered about her mother and the trouble, had tried to draw her out a few times on the drive without success.

"Do you get homesick yet, Melinda?"

"Oh God no."

"Where is home?"

"Ugh, Manyaunk. Pennsylvannia."

The girl looked as if she'd tasted something bitter. "Near Philly. Philadelphia."

"Do you miss your friends?"

Melinda fidgeted with the cutlery. "I haven't really got any to miss."

Then her face brightened.

"There is one, Amanda Peters. She's really cool and wants me to join the drama club. Soon's I get back."

"Well," said Elise, "that sounds like a very nice plan."

"At least I think Amanda likes me. I don't know why she would. She's real pretty and real popular and she's always got lots of boys checking her out."

"Well, perhaps she might direct some boys your way."

Melinda frowned at this and sighed. "I'm afraid I'm just bound to live in her shadow."

"Oh nonsense."

"No really. I'm shy. I have a hard time figuring out what to say."

"Well, you certainly do alright as I see. You know a lot for a girl your age. You can talk to them about books, about things like we talk about Melinda."

"No I can't. Boys at our school are all stuck on themselves and not much more besides."

"I think if you do drama, you will get to be in front of a lot of people on the stage. This takes courage. This is certain to make you become less shy."

142

"Oh, I don't know. I'm goofy and awkward. And I'm no beauty queen either."

"Nonsense," Elise reached across and squeezed the girl's hand. "You must be*lieve* in yourself better. I'm sure it's not too long you get a boyfriend."

"Well," Melinda sighed, "all I can say is he better be nice."

They finished lunch and Melinda's spirits brightened at sensing the day was still young and they would be spending a long afternoon in an art museum.

The museum's collection was remarkable and surrealistic in its orientation and they took their time viewing the eccentric painter's dreamy vision expressed onto canvas. Melinda thought these were obscurities she would be unable to conjure up even in her wildest imaginings. She stood for a long time in front of *Enchanted Beach with Three Fluid Graces*, entranced by three female forms who seemed to disappear into the sand as if washed away by ocean waves or melted in the sun. Elise stood next to her and they studied the painting, speaking in half-whispers.

"The artist," Elise said, "is so unlike all others."

"In what way?"

"I mean, for most people, it is not right, this tendency to dwell on oneself too much. To be self-absorbed is-is… I'm sorry, I don't know the word in English. But it is anyway considered quite rude to most."

"Like, narcissistic?"

"Yes, in a way. But for the artist, to, how to say… plunge the depths of the soul, to go inside oneself, this is in fact a *duty*. It is a necessity. There lays the pool from which to draw the water for one's creations. The artist must forego all else in order to truly do justice to their gift."

"Well, I mean, they do bring something back don't they? For everybody I mean."

"Yes," said Elise, "this is the point. They bring something back. They are given a covenant, it is almost a sacred trust. But they live in their own world, they must remain inside their own thoughts for so much time, it is hard to share that world with others."

"Until the work is finished."

"Yes, then they might share that. But to them their work is never finished."

They wandered to another room where, projected onto a wall screen, was the famous dream sequence Dali had designed in for Hitchcock's film *Spellbound*. Melinda sat mesmerized and they watched it for two more go-rounds. She said to Elise, it really is just like a dream.

"Do you get dreams like this ever?"

"I *wish*," Melinda groaned.

"What do you dream about?"

"Well, people chasing me. I get that a lot. I also get dreams where I'm stuck and can't get out. Like on the golf cart last night. You should have seen that woman coming out of the mist. It was a little like that." Melinda pointed at the frenzied man in the film.

"That must have been very frightening."

"What do you suppose is wrong with that lady?"

"Well," Elise said, "people get old, sometimes they lose their faculties."

"Well, then why hasn't my Nana?"

"It's different for different people."

"Nana's as sharp as a tack."

"That's very lucky."

"How's your aunt doing?"

"She, ah,"– Elise measured her words. "We hope she gets better."

"But she's not doing too good?"

"I don't know. Mama and me, we worry."

"That sucks."

"That what?"

"Sucks. It means like, it's not good."

"Oh, okay. Yes. But it's a part of life. Come on, Melinda, we go. Maybe there's something in the gift shop you like eh? I'd like to buy a memory to take back with me."

They combed through the shop. Her mom had crushed a twenty-dollar bill into the pocketbook. Melinda kept changing her mind between coffee cups, pencils, pens, posters, books, playing cards and other knick knacks. At last she went to the discount table, settling on a 2004 agenda calendar featuring Dali paintings. For her mom.

*

Pub Night. Happy hour. Half price drinks. Drink to forget. Drink for nothing else better to do. Raise a glass and make a toast. Drink to the memory of a loved one. A chance to let your hair down. A chance to cast aside differences, in a unified senior kinda way. A chance to laugh and joke with your fellow man in a cool, fraternal slap-on-the-back kinda way. A chance to commune with the spirits. Pub Night.

Frank arrived early on the golf cart with Betty Molnar. Libby was locked in, and he wasn't sure if she even realized it. After he'd changed the third and final doorknob, at the back of the house (that one was a real doozy), he'd changed and started getting ready for Pub Night. Libby said, Frank let me come with you. I can handle myself. Let me come to Pub Night. But Frank waved a dismissive hand at the air, I'll tell you Libby, he said, it's getting so boring I'm having second thoughts about going myself, y'know? She stomped her foot and skulked off to the bedroom. Frank said, what's wrong honey? He hesitated at the doorway and Libby lay face down on the bed, kicking her feet up and down.

"I want to go," came a muffled reply, her face buried in the pillow.

"Tell you what, hon. Tommy and Debbie, you know, the D'Antonios? You remember them. They're out of town until next week, and they really want to see you. This week, nobody's gonna be there. I won't be late, believe me."

"Everybody's gonna be there!" Libby's urgent words were smothered by the pillow. Frank said, "Next week, I promise. You got the TV all to yourself."

Now he was at the club shaking hands with Tommy and Debbie D'Antonio, who were already a few drinks in at the bar and he wasn't having too bad of a time, standing there ordering a pitcher. Betty waved them over to a table near the wall on the far side of the large room. Frank poured the beer, the music started and Tommy wanted to know when are we gonna be on the links again Alsatian, you about killed me with that show of yours the last go round.

"And just where are you hiding that wife of yours," Debbie wanted to know.

Frank shrugged and told them he thought it would be at least until Saturday before the links would be dry enough for golf. Wet wet wet, was what Frank said.

"Well," said Tommy, raising his glass, "let's just drink to the next round of golf and the next exciting episode of the Frank Alsatian Show."

On the heels of this Gerry Hagoden snuck up behind Frank and clapped him on the shoulders. "Hey pal," he said. "Glad to hear the good news."

"What good news?" Debbie D'Antonio looked inquisitively between the two.

"Libby's pregnant," Tommy quipped.

"I mean," said Gerry, "the good news is Frank hasn't retired yet. From golf, that is." Gerry guffawed and slapped at the table. To Debbie D'Antonio his enthusiasm seemed a little overdone.

"What are you boys trying to hide," she said. "You scoring drugs behind our backs or something?"

This joke made Gerry slightly uneasy in light of what he'd been up to over at the Gastons a few nights ago. Had word of it spread around the party, reached the ears of the D'Antonios?

"Well he better *not* be," sounded a raspy new voice. It was Shirley Hagoden, chewing gum and getting ready to switch over to cigarettes. She winked at Frank as if to convey that it was all good, although she disagreed with him about almost everything under the sun.

"Hey girl," said Debbie to Shirley, "are we going to dance tonight or what?"

Shirley made a little jiggle and nodded an eager response at the bartender, who was holding and pointing to an empty pitcher, her face a question mark.

"Let me tell you something," Frank was saying to Tommy while pointing at Gerry, "he farts again in the middle of play and I'm gonna personally plug him up for good."

Debbie howled at this. Betty Molnar regarded Gerry with a mellifluous, high-pitched and insidious cackle. Gerry blushed. Frank handed him a plastic cup of beer, still shaking his head, while the others frowned at Gerry, who merely jabbed a finger at his chest and shook his head in abject denial. The hell if he'd be talking to Frank Alsatian about the boats or anything else tonight.

Anyway here came Ron Shutmeyer, perhaps a good candidate for an ear-bending about his broadening knowledge of recreational boats.

"Where's *your* wife," said Debbie to Ron, casting a furtive glance at Frank.

"Not feeling well." Ron said, "She might come over later."

"Well," she winked, "we'll just have to keep an eye on ya."

Ron Shutmeyer gave a tentative laugh and rolled his eyes at this. He was buoyant as ever, on his feet, it was as if he were perpetually looking around for something to do. Well, it was all right here under his nose, all of it and the DJ, a member of the security staff, announced that tonight was the fifties sock hop competition and the dancers would just have to *ah show us your stuff and don't forget to dress the part*. As he was saying this, a couple happened upon the main room. The lady wore bobby socks and saddle shoes and a long pleated skirt, and her beau had on a pair of denims cuffed at the bottom, black shoes and a white tee shirt, rolled up in the sleeve was a genuine pack of red-box Marlboros. It was Philip and Sugar Gaston and they weren't the first to arrive in costume but definitely the most remarkable. Philip had only a near crew cut to work with but he'd found a way to grease it up a little. Sugar's hair was pulled back in a ponytail and she had on more makeup than usual.

Gerry eyed the incoming Gastons with some trepidation, but the place was packed tonight and he doubted they'd gravitate in any way toward the orbit of Frank's camp. Besides, their table up against the far wall was by now pretty well buried. He glanced at Frank and it looked as if Frank was hardly up to holding court on politics tonight. In fact Frank looked pretty morose, glancing across the table with his arms folded at Betty Molnar, who was at that moment sounding off about home owners association fees going up, unjustly of course, along with Hillsborough County property taxes. The place to live, she'd heard, was Pinellas County. Frank looked on and barely nodded his head as Betty elaborated on rising taxes and all those damned entitlement programs the Democrats insisted on funding, just kept right on funding while people who worked and slaved all their lives could pay more and more in so the moochers could mooch a little more and so forth and so on. To this Frank appeared remote, he didn't attempt to interject, embellish or otherwise alter in any way Betty Molnar's running monologue. He gave the occasional obliging nod. He hunched over the table. To Gerry he looked haggard and gaunt.

Shirley by contrast was vibrant, bouncing on her feet and having no trouble in keeping a conversation flowing, however mundane the stream. Shirley had entered the Hagodens into the dance contest and Gerry indulged his wife's whim. Shirley had no retro costuming from which to draw in her own wardrobe, and while the rest of the contestants, totaling five couples, had made the rounds of the local thrifts for appropriate garb, Shirley had merely donned an old pair of saddle shoes and tied her frazzled hair up in the one usable fashion accessory from home, a polka dot bow. Gerry wore a golf shirt, khaki shorts, and tennis shoes. His socks were pulled up all the way to his knees, Frank thought he looked like a jerk and told him so.

"What, *why?*" Gerry was perplexed.

"I mean tug those socks down a little. You look like a guy who's not playing with a full deck."

"And just why's that?"

"I don't know," said Frank, "you just do. With the socks that way. Fix em' before you hit the dance floor."

"Wadda you care?"

Frank shrugged, said, "I dunno. Guess I don't want to be made a laughing stock for the company I keep. Kinda like guilt by association."

"You mean like Libby."

It was out of his mouth before he knew it and he immediately regretted it. "Sorry Frank. What I meant was—"

"Yeah," Frank glared at him, "I know damn well what you meant."

Ron Shutmeyer got restless and wandered off somewhere. Debbie D'Antonio was already downing her third gin and tonic and glancing around for a place to seek refuge from the steady stream of vitriol issuing from Betty Molnar, who failed to heed any of Debbie's subtle attempts to alter the course of the conversation. She watched Melinda enter from the lobby at the other side of the room, a straw bag slung over her shoulder and on her heels a woman Debbie recognized as the girl's mother. The girl carried herself with a studied comportment, keeping her head up straight, an obvious if affected air of sophistication. Debbie watched with a mild amusement as the girl attempted to insinuate herself smoothly into the older crowd. Because as much as Melinda was determined to project herself as a grownup, Debbie D'Antonio saw all grownups as big kids with wider vocabularies and nagging health and money issues– and this was never more obvious to her than at the Pub Night, when alcohol loosened not only tongues but bodies, and the body language– everyone seemed to move about with extra animation. The girl's body language indicated to Debbie that she had not wished to arrive as one half of a pair– the mother in tow was clearly not a bragging point.

Melinda in fact had her bathing suit, a towel and a book in the bag. Her secret plan was to drop her mother into a room of strangers, a proverbial tank of piranhas, and then head for the outdoor swimming pool. She had her own grownup world and there was no place for her mother in it– she absolutely did not wish her mother to poison it with her authoritative presence as the guardian and chaperone she'd become since her arrival the previous evening. The pool was open until nine and she told her mother she'd meet her at the cart. She wasn't taking any chances.

It was Sugar Gaston who would serve to foil this plan– Sugar sweet Sugar, stepping up fresh from the preliminary round of the fifties sock hop dance competition and grabbing Melinda's arm, bag and all, to guide the girl through the obstacle course of bodies to the dance floor. Melinda reveled in the attention and at the same time hoped she could curtail it soon enough and make her escape to the pool. But it quickly became apparent this was not to be, Melinda was after all a novelty among the grownups, and most if not all of the social animals with whom she'd made the rounds last Saturday night at the Gastons' dinner party were out in force tonight. The Hagodens remained on the dance floor, Shirley was doing the twist with every ounce of energy she could muster, Gerry was running at half speed. Melinda got pulled into the twist. She hated the twist, in fact she hated *dancing*. She hated dancing and her mother knew this, and so this knowledge quickly rendered her communion with the participants a farce, out there doing the twist with people four and five times her age. She was laughing with Sugar, she was laughing with Shirley, she was laughing with strangers, her eyes all the while darting to the lobby and willing Elise not to appear. Gerry Hagoden's heart wasn't really in the twist either– he was still stinging from that thing he'd said to Frank, that callous barb about Libby, as if he'd fired those brutal words not at Frank but himself. He glanced from time to time over at Frank sitting alone at the table and suddenly there was no room for dancing or partying in Gerry Hagoden's heavy heart. Shirley was getting into it pretty good with Philip Gaston, who was going low to the floor, swinging his tanned arms, the cigarette pack bulging out of his tee shirt. At last the twist was winding down and the DJ announced that the next elimination round was coming up soon. But now, the King! And suddenly Elvis Presley was singing *you ain't nuthin' but a hound dog*, and the dance floor was quickly overwhelmed with newcomers.

Gerry cut a path to the bar, procuring a fresh pitcher and bringing it over to Frank. *Go ahead*, he muttered reprovingly to himself, *help a man drown in his sorrows*.

"Hey," he said, pouring beer into Frank's plastic cup, "I'm really ah sorry about what I said. It was a dumb thing to say."

"Don't worry about it."

"Have you thought any about it? I mean about what you're gonna do."

Frank gave him a sharp glance that indicated shelve that conversation for another time another place.

"Right, gotcha," Gerry nodded, sensing they were back on conspiratorial terms. Then he said, "Hey, guess what I'm thinking of buying?"

In the meantime, to Debbie D'Antonio's great relief Betty Molnar had shifted conversational gears, although now it was all about nagging aches and pains. "Well," she was saying, "there's one thing I'll say for Edna Norton. You never hear her complain about a single thing. Not one single thing. Unlike Betty Dixon,"– she rolled her eyes– "I get an earful about every last morsel of her pain. It's *oh my arthritis is attacking me today, I get it in my knees* she says, *in my hands* she says, *right to the core of my hips* she says. *I get heartburn, I get migraines*, she says. To listen to that woman you'd think she spent her nights in a torture chamber."

"Maybe in a sense she does," said Debbie, and Betty waved a dismissive hand.

"Oh God," she said, "these people don't realize how good they have it. Complaining only draws attention to the problem so why complain," she complained.

Melinda had in the meantime been exchanging a few brief pleasantries while watching her mother– who had by now made it to the far wall and stood against it fidgeting, her fingers running along her purse in that way Melinda had come to know all too well.

The girl was just hatching an escape plan from the dance floor when the French ladies entered from the double glass doors behind the DJ.

Frank also noticed them immediately. While Melinda's primary concern was Elise, Frank's attention was drawn fully to Marion. She was not in costume for the sock hop night– in fact she was dressed plainly enough in a solid blue long sleeve shirt and white jeans, a turquoise necklace and matching bracelet– but to his eyes she appeared more marvelous than ever before. He made up his mind right then and there, later when the silly dance contest was out of the way, they would dance again. Gerry's eager words about recreational boats were suddenly falling on deaf ears as Frank's eyes drank in the sight of Marion Legrand– beside her daughter, glancing around nervously, her face at last brightening with the first sign of recognition, pointing to and waving at the girl on the dance floor. At the same time Sugar returned her attentions to the girl, tugging at her windbreaker and shouting above the noise, *c'mon, show us your stuff,* as *Hound Dog* wound down and segued into *At The Hop,* another up-tempo ditty by Danny and the Juniors. Melinda wasn't going to get off that easy.

Shirley Hagoden took a little break from the dancing and greeted the ladies in front of the double doors on her way out. She asked about Mimi, and they said she was playing rummy with her neighbor.

"So," she winked and patted Elise's arm, "girls night out, eh?"

Elise smiled and looked over Shirley's shoulder at the dance floor, at the girl.

"Well," said Shirley, "I'm glad you all came out for fun. Take your mind off things. Come join us at our table," she said, pointing toward Frank and Gerry, and both were caught staring.

"Oh thank you Shirley," said Marion, waving over at two grown men both blushing.

"Never mind. Now get yourselves a drink."

With that, Shirley Hagoden pushed through the double doors and out into the night air for a cigarette. She found Edna Norton and Tommy D'Antonio sitting across from one another at one of the cast iron patio tables and pulled up a chair.

"We were just talking," said Tommy, "about talking to ourselves. I've started this weird habit lately and I just can't seem

151

to stop it. I mean like, talking out loud to yourself? Y'know, with nobody else present."

"I've been talking to myself for forty years," said Shirley. "Alone or not."

"Well," Edna Norton shrugged, "if you can't talk to yourself who *can* you talk to?"

Tommy stubbed his cigarette in the sand of the miniature aluminum pail ashtray. "Well," he said, "I'll leave you two to talk to yourselves. Just don't let the cat outta the bag. About me talking to myself that is," he said, and at their chuckling brought a finger to his lips.

Back inside, Sharon was talking to herself. *I won't stay very long, I'll just have a drink and leave, just one little social drink and leave. Maybe I'll go sit out by the pool and hang out with Melinda. No no, she might feel I'm cramping her style. Well, I guess I could wander around the club, read a magazine in the lounge, check out the weight room, maybe tool around on the golf cart a little. Oh, why do I feel like such a fish out of water? Kinda like a freshman at the senior prom. I don't know any of these people.*

She sidled up to the bar, a line of tall chairs all around it and none of them empty. There were tables with empty chairs, but Sharon Rutherford was not one to go introducing herself to a group of strangers, she could not embolden herself enough right now to inquire *is this seat taken.* So she got her whiskey and ginger ale and stood with her back to the bar facing the dance floor, a requisite smile painted on her face. It wasn't long before a stocky middle-aged guy with greying curly hair and a moustache started at small talk.

"You just down for a break from winter or what?"

"Yes," she said.

"Where from," he asked, wiping at his moustache.

"Philadelphia area. How bout you? Warm weather lure you?"

"Oh, no. My wife and I used to come down just to visit my father-in-law. This year we took the plunge ourselves."

"Retired?"

"Yep."

"You look pretty young to be retired. If you don't mind me saying."

"Mind a compliment on age? Never. No, actually I'm fifty-three. Started at GM right outta high school. Eighteen years old."

"Wow."

152

Sharon looked at the pair of twinkling blue eyes beneath furry eyebrows and thought, this man is happy as a clam to be retired with so many years in front of him. She knew there'd be many more working years for herself beyond fifty. Why didn't she go straight to work for a big company, instead of building a business career of sorts, rolling over 401ks, with a resume filled invariably with job titles that included the word assistant?

"And how about your wife?"

"She's retired. She worked another year after I quit. Got less years, but she was happy to just bite the bullet and get out."

Sharon smiled and nodded and said that's great. "Good for you two."

The guy stuck out his hand. "I'm Ron."

"Sharon," she said, giving his hand a brief and firm shake. "Nice to meet you."

"So," he said, "who are you visiting?"

"My great-grandmother, if you can believe that."

Ron Shutmeyer snapped his fingers and then tapped his forehead. "Um, Flora, right?"

"Yes," Sharon was a little taken aback, "that's right."

"Is that your daughter," he asked, nodding at Melinda, who was working her way towards the hallway to the pool.

"Yep, that's my little teenage wonder."

"She's a good kid," Ron waved at Melinda, but the girl's eyes were fixed in front of her, entirely focused on negotiating the shortest possible route to the exit.

"She can be."

"Oh, she's very intelligent. Vanessa, that's my wife, she's real ah- well she can kinda read people real good, y'know? She thinks your daughter's smart as a whip. Like way beyond her years."

"Well," said Sharon, "thanks, I know she is. It'd just be nice if she'd apply herself more at school."

"Ah," said Ron Shutmeyer, beaming, an expression Sharon was beginning to think was fixed. "School isn't everything."

She gave not exactly what you'd call a convincing nod of agreement.

Across the room, Frank sat and drank. His wife safely barricaded at home, the alcohol took the edge off and Frank wasted no time inviting Marion onto the dance floor. But no sooner had they begun to strut their stuff to *Rag Doll* by Frankie

Valli and the Four Seasons, than the DJ suddenly faded the music to summon the sock hop contestants. Frank grimaced at the truncated dance, now he'd have to ask the same thing twice. He sensed other eyes pressing upon him as he guided Marion gently by the elbow back to the table. Two weeks in a row, same lady, and people would be talking because people were people and that's just what they did.

Back at the table, everyone was gathering their things and preparing to migrate outside to the patio. It was a warm summer night and Shirley Hagoden, an early elimination from the dance contest, wanted to smoke without having to relocate at each new urge for a cigarette, the frequency of which increased with every sip of beer. Gerry lingered to watch the final round of the dance competition. It was the Gastons versus Patty whats-her-name, a well-known flirt, and her beau of the moment whose name Gerry was equally unable to recall. Patty was just a little too stuck on herself for a lot of people's liking, Patty fancied herself and had herself all dolled up in the white pleated skirt, saddle shoes and bobby socks and the letter sweater– comporting herself with a commanding presence that said this was her turf. The Gastons were dressed and dancing in a style clearly not representative of their own generation. To his own surprise, Gerry found himself rooting for the Gastons.

The Gastons clasped hands and leaned back on their heels, perfectly still, trusting the weight of their bodies for balance and support and gazing into each other's eyes in a manner Gerry thought absurdly romantic for a married couple, waiting for the music to start. It did, Frankie Ford singing *won't you let me take you on a sea cruise*, and all at once the Gastons came to life. So did Patty whats-her-name and her exuberant old stud whose socks, Gerry noticed with some amusement, were pulled taut right up to the knees. The guy, Gerry thought while checking his own socks that he'd rolled down, looked like a jerk.

The Gastons worked their magic– Philip twirled his wife with both command and flair, their bodies met and separated with a sure fluidity, with what you might call the style and grace of swans. They both charmed and dazzled and the crowded room responded, clapping in rhythm and urging them on to dizzying heights. Even Gerry found himself unable to keep from tapping his foot and clapping his hands and robustly cheering on the

Gastons. Philip finished in one fantastic flourish, his wife draped over one bended knee, both of them panting and locking eyes in the same manner which they began. The DJ, whose judgment had up to now been the sole determinant of winners and losers, announced that he would let the audience decide this one. The couple who got the loudest cheers would walk away with the trophy, a recycled marble and plastic faux brass thing with a piece of paper overriding the gold-engraved plate on the base with the typed words, Sunny Glen Palms Annual Sock Hop Champions. First Patty whats-her-name and her beau, whose name Gerry once again missed, got a modest applause from the room. This was followed by an overwhelmingly thunderous applause for the Canadians who raised up joined hands, waving and laughing and Gerry laughed just a little too— Patty was trying to appear gracious and every bit taking it in stride, but he knew that underneath all the effort of saving face she was gritting her teeth. She took any matter of competition entirely too seriously and this was why Gerry, more so than his wife, took an instant dislike to Patty whats-her-name, who was single and repeatedly broadcasted this status, habitually threw herself at men whose interest invariably seemed to dwindle.

A line was forming at the bar and Gerry went over to fetch a pitcher. On the way, he almost collided with Kenny Fitzroy, and when they'd each recovered their personal space he regarded his sometime golf partner.

"You feeling better Kenny?"

Fitzroy nodded and stood uncharacteristically mute. He was thin and wiry and under bushy eyebrows had shifty eyes that darted this way and that. He had a nervous tic that caused his face to spasm. Kenny always wore the same outfit— a golf shirt, jeans and tennis shoes that were far beyond their prime. His hair was thinning and balding on top and his teeth were yellow and you saw them a lot because Kenny Fitzroy very much liked to hear himself talk.

"We're sitting outside," Gerry said, sidling up to the bar while indicating the door that exited onto the patio by the man-made lake. Kenny Fitzroy didn't acknowledge Gerry's invitation, but remained pinned to his side throughout the whole business of ordering pitchers of Miller Lite.

"Well," Kenny's eyes lit up as if he'd hit an on switch, "this whole flu business is really going around I guess. I've had the flu more than a few times in my life but this one was the worst man, the worst Gerry, it gave me a hacking cough, fever, up three four times a night to lean over the bowl and do you know what. God, I thought there was no end in sight to it, but I'll tell you what I guess I didn't miss much golf eh? All that rain, guess if I had to pick a time to get deathly ill it'd be last week. I did get a chance to catch up on some primo music stuff. None of this garbage that's out there now, oh no. I dug out my VHS collection and got right down to watching that rock and roll collection I got myself for Christmas. Now that was some music. Man, the Beach Boys, the Beatles, the Stones, Creedence Clearwater..."

Gerry had only a vague notion and little interest in what Kenny Fitzroy was talking about. He'd ordered two extra pitchers and only after he nodded a second time towards them in the middle of Kenny's stream of dialogue did Fitzroy figure to pick them up and he trailed behind Gerry towards the doors to the patio, the barrage of words now directed at Gerry's back.

They had two tables pulled together and Frank had begun to turn buoyant and talkative, he looked like his old self again, and that made Gerry a little anxious. When they pulled up beside Frank's table and set the pitchers down, Frank regarded Fitzroy, who was still directing his verbal onslaught exclusively to Gerry in lieu of making any effort at greeting those at the table or yielding to any conversation in progress. Fitzroy's chatter always grated on Frank Alsatian's nerves, and Gerry knew this. In fact, the inclusion of Fitzroy on their regular golf outings to make teams was Gerry's doing, it was Gerry's idea, and Frank was rapidly tiring of Fitzroy, there was little shelf life with guys like Kenny Fitzroy in Frank's social cupboard. Kenny was childless and unmarried. Try as he might Frank could not conjure up an amenable partner, a soul mate for Kenny, unless of course she was completely deaf. Kenny spoke the extended monologues of the lonely. Kenny's retirement setup had befallen him entirely from the proceeds of an inheritance from a mother he'd lived remote from, geographically and by all indications emotionally, for all he mentioned her. Kenny Fitzroy had long stories and you never heard the end of them. The only way to curtail them was to cut him off rudely, raise your voice louder than his and abruptly slam the floodgate. You had to head it off the way a sentry would a charging army- by raising a club and beating it back. But neither Gerry Hagoden, nor Tommy

D'Antonio, nor anyone else had the heart to do it. The only one for the job was Frank Alsatian.

Kenny Fitzroy nodded vaguely at everyone, and their light and easy banter was overtaken by his urgent insistence to Gerry at first and then the broader audience before him that beyond a doubt nothing fresh, nothing innovative, nothing of any lasting significance had emerged from the music world since the Beach Boys, the Beatles, the Grateful Dead and a scattered few of their peers. All music since then was a mere rehash of that which came before it, according to Kenny Fitzroy. It's like baking a cake from a cake he said and the group met his remarks with that glazed-over look a professor gets one hour into a lecture without a restroom break. Edna Norton looked from the animated speaker to a languid Frank, taking measure of Frank's growing unease.

Melinda Jane Rutherford had been intercepted on her way out to the pool by Elise, who'd steered her right back to the very place from which she'd only just escaped, and now here she found herself at the overflow table which adjoined the one over which Frank held reign. Melinda Jane Rutherford, one leg crossed over the other, twirling her hair and casting glances across the patio at the door from the club, on the lookout for her mother.

"I mean the music you hear nowadays," Fitzroy prattled on absent any nods of assent, "lacks any vitality, it's disingenuous, it's a bunch of self-indulgent, monotonous tripe. There's no melody, there's no, no... *beauty* in it. The genuine article stopped somewhere in the seventies..."– here he appealed to Gerry, but Gerry Hagoden merely shuffled his feet and stared at the ground and wished someone else would take the bull by the horns and steer the conversation in another direction.

Melinda wondered if this guy ever came up for air. He was beginning to get on her fourteen-year-old nerves and she began to speak, politely, conversationally at first, then a tad more spirited, and at last with an authoritative tone beyond her years. "Excuse me, sir, but I have to take exception there!"

Everyone turned their attention to Melinda, even Frank Alsatian was struck by the girl's moxie, her steady command in both delivery and countenance. She brushed her rust colored hair across her forehead and stared straight down at the table directly in front of her. "I mean you're making a blanket statement on music and musicians as a whole? Like, one broad sweeping statement, and with just a few words you dispel any notion of value, you dismiss out of hand any of the beautiful and, and... wonderful, um like, sound creations that are underway right now, right this instant? To do so is pretty ignorant. N-no offense sir, she brought her gaze upon a muted Fitzroy, but I mean ignorant only in the way of lacking knowledge, awareness. I mean, *who* or *what* do you presume to be? All-knowing? God?"

"I didn't mean that,"– Fitzroy tried to interject– "I was only saying–"

She cut him off immediately. "You know, there's a ton of inventive and beautiful music out there, and I'm sure you've never heard any of the bands I listen to. And you'd probably hate them anyway, but it doesn't in any way invalidate the way they can move me, or anyone else for that matter. It's all subjective."

"Sure but–"

"I mean, what you're suggesting goes against nature itself anyway. Beautiful and ugly things are created ad infinitum, it's dynamic, it's perpetual, it never ends–"

"I'm not saying–"

"The only way you could presume to make such opinions would be if you had listened to everything on this planet created since time began up until now, disrupting your flawlessly perfect Beatles ideal or seventies or... whatever."

Melinda at last twirled her hair and said, just sayin.

Fitzroy stared hard at the table in front of him, his brow furrowed, as if plying his mental faculties to assemble a response.

"Well," said Frank, sneering and tilting his plastic beer cup at Fitzroy. "Guess our little friend here just got your number pal."

Everyone laughed then, except Melinda, who blushed and shrugged her shoulders and repeated, just sayin. And then Ron Shutmeyer's hairy arm pushed open the door to the patio and Sharon ducked underneath it. Melinda got up from the table, this time determined not to let anything stand between her and the swimming pool– there was a path around the building just beyond where the grille was set up and she scooped her bag and made a beeline for it. It was beginning to get dark.

Fitzroy, momentarily deflated, looked appealingly towards Gerry Hagoden as if to bend his ear once more. In avoiding eye contact with Kenny, Gerry found himself stuck with the only alternative and it was Frank Alsatian. The girl, though gone without so much as a nod to the table, seemed to have brought Frank to life and he was now going full bore about the upcoming election and how Clinton was raising his sissy voice about the war and how John Kerry was a phony and the truth would out with the Swiftboat investigation.

"What I don't get," said Kenny Fitzroy, plunging headfirst into this burgeoning conversation, "is how you right-wingers can stand behind a guy whose rich daddy got him some cushy post in the Texas Air Guard that he shamelessly avoided, I mean Jesus, the guy can't even read, a damned C student and probably those Cs were dredged up from a muddy river of Ds and Fs by a few phone calls from Poppy the legacy. And then Kerry goes and serves and what do you meatheads go and do but make up stories about it and vilify his service?"

Now this really got Frank's ire and he leaned in and Gerry could tell right away it was going to get personal.

"You *jerk*," Frank said levelly, "you idiot."

Fitzroy kept right on talking and at last Frank's fist came crashing down on the table. He was red in the face, and Gerry said take it easy, take it easy pal, but it was past the point of no return and Frank was hollering at an already chastened Kenny Fitzroy.

"You liberals just can't stand the truth! I'm not saying the man's perfect, but goddammit he's our commander in chief, you got that? The president by God, and for you—"

"Take it easy Frank, Gerry repeated, you're getting all worked up and—"

"And for you to say he's a liar, that the vice president is a— what did you call him last time out on the links? A thug? A *thug!* Why don't you just shut your big California left coast mouth, you little child! Live in the real world, damn you!"

"I *am* in the real world. It's you right-wing nuts that are being naïve—"

"Shut your fucking mouth you moron!"

"Why can't you debate without resorting to name-calling?" Fitzroy shrugged, trying hard to appear cool calm and collected, but nonetheless prepared to make a run for it if he had to.

"You goddamned *socialist pig!*"

Shirley Hagoden stubbed her cigarette out determinedly and said, "Shut the hell up, shut the *hell* up both of you. We come here to have a good time and now this horseshit. Ya wanna do us all a favor? Stay home and watch TV."

That was the end of that.

Frank grumbled, crushing his beer cup in his hand. Now he'd done it. There'd be no second dance with the pretty French lady, because Frank lost his composure, he'd exhibited irrational behavior in her presence and he already knew that her daughter had some serious philosophical differences with him and took exception to most if-not-all of his strongly-held convictions, his core values. He'd really done it, and he scowled at Kenny Fitzroy, the catalyst for his disgraceful outburst.

"Get outta here," he said. "Clear off."

Kenny Fitzroy didn't hesitate a second– he just got up and without looking over his shoulder, walked to the glass doors and into the Club, and Gerry Hagoden was sure they'd be looking for a new golf partner, soon as the water evaporated from the greens.

*

Poolside. Melinda shucked herself out of her shorts and readied herself to plunge headfirst into the deep end, despite the No Diving signs that littered the pool deck area. There was not a soul in sight and that pleased her, it pleased her very much. She'd have liked it if she could have shed herself of all clothing, she craved that delightful, liberating spirit that only nakedness seemed able to evoke.

The water was delightfully warm and for a while the girl floated on her back, looking at the clear night sky and dismissing from her mind any of the claustrophobic thoughts creeping in on her due to her mother's presence and the impending onslaught of relatives just a mere few hours away. There were supposed to be more than a hundred guests, more than Nana's years, more than Melinda cared to be around. Some of these relations she'd never met. She'd been anxious about all that but now there was only the dark dome above her and the tiny glittering stars decorating it. The water was like a liquid blanket and Melinda was snug in it. She closed her eyes and drifted for a while and then she heard the sound of muffled voices, at first far away but now getting closer to her, breaking the peace and calm amidst the lapping waters. She glanced over her shoulder toward the clubhouse. A man approached, his figure silhouetted against the floodlights, with a woman in tow. The man crouched by the poolside, testing the water with his fingers. It was Philip Gaston.

"Sorry," he said, "didn't mean to break the spell."

"That's quite alright."

"Nice evening."

"Yes."

He took a pull from his cigarette and then Sugar waved and whispered, "Mind if we join you?"

"No. Come on in. Water's warm."

"Well," said Philip, "I'm gonna get our suits from the jeep." Sugar shot him a funny look, as if perplexed at the suggestion of clothing. Melinda floated on her back while Sugar removed one of her flats and ran her toes through the water.

"Do you believe in God," Melinda asked.

"Me?"

"I mean like, do you believe in a higher power, something greater than us mere mortals? Something that can like, influence events."

"Sometimes," said Sugar, "sometimes I think I might. But it really doesn't make much difference one way or the other. We're all still here enjoying ourselves."

"And suffering."

"Well, one does one's best to limit that."

Philip returned in his Speedo and threw Sugar her one-piece swimsuit. She glanced around in all directions, then pulled her shirt over her shoulders and shimmied out of her skirt. In an instant she stood naked, and Melinda looked sheepishly the other way until Sugar had donned her swimsuit, grabbed hold of the ladder and lowered herself into the pool. Melinda continued to move about gracefully, bouncing her toes on the pool bottom like a ballerina and spreading her arms like wings in slow motion, lightness throughout the weight of water. This was the first time for Melinda to be alone with the Gastons, and while they exuded calm and relaxation, Melinda was not sure why she wasn't completely at ease around them. She wondered with some anxiety whether her mother had come to be introduced to Elise and Marion.

"Honey," said Philip to Sugar, "did ya let the dogs in before we left?"

161

Sugar looked contemplatively at the water in front of her, making swirls with her arms. "I think I forgot. Wait, wait… No, that was last night. No dear, I think I positively forgot to bring the dogs in tonight. Shit," she said, "that neighbor will be reading us the riot act tomorrow."

"Aw, to hell with those scoundrels," said Philip, lowering himself into the water with slow, tentative steps.

"They don't like it when our dogs get out," Sugar elaborated to Melinda.

"And poop in their yard," said Philip.

"And bark."

"Honey," said Philip, "our dogs don't bark."

"Well," Sugar said distractedly, "not much anyway." The three swam in silence a good while and Sugar draped her arms over her husband's shoulders and then his neck as he swam for the ladder. They hauled themselves out and began to towel dry. Melinda soon joined them and the three of them huddled on the chaise lounges, shivering a little. Philip lit a cigarette. "Honey, we still have to get a gift for Flora."

"Yes we do," said Sugar, starting toward the restroom. Philip sprawled out on one of the lounge chairs, pulling on his cigarette. "Have any of your guests arrived yet Melinda?"

"No, not until tomorrow. Most of them are coming for the weekend only."

"What about your mom?"

"She's here already."

"You don't sound very excited."

"Should I be?"

"I don't know."

"Anyway, Nana seems worried."

"Well it's not every day you turn a hundred I guess."

"No, that's not it. I think it's about the money."

"The *money?*" Philip leaned forward on one elbow. "What do you mean, the *money?*"

"The money to pay for the party. I don't really know. But I think the Business Office keeps calling her and making her really nervous."

Philip puzzled over this. He said, "She told me that one of your relations— I don't know, maybe it was a great-grandson or somebody, was footing the bill? Something like that."

"Who?"

"I don't know. I don't remember."

"I just hope it's not uncle Nathan. If it's my uncle Nathan, he sure isn't footing any bill anymore."

"Why's that?"

"He sorta had a meltdown. A corporate meltdown."

"*Oh?*"

"I heard my mom talking to my aunt Susan about it. Aunt Susan– she said his house was under water. But not like a flood or anything. I don't know what she means by that. What does that mean, *under water?*"

"Means he's got more in it than it'd sell for."

"Huh?"

"He's got more debt than the fair market value."

Melinda's eyes glazed over. "*Any*way," she said, "my mother says he's having a midlife crisis. The worst kind. Did you have a midlife crisis?"

"Me? I had an *early* life crisis. We were dirt poor. I got my life crisis out of the way pretty early I guess. Now I have so much goddamn money I don't know what to do with it."

*

It was starting to get a little chilly out there on the patio. Everyone began to migrate back inside as the staff shut down the grill and began to tidy up, yet a good number lingered at Pub Night. Gerry was dancing cheek to cheek with Marion Legrand, his hand placed gingerly on the small of her back. He couldn't remember the last time he'd occasioned to dance cheek to cheek with a lady, and his wife, watching from the sidelines, couldn't either. All Shirley knew was her husband's enthusiasm for the dance floor that evening had waned with their elimination from the sock hop contest– but now it seemed to have been reignited as the DJ shelved the up-tempo numbers and the music selection was unmoored from the fast crashing waves at the shoreline to the deeper sea of the slow dance. It was in these still waters that Gerry and Marion suddenly found themselves treading carefully, methodically, and exclusively– the pub crowd having graduated from the competitive urgency of the sock hop to the easy idling of social engagement. Just as the gist of the evening had shifted from one of moving the limbs to that of moving the mouth here was Gerry Hagoden shuffling his feet with some trepidation, with a marked clumsiness against the more graceful movement of his partner. The woman he held wore the unremarkable garments of casual dress, but to Shirley Hagoden, Marion Legrand might as well have been attired in a slinky black velvet evening gown with sequins about the low neckline and sleeves and it may just as well have been diamonds or pearls rather than the bulky turquoise on the necklace around her slender if somewhat wrinkled neck. Gerry's lips were moving, saying something to this exquisite and refined French woman, and Shirley wondered if the French woman could understand half of what her husband whispered at such close proximity. Where Gerry had a good few inches on Shirley in height, Marion, she noticed, measured almost equally. Betty Molnar was groaning about the ruckus the contracted Mexican landscaping crew managed to make when they came to cut the grass and trim the hedges, and Frank Alsatian was sulking again and pouring himself another one out of the pitcher. When Betty realized that her audience was only half listening she straightened the sleeves of her blouse distractedly, glanced at her watch and drummed her fingers at the table. At other tables people talked and glanced occasionally at the pair of slow dancers.

Gerry felt the slow dance take years off his body, he got that heart in mouth feeling a younger man might feel at the first pangs of love, when the object of desire moves from a distant target to a close-up that makes the knees buckle a bit. He was whispering slowly to her about the boats and this seemed to evoke childhood memories for her of magnificent sailing vessels along the sandy beaches of southern France, and the breezy regattas to which she was often a keen spectator. In her enthusiasm she drummed her fingers in cadence with her words on his back, then brushed them along it with an urgency to match the excitement behind her words of broken English and it was thus that he became what you might say caught in the spell. While Marion's hand wandered carelessly along the regions of Gerry's back, Gerry's mind wandered from the abstraction of beautiful boats to the intimacy of the moment. While the rest of the room glanced occasionally with a mild interest, this new couple had Shirley Hagoden's complete and undivided attention.

Frank Alsatian saw what happened next and it snapped him out of his funk with a lightening bolt of jealousy. There were a few witnesses from other vantage points, some of whom would swear their lips had never touched, that they'd merely grazed cheeks, but you couldn't convince Shirley Hagoden of that. Not so from her point of view. What her sharp eyes saw was known by no other term than a kiss, and not a peck, but one which would have lingered had the French woman not recoiled from it somewhat playfully, rearing her head back but breaking neither eye contact nor embrace. What Shirley Hagoden's crimson eyes saw was her husband Gerry kiss, with an alarming determination, the lips of another woman.

*

The double doors from the club at the other end of the pool opened and four figures emerged onto the deck, silhouetted against the floodlights. They spotted the silhouettes at the other end and approached. When they'd neared enough, Melinda could discern Ron and Vanessa Shutmeyer with an unfamiliar skinny younger guy, and then she recognized with no small measure of chagrin, her own mother.

"Look," said Vanessa Shutmeyer, pointing at Melinda, "there's your daughter!"

Melinda made a crooked smile at this, shrugging her shoulders in a sort of mock affability. These weren't the friends and this wasn't the night for her mother and her to share. She begrudgingly resigned herself to call it quits. She suddenly wanted to be around other kids, for a little while she didn't want to be Melinda Jane Rutherford, for just a little while anyway. Where were the kids though? Back to school after Christmas holidays. They'd jumped ship just when she'd climbed aboard. A mutiny on Melinda.

Ron Shutmeyer was bouncing on his heels and beginning to unravel some breaking news, a story fresh from the South Club dance floor, *you won't believe this* he said to Philip Gaston, but Gaston remained pensive, rubbing his goatee distractedly.

"Mom," said Melinda, "I want to go home and read. You can have the golf cart."

"No honey, I think I'll go with you."

"Nonsense," Sugar Gaston said to Sharon, "you are going to stay and hang out with us. We'll take you home."

Sharon looked imploringly at her daughter, but Melinda was already gathering her belongings and hefting them into the large beach bag.

"Yeah," said Ron Shutmeyer, "why don't you hang out with us awhile."

"Alright," Sharon shrugged.

Melinda said goodnight to everyone and started for the path to the parking lot. Shutmeyer took up his story again, about Gerry Hagoden and the kiss, but Philip raised a finger and said, hold on a minute. He wiggled his feet into his sandals and started towards the parking lot and Melinda, calling over his shoulder for Shutmeyer to hold that thought. When he got to the parking lot, Melinda was just getting ready to back the golf cart out of its spot. "Wait up girl," he said. "Wait."

"What is it?"

"I have something for you." He went to the jeep, opened the glove box and rummaged around until at last he fished the leather bound book and undid the clasp. He returned to the golf cart and climbed in beside Melinda. "You got a pen?"

Melinda pointed at the compartment in front of him. "In there."

He extracted a ballpoint pen and scratched it at a finger to get the ink going. Melinda could hear his labored breathing which seemed to accentuate, against the quiet, some measure of gravity in the matter at hand. He scrawled something at the little book in his lap.

"Here you go."

He tore away at the perforation and then, lodged between his index and forefinger, was a check. Melinda regarded a yellow document with fancy gold bordering, on the header it read Phillip and Margaret Gaston. His signature had a playful, buoyant flair to it. The rest of the check was unwritten. A blank check.

"That's for your Nana."

"No, no! You don't have to do that. Really."

"It's our birthday present to her."

The girl frowned at the check, tapping it lightly. She went to pass it back to Philip but he merely shook his hands at it.

"Just take it. Trust me, Flora doesn't need the stress right now. Tell her to march it down to the business office. Just fill it out for whatever amount they need."

"But—"

"Later alligator," he said, clambering out of the golf cart and calling over his shoulder, "Gonna be one hell of a party."

She watched him right up until he disappeared from view, shaking her head and drumming her fingers on the check.

*

Back inside the club, Gerry Hagoden had himself a little explaining to do. News of his transgression had spread about the room like wildfire from those few who'd witnessed it. The din of conversation lowered, the dance floor emptied, the makeshift DJ began dissembling the sound system, the staff had begun wiping down tables with a new urgency and Pub Night had come to a grinding halt.

Gerry had some explaining to do alright, but those due an explanation had quickly deserted. Marion and Elise had left without so much as a nod in his direction. The remaining crowd were mostly strangers to him and he felt their eyes upon him, their faces betraying their amusement. He lowered his eyes as if he were before judge and jury right there that night at the South Club, but the prosecution had vacated the courtroom along with the chief witness. He was walking home tonight but that was fine by him. Right then he could really use a walk.

*

The checkbook wasn't the only thing Philip Gaston had extracted from the glove box. He's slid into his khaki cargo pants pocket an Altoids breath mint tin containing a plastic baggie of high-quality hydroponic marijuana. He sauntered back onto the pool deck to rejoin both the group and Ron Shutmeyer's story. But Shutmeyer, still bobbing and weaving in his tennis shoes, had finished that one and had already begun sculpting another.

"So," he was saying, "there we are, my wife and I, no keys, drunker'n skunks, just wanting to get back inside our room, it's like three o'clock in the morning, okay?"

167

"But we can't find the concierge," Vanessa chimed in.

"The concierge?" Sugar Gaston looked on incredulously.

"Right," said the skinny guy standing next to Sharon. "A sleazy roadside motel with a broken ice machine and now we get the *concierge*."

After a few snickers and knee slaps, Ron resumed the story. "So what do we do? We go banging on the office door even though the lights are out, try and get an extra key or something–"

"And then," Vanessa said, "the light comes on and here's this disheveled-looking lady all, you know, curlers in her hair, cigarette dangling from her mouth–"

"What, Gaston interrupted, was she doing at three in the morning with curlers in her hair?"

"Beats me," Vanessa shrugged.

"So," Ron continued, "she answers the door and tells us the manager, I'm guessing her boyfriend or whatever, isn't around but then we hear this, like, commotion... around back–"

"And Ron wants to go check it out, right? I tell him you're crazy hon, but I'm sure not gonna to let you go by yourself–"

"When *was* this," Sugar asked.

"Just last month," said Ron, "up in Pensacola. So anyway, we decide to go around the side of the building, there's this alley, see, and across from it there's a sort of open lot. And there's our guy, can of Bud in one hand and a cigarette in the other."

Vanessa shook with laughter, grabbing the skinny guy by the elbow to steady herself. "You wouldn't believe it if you saw it."

"What, what?" The skinny guy beamed.

"He was barking at the dog."

"Barking at the dog?" Gaston repeated and the bunch of them burst into fits of laughter right there by the poolside and suddenly Sharon felt the glow of kinship like a breath of fresh air, like it might be possible after all to have a good time. It was getting near nine, the pool was about to close, and here they were shaking in collective mirth. Gaston had an idea. "I've got some silly smoke," he said. "Why not go for a late night soak in the secret hot tub?"

"Sounds good," said Ron, still bouncing from one heel to the other.

"So where's this secret hot tub," asked Sharon.

"It's over at the Latham Court pool."

"I didn't know they had a pool over there," said Vanessa.

"We've been going there for years," Sugar said. "You just have to be *vewwy vewwy kwuiet*," she intimated conspiratorially in an Elmer Fudd voice.

"Okay," said Vanessa, "so how we gonna get there, walk?"

"Too far," said Sugar, glancing at her husband. "Let's all pile in the jeep."

"Sounds like fun," said Sharon.

So they all piled in the jeep. Vanessa Shutmeyer dropped into her husband's lap and Sharon imagined a long and happy marriage. What would that be like, she wondered to herself, and then there was nothing to do except self-consciously place her bottom in the lap of the skinny guy who's name she'd forgotten. She worried about her body weight and tried to play down a compromising position, giggling along with the Shutmeyers and the Gastons. They came to a stop sign and then from the passenger seat, Sugar hiked up her skirt and lowered her panties half-standing half-crouching to moon both those in the cramped backseat and the car behind them. This sparked an explosion of raucous laughter and applause from the backseaters. There seemed to be no shortage of applause for Sugar Gaston this night. A warm surge erupted in Sharon as her sides shook with laughter, a lightness of being she could not remember last having felt. The girls-nights-out back home were mannered and cordial at best– this was a completely different ball of wax. She was beginning to feel like a teenager. She looked from one mirthful face to the next, still clutching the back of the seat and keeping her shoulders straight to keep from falling into the arms of a stranger. Gaston switched off the headlights as they turned into an empty little parking lot, Sugar turning around to face the backseaters and bring a finger emphatically to her lips, although the others had already begun to stifle their chatter. Gaston killed the engine and the jeep coasted into the last parking spot, sheltered from the glow of streetlights by the overhanging branches of a cypress tree.

Laughing and shushing each other at the same time, they clambered out of the jeep and followed the Gastons towards a chain-link fence that stood about four feet tall. Both Gastons turned around, finger pressed to lips to shush Ron Shutmeyer, who seemed incapable of containing his voice to a whisper. Philip Gaston gripped the top of the fence and vaulted himself over, then extended a hand to assist his wife. One by one he guided the others, his hands knitted with laced fingers to form a step to bear them each over. In daylight the pool benefited from the shade of a good stand of surrounding pines and cypresses– at night their branches cast eerie shadows in the moonlight. They all followed Philip Gaston to a little pagoda, underneath it a modest hot tub. Everyone grew silent and almost reverent, as if they'd happened upon some church and found themselves smack dab in the middle of some arcane and sacrosanct ceremony. Crickets sang, a night choir from all sides. "I don't have a suit," Sharon said.

"Neither do we," said Gaston, climbing out of his khakis while Sugar began to shed her own garments. Just like that she was naked before everyone, and then she walked on tippy toes away from the hot tub toward the pool, which was bathed in moonlight. Sugar's body looked pale and almost blue in the dim light to Sharon as she tested the water with her toes, then lowered herself one bit at a time into the water. Gaston, stripped down to a Speedo, fetched a lighter, a small pipe and the tin from his shorts. Here goes, he said, flipping a switch on one of the pagoda's posts and bringing to life the hot tub, its jets now blowing full steam. Stepping out of the Speedo, he lowered himself into the bubbling waters. Ron shot his wife a *why not* glance and soon the Shutmeyers were liberating themselves of all clothing.

"What about it John," said Philip Gaston, glancing up from the bowl where he'd packed the marijuana tidily with the focused attention a taxidermist might render a precious and endangered species of fowl. "Thought you were an old pro at this by now."

"I'm all for it," the skinny guy beamed, undoing his belt and dropping his drawers, and then Sharon was the only one left fully clothed, perched on the bench at the perimeter of the pagoda. She was of two minds. On the one hand, if she stuck around fully clothed, would she not seem a prudish bore, an awful fuddy-duddy, or worse still a voyeur of sorts? On the other hand, she couldn't bring herself to unveil what she regarded to be a not altogether attractive body. She'd had little opportunity to avail herself of the sun enough to tan her pasty white and freckled skin. And she was on the plump side– she cringed at the thought of their eyes falling on the folds under her breasts, the sagging flesh under her arms. Dark as it was, this just wasn't the place. It was too intimate. She wished there were a hundred more people walking around naked so she could just blend in.

But here was the young skinny guy pulling a tee shirt over his head and then his boxers were off and she purposely looked the other way, out towards the edge of the little park where it met the property line of the nearest neighbor. She suddenly registered a light coming on– she waved at Gaston and pointed at the house. Perhaps this might just put a damper on the nakedness and spare her any embarrassment. But then again, it was just a light coming on. The screen door remained closed and there was no evidence of anyone on the porch. They all resumed their chatter, Ron ever failing to master the art of the whisper. He was at ease sitting beside his wife, telling another story from their Pensacola trip, something about them taking a wrong turn into a strip club. The young skinny guy had a nice easy laugh and Philip also grinned while passing the bowl to Vanessa. Sharon agonized.

She glanced over at the pool and there was Sugar, floating on her back and listening to the night chorus of crickets, as naked as the day she was born. There was something about the serenity of the image that slowed Sharon's pulse, and then she found herself beginning to untie her tennis shoes, tugging off the ankle socks and continuing to undress, glancing sideways to see if anyone was looking, but they only looked between themselves there at close quarters in the hot tub. Next thing she knew she was lowering herself naked between Vanessa Shutmeyer and the young skinny guy, soon up to her neck, gratefully hidden under the waterline and beneath the bubbles.

The young skinny guy's name was John and soon they were talking to each other as if they were fully clothed, or as if it were perfectly natural to be sitting stark naked next to one another, separated by mere water. "You should play volleyball with us," John said. "Ten o'clock tomorrow morning at the South Club."

"I'm not very good."

"Oh, it won't matter," he assured her.

"So what do you do besides, John?"

"I guess I'm a dropout," he said.

"You mean like a high school dropout?"

"No, no I've got an undergrad degree. I mean a corporate dropout."

"John's back visiting his Mom for a spell," Philip injected, his voice strained from holding in the smoke from his last hit on the pipe. "I'd say this guy's really injected some good ole youthful enthusiasm into the place."

"A *corporate* dropout," Sharon echoed. "Wow."

"Yeah," he sighed, "quit my accounting job at Dupont and just sort of... drifted, I guess. For a while."

"Drifted like where?"

"Europe."

"Wow," Sharon said, "that's pretty cool."

"Yeah, well I got a chance to travel, you know?"

"What all did you do?"

"At first I just took the Eurorail and, you know, just sorta hung out at hostels. Worked on organic farms a bunch and taught English second language, the first year."

"The first year?"

"Yeah."

"How long've you been a dropout John?"

"About seven years."

Sharon digested this piece of information and then said, her voice seeming to herself to come from somewhere entirely else, "Do you wanna go for a swim in the pool?"

"Sure," said John, "why not?"

He stepped out of the hot tub and reached for her hand. The idea that social decorum was respectable even in the nude amused Sharon and she giggled a little. She cupped her hands protectively between her legs, goose-stepping along the concrete path to the pool. At the same time Sugar was heading toward the steps at the shallow end.

"Has he got that pipe going yet," she wanted to know.

"Yeah," said John, "it's well underway."

Sharon wondered whether she'd oblige when it came her turn and the pipe was proffered her. She wasn't sure. She swam and let her mind wander. If she'd drifted, if she'd never met her ex-husband at a happy hour, if Melinda hadn't been born, would she have decided one day to just up and leave? To just shirk responsibility and walk away from all the tension of a career path and the mundane reality of the workplace? Would she have had the guts?

They swam around in the pool a little longer and then Sharon stepped out and the night air was crisp and she shivered and stepped lively towards the path to the pagoda and lowered herself back into the hot tub. Her tensed muscles immediately relaxed in the warmer water. It was like a giant bubble bath. Then without warning, the jets stopped spewing water and everything went silent.

"John!" Philip called out, his wife shushing him. "Turn on that power, dude. Hit the switch. Hit the magic switch."

"The *magic switch*," Ron mimicked and then there was some giggling, sniggering. Sharon relaxed and then a light came on from next door. They all got quiet and sank lower into the tub. Next thing a white vehicle with Security stamped on its doors came slowly down the street just beyond the bushes. Sharon looked over her shoulder and shuddered at the thought of being found out, reported, getting in trouble in front of her Nana, not to mention her own daughter. The vehicle slowed by the entrance to the parking lot and then to everyone's great relief, it continued on. Sharon looked next door and saw the silhouette of a man on the screened porch. She pointed over her shoulder and brought a finger to her lips. The light went out and then they slowly, quietly, cautiously went about resuming conversations, Ron Shutmeyer still unable to confine his voice to a whisper. The bowl was repacked and lit by Philip. He passed it not right but left this time, to Sharon. She started to pass it over to John, then thought why not? Why not join in carefully, with just a little pull. A light pull, maybe even a sort of fake pull, that'd be the trick. She'd pace herself, because the truth was Sharon Rutherford was a light-weight when it came to smoking pot. She always was, and now it had been several years since she'd had occasion to be around it and she knew her tolerance would be very low and she had just better take it easy. Sharon relaxed a little and began to savor the company. By the second go-round she took a deep pull from the little pipe. She wiggled her feet and sensed it would be a long time until she could trust herself to properly stand up. Sugar was saying to Ron Shutmeyer, we gotta get you two on a nude cruise. Ron said no way man, and Vanessa said why not?

"I dunno," said Ron, "I just can't see myself walking around butt naked in front of a bunch of people."

"You're doing it now."

"Yeah, I know, but this is different. We know everybody."

"For me," said John, "it's harder walking nude around people I know than total strangers."

Sharon nodded, but could find no words. It dawned on her then— the effort of articulation, the effort to make sense, she was always finding herself having to make sense. As a parent, as an assistant administrator, as a client to a divorce attorney, as a sister talking to her suicidal brother Nathan, as whatever role she found herself thrust into. Right now, absent a role, she couldn't make any sense. Not one damn bit of sense. She knew it. She knew it like she knew her own name. The conversation around her became a background noise as she turned her head in all directions, a sentry on the lookout for any sign of invasion to this late night gathering of middle-aged naked people in a typically sedate over-fifty-five retirement community. At last she settled on studying the faces of those around her and when she laughed it wasn't so much at the words but the expressions that came with the delivery of them. Animated or solemn, the faces themselves gave her a fit of giggles. Everyone was laughing at intervals anyway, and after a while she returned her focus to the words. In the meantime was it her imagination or was Philip Gaston playing footsies with her underneath the water? What at first she might have took for an inadvertent and unconscious touching of the feet became clearly a bout of footsies and that only served to accelerate a return to verbal cognition. She also could see Sugar Gaston having turned herself in such a way so as to fix her eyes on Ron Shutmeyer and Sharon thought my God these people are swingers, real live swingers and she returned her attention to the skinny guy on the other side of her.

"I don't think," John was saying, "I could ever work for somebody else ever again."

"You better hope you can be so lucky," said Philip Gaston. "You never know what the future has in store. What about you Sharon? What do you do?"

"I'm an administrator— er… assistant administrator at a fortune cookie… um sorry,"– here her voice began to give way to laughter– "I mean Fortune *five hundred* company—"

To this everyone burst out laughing and it was beginning to get loud, *really loud* out there in the hot tub, not too far from the residences of some Sunny Glen Palmers. But they could not contain themselves at that last one, Sharon thought she might wet her pants from laughing if she'd had any on. Not now, she strained to fight back the urge to pee like a little girl in a kiddie pool and at last she could stand it no longer, she raised herself out of the hot tub and hotfooted it across the concrete to the wet grass and the bushes beyond. If anyone had told her yesterday on the flight down in her starched business attire, with her briefcase and her laptop— that she'd be running soaking wet, naked and giggling to herself to pee in the bushes just one day later, she'd have guessed they were certifiably insane. She plunged into the miniature-landscaped woods with their deep shadows and she was glad of the darkness. But in that same cloak of obscurity lay the random aspect of the evening. Events were unfolding in a haphazard manner and she was not sure she altogether liked it. She finished her business and darted to the hot tub with one hand between her legs and the other covering her breasts. This amused the whole bunch in the hot tub and she could see why– after all, if you made up your mind to go and get naked, what was the sense in covering up the private parts that clothes hid? She was blushing and she knew it as, shivering, she dropped herself somewhat ungracefully out of the crisp night air and into the bubbling hot water. Ron Shutmeyer and his wife stood up with no effort to conceal their privates and started for the swimming pool. Sugar Gaston and John were gazing upon one another and connecting on some level beneath the waterline, and Philip Gaston now went beyond footsies and there was no mistaking that his hand had found its way to Sharon's calf and then over her knee and to her thigh, where it rested now. She offered no resistance. It felt strange to her– no man had touched her in any way since her divorce. It was flattering and it was frightening. She turned her head towards John and intended to engage the young man in a conversation about his restlessness and unconventional choices in life, but John was now fully engrossed in Sugar Gaston, their eyes locked and laughing softly at something for which the two seemed to share exclusively, some ancient and sublime truth. Philip Gaston had moved closer and Sharon could feel her body stiffen. The Shutmeyers were splashing at one another and then she could glimpse Ron mauling Vanessa, and she could see the night was going to get frisky.

"How long have you been retired," she said to slow Philip's advance.

"Oh," he said, "I dunno. Long enough to forget how long I guess."

"How did you manage? If you don't mind me asking."

"No I don't. We started several surgical clinics all over Toronto. Somehow I got the bright idea there was a demographic of patients might want to book their appointments and surgeries at night. When they didn't have to take time off from work and so forth. It just exploded faster than I could even keep up with. Then we just worked our butts off."

Sharon nodded and Philip leaned in for what she was sure was a kiss. She raised a hand up to her mouth. "I'm just recently divorced," she lied.

"I'm still married," he said.

"I'm just not exactly the touchy feely type."

"Suit yourself," he said in a not at all disagreeable tone. Sharon didn't know quite where to go from there– the other two in the hot tub were still engaged in some private reverie with the rest of the world tuned out.

"This," she said to the water, "feels nice though. Thanks for letting me tag along."

It got real quiet. Just the sound of the bubbling water, the streaming jets and the crickets. Then the Shutmeyers came noisily up the path towards them, Vanessa limping behind Ron.

"What'd you do," Philip chortled, "stub your toe?"

"Gotta get her back," said Ron, "bleedin pretty bad."

"Oh shit, let Doctor Gaston have a little look-see."

Ron was again bouncing on his heels. He glanced across the pool at the pavilion. "D'you think they've got a first aid kit or something over there?"

"I dunno," said Philip, "I doubt it."

"Well," said Ron, clambering into his shorts, "I'll go have a look."

"We should go," Vanessa whimpered, naked and shivering.

"Let me go see if we can get a band aid on that right now honey," Ron took off for the recreation area and the pavilion.

Sugar, still sunk up to her neck in the tub, had somewhat come out from under her spell and pointed to the bench. Towel, towel, take our towel, girl. Towel towel, towel, she kept repeating drunkenly even after Vanessa had snared it from the bench and begun drying herself, standing on one leg until Philip said let me see the foot, oh yeah it's a bleeder alright, there there.

Ron returned empty handed. "Nothing," he said. "No luck. There's a whole bunch of cabinets, and one of em's got a first aid sticker on it, but they're locked, every damn one of em."

"Alright," said Philip, "let's wrap it in a sock and get going."

"Aw," said Sugar, "I don't wanna go. I'm staying here, with John. He'll protect me from all the wild animals."

"Okay," said Philip, "let me take these kids back and—"

"I think I'm gonna call it a night myself," Sharon stood up and stepped out of the hot tub. There was one other towel on the bench and she helped herself to it. Ron was making a tourniquet of his wife's tube sock and speaking to her in soft reassuring tones. John climbed out of the tub next and before long it was all six of them clothed and heading for the chain link fence, Ron supporting his wife, who hobbled along beside him with one arm draped around his neck. Getting Vanessa Shutmeyer over the chain-link fence was no small feat, Ron prodding her up and then scrambling over to help Philip and John on the receiving end. All the while, everyone was hooting and hollering and cheering her on. Despite Sharon's best efforts to shush the others between her own bouts of the giggles, it got loud enough for the lights to come on from a house across the street from the parking lot. A figure approached them tentatively, shining a flashlight.

Philip shielded his eyes and said, "You Security?"

"No."

"Well thank goodness for that. Now turn that damn light off and let us attend to this poor woman's broken toe."

"It's not broken, I think I just stubbed it—"

"Ssshh," said Philip.

They could see the man now in his button pajamas, with knee-high rubber boots, rain gear. It made for an odd costume. "The pool is closed after dark you know," he said. "So's the hot tub."

"And so is this conversation," said Philip. He turned and began walking towards the jeep, calling over his shoulder, "C'mon let's get outta here. Before he calls security."

"I'll call them, the man with the flashlight asserted. I'll call in your tag numbers."

"Aw leave us alone, we were just having fun," Sugar said as she helped Vanessa back onto her husband's lap. "We weren't bothering anybody."

"We could hear you loud and clear," said the man.

"I'm sorry about that." said John, "We promise you won't anymore." Philip started the jeep and Sharon flopped into John's lap and hoped to God they didn't get reported on, what on earth would she say to her daughter?

Now the man had his cell phone out and was dialing. Philip drove with the headlights off and just when they'd got past him and were turning onto the street Sugar had her skirt down again and gave it to the guy, a full moon. Philip merely glanced at his wife's bare ass and chortled, shook his head and switched on the headlights.

"Do you think we'll get reported," Sharon asked.

"Only way they can boot the Gastons out," Philip chuckled, "is if we fail to pay our association fees."

The security truck snuck up behind them at the stop sign. Sharon shivered as the blue light flashed across the jeep. Philip cursed under his breath. The security guard approached, the flashlight beam playing along this way and that on the jeep. The taut face that appeared in the window frame was adorned with a close-cropped beard and mustache and a no-nonsense look. "You a resident here?"

Philip pointed at the sticker on the windshield.

"Philip Gaston. My lovely wife Margaret."

"You can call me Sugar," Sugar advised him playfully.

"I see," he sneered, pulling out a clipboard. "Address?"

The Gastons and then the Shutmeyers gave their names and address.

"What about you," the guy leaned in and gave John a piercing glance.

"He's our guest. He's staying with us."

"And *her?*"

Sharon averted her eyes from the security guard's piercing stare.

"She's our guest too."

"Names?"

They gave their names and the man jotted them down carefully, even had them spell them out.

"What were you doing in the Latham Club parking lot at this hour?"

"Just a little harmless fun," said Philip.

"Yeah well, let me run your plates and we'll just see if you are who you say you are." He glared one by one at the jeep's occupants before he walked back to his own jeep.

"Knock yourself out," Philip replied and when the man had returned, with a bumptious nonchalance, to the security truck he muttered to himself, "Goddammit, give someone a little bit of authority and just watch how it goes right to their head."

Whatever buzz Sharon had on was completely stripped by the circumstances. She imagined having to explain herself before both Nana and Melinda, losing complete credibility with a single bad judgment call. Why had she agreed to go along for the ride?

The man skulked back to the jeep, taking his time. "Okay," he said, handing Philip his license back. "You have a formal complaint against you. Pool and hot tub close at nine, got it?"

Mute silence.

"Got it?"

"I believe you've made it abundantly clear. Now we'll just be going."

"Mr. Gaston. There is a formal written report on this incident. You have been warned. In the event there should be another such incident—"

"Look," said Philip, "we've committed no crime. I'm not going to waste my time arguing policy with you. It's very late and it's past our bedtime. Good night."

"Security will provide you a copy of the incident report…"

The man's words trailed away as Philip put the jeep in drive and cruised away slowly, looking at the rear view mirror and saying, *bite me.*

They went first to the Gastons to tend to Vanessa's toe. While Sugar corralled Vanessa into the bathroom and fussed with antiseptics, Philip made a round of gin and tonics for everyone. Sharon adamantly refused, then gave in and accepted the fizzling glass. *This night just might never end,* she thought.

Philip switched on the stereo. Sugar and Vanessa returned to the living room and before long all six of the revelers were dancing in a frenzy to the American Graffiti soundtrack. Pillows were upturned, dancing partners swapped, glasses clinked, and Sharon surprised herself with some of her own dance moves.

Their ecstatic jubilee was brought to a crashing halt when Ron Shutmeyer fell straight back into the bookshelf that housed the stereo system. Philip was immediately doubled over, laughing so hard he began to gasp for air. John didn't see any of it as he was riffling through the Gastons' CD collection. He helped Ron straighten out the stereo and the books and then said, "I'm gonna put on the Who."

"Wait," Philip said. "Let an old man catch his breath.""

Think we can leave our car at the South Club," Ron asked Philip and Philip shrugged, "don't see why not, what're they gonna do, tow it?"

"We better get it honey," said Vanessa, yawning and looking at her watch. "It's almost two thirty."

This announcement startled Sharon, who had it pegged for somewhere around midnight. The time had sure flown by and she wondered if Melinda was waiting up for her. "I've- I've really got to go," she said, gulping down the gin and tonic and setting the glass on the table with a ping as if to emphasize the point.

"We'll drop you home," said Ron.

"Tell you what," said Philip. "I'll run you all up to the South Club in the truck. That jerk may have called in the dogs on the jeep. Waddya think honey?" Philip called over to his wife on the sofa, but Sugar was sound asleep with her head back, snoring lightly at the ceiling.

By the time Sharon had navigated Ron Shutmeyer to her great-grandmother's house in the Coco Palm Circle cul-de-sac the black sky had already begun to turn a shade of blue and the birds were starting to wake up and chirp. She thanked them and wished Vanessa good luck with the toe and then waved at them before she let herself in by the side or front door depending on how you looked at it. She was more than a little relieved to find it unlocked and taking off her flats, she tiptoed across the kitchen to the tiny bathroom. She could see the light was off in the guestroom that she and her daughter shared, and she was grateful for this. She went to switch on the light in the bathroom and got the noisy exhaust fan instead. She swore under her breath, switching it off and fumbling for the right switch. While she brushed her teeth, she reminisced about getting ready for bed with her cousins on the family vacations she'd been on up in Lake Hopatcong when she was her daughter's age. How careless and unencumbered she'd been, little Sharon. Two weeks of canoeing, board games with extended family, everyone turning in for bed in the shared cabins, the grownups in one and the kids in the other. She and her cousin Ann made forts by day and at night would read by flashlight under the sheets, her brother shushing them and telling them to go to sleep. How innocent and spontaneous those idyllic summer lake vacations were– the long dock from which they'd drop the inner tubes and then jump in after them. She wished her daughter had been afforded similar childhood experiences. Their family had gotten too small and everyone worked far too much– two week vacations were unheard of these days. She shook her head and placed her hand gingerly on the doorknob of the guest room, turning it with some hesitation, then crept into the room and groped around for the small suitcase that contained her pajamas. All at once the image of the man with the flashlight in his silly pajamas with the knee-high rubber boots came to mind and she had to cover her mouth to keep from laughing out loud. She riffled through her clothes, methodically at first and then a little more determinedly until her hands fell upon familiar silk pajamas.

"Mom?" Melinda's voice croaked, breaking the silence.

"Oh shit," whispered Sharon, "I was hoping not to wake you up."

"Everything alright?"

"Yes. Everything's alright. Go back to sleep."

"What are you doing?"

"I just got up to go to the bathroom."

"But you're dressed." Melinda was up on one elbow now, head cradled in her palm.

"I know. Kind of a late night for your boring old mother."

"Where were you," Melinda rubbed her eyes and yawned, "I mean out this late."

Sharon weighed the question while shaking off her jeans and thrusting her legs into the pajamas, then hoisting her long sleeve shirt over her head, unclasping her bra and then hastily buttoning her pajama top. The room felt stuffy to her. "You hot in here?"

"Not really."

Sharon was suddenly overcome with a longing to be close to the daughter she felt had slipped through her hands, her busy working hands. "I know I'm not perfect," she said, "I know it hasn't been easy on you, any of this. Your dad and I. My work schedule."

"It's okay," said Melinda sleepily, flattening herself once again on her back.

Sharon stood over her daughter. "I love you honey. I really love you and I'm sorry about everything."

"It's late," the girl said. "You need to get some sleep."

Sharon kissed Melinda lightly on the forehead and then climbed into bed, pulling the sheet over her. For a long while she lay on her back and listened to the sound of her daughter's light breathing as the girl drifted easily back into a deep sleep. Sharon lay and thought a while about her serious and bookish daughter and recalled the unbridled silliness that played a hand in her own childhood. Light began to creep through the blinds. She thought about sleeping tablets, but she was too exhausted to get up and dig them out. She glanced across the room at the other twin bed and the form that lay blanketed on it. Melinda had rolled onto her side—her face had a calm and composed expression that looked strangely alien to Sharon, as if it were not her own but someone else's child she beheld. Her daughter's look of undisturbed peace the same as one Sharon might have had at that age, drifting about the still waters of Lake Hopatcong inside her inner tube with eyes closed, bathed in the soft rays of the summer sun.

6

Friday. Another day born out of the darkness of night. Just another day for the collective of retired people whose next-door neighbors were a luck of the draw, a crapshoot– a proverbial hodgepodge thrown together from across fifty states to pattern a community on a block of land which not too long ago had been a swampy undeveloped natural refuge with creeks and cypresses, the exclusive domain of herons and alligators. The land had now been overrun with buildings and golf greens, but the indigenous species hadn't exhibited any signs of resentment– there were no known instances of any aggressive behavior resulting in any harm or injury to human dwellers. Those diehards that remained lurked about in what little was left now of the land's natural state, mere clutters of mini-forest along the pathways of the golf greens left intact for the scenic benefit of the members of the community known as Sunny Glen Palms.

Gerry Hagoden was supposed to go meet the boys for a round of golf, but that was a rather tenuous prospect as the sun began to rise at 7:15. The first question mark was Kenny Fitzroy, considering the way Frank had run him off the previous evening. The second question mark was Hagoden himself, who may as well have been an alligator, laying there on the couch and rubbing his eyes out of an uneasy sleep. Before he even opened his eyes, when consciousness only began to bore a hole through the sleep darkness, the day had already begun to present an uneasy ambiguity. Yes, he may as well have been an alligator– he had done no bodily harm to anyone, but he sure as hell had hurt his wife's feelings. Last night he'd walked home with sunken spirits, and after several minutes of knocking on the door and skulking about outside on the sidewalk, he heard the click of the deadbolt being undone and she'd let him in the house wordlessly, pointing at the sofa which she'd already made up. She retreated to the bedroom, emerging briefly to heave a pillow at the sofa, she flung it so hard it bounced off and landed on the floor.

Now it was morning and he knew they'd have words, he just knew it. He thought briefly about Marion, picturing the easy morning he could imagine was under way just across the street– a

183

morning of croissants, savory French-pressed coffees and light banter. He wondered if the incident that had only served to bring disharmony into his marital affairs, which menacingly plagued his unrested mind, was being bandied about just a few hundred yards away with the most playful nonchalance.

Hearing his wife emerge from the bathroom and begin to fidget in the kitchen he squeezed his eyes shut and willed himself away— back to the darkness of sleep or maybe far away on one of his walks. Wished he were out along the golf cart paths beside the greenways, eyeing the remnants of nature, or along one of those quiet streets off of Hammersmith, wished he were there admiring the perfectly manicured lawns of the houses that lined the street, fabricating stories about their occupants while he whistled and walked, whistled and walked.

He got up, scratched himself, and passed by his wife on his way to the bathroom without any exchange of good morning. Gerry peed and reflected with mounting anxiety that their son, daughter-in-law and grandkids were arriving tomorrow morning. This meant they had roughly twenty-four hours to try and make some headway on this unusual, disruptive and badly timed marital problem. In the mirror he studied his puffy eyes and unshaven face and then splashed cold water at it. He climbed back into the same khakis he hung on the back of the door last night and then stepped tentatively into the kitchen. He poured himself a modest cup of coffee from an untypically meager pot and glanced over at his wife on the screened porch reading the Tampa Tribune, a pair of reading glasses perched on her nose. Gerry switched on the television to fill the room with noise and sat for a while. Shirley commenced to snap the pages of the newspaper with exaggerated briskness, as Gerry watched smiling anchors bring in the morning news. More troops deployed over to Iraq, the Dow Jones closing yesterday with a slight upturn. He switched to Good Morning America. More buoyant optimistic faces doing their best to paint a rosy picture on things while Gerry sipped absentmindedly at the bland coffee, half-listening. At last he drained the cup and cleared his throat.

"Honey," he called. "Sugarcakes?"

Shirley lowered the newspaper enough to glare at him briefly, then brought the paper back up under her nose.

"We have to talk," he said, somewhat hesitantly.

Shirley riffled the pages of the newspaper and flung it at the wicker table in front of her. "*Talk*," she said, "talk about *what?*"

"I'm sorry," he said, his eyes welling up and feeling a frog in his throat. "I am truly sorry for what happened last night."

"Really," she said, "is that all you've got to say for yourself?"

"It's about all I can think of."

Shirley heaved a sigh of exasperation. "Well," she said, "I'm sorry but that's just not good enough."

Gerry gripped the sofa and pushed himself up. "Well," he said, "suit yourself then."

"*Suit myself*," she snapped, "*suit myself then*. Oh sure, go on, romance and kiss a woman right there in front of my eyes, right there before the entire community—"

"I said I was sorry. And it wasn't the entire community."

"Well it may as well have been. It may as well have been Gerry Hagoden, because pretty soon they'll all be talking! They'll all be talking and I'll be the laughing stock of Sunny Glen Palms. And all on account of your reckless behavior."

For a good while nobody said anything, there were only the giddy voices of Good Morning America from the television.

"I don't know," said Gerry finally, "what more I can say. I said I was sorry."

"*Sorry!*" Shirley jumped to her feet and when she landed on the floor it shook the sliding glass doors and a few of the stained glass window ornaments spilled from the doors onto the carpet.

"Maybe you can tell me this, Romeo! Maybe you can tell me what on earth possessed you to go and, and kiss, in *public*, on display right there in front of the whole room, some *hussy*, some flirtatious *bitch*—"

"*She is not a bitch!*" Gerry's voice thundered before he could stop it.

"Oh isn't *this* something." said Shirley to the floor almost at a whisper, "Look at my faithful husband, coming to the defense of his lover."

"I only meant it wasn't her fault."

"Oh? And just whose fault was it then?"

"I take full responsibility. I'm the one kissed *her*, not the other way around."

"*Well* now, at least we're getting somewhere, he admits the dirty deed." Shirley stood with her hands on her hips, nodding her head emphatically and looking directly at her husband. "And while we've got you talking, maybe you can tell me just what made you,"– here her voice trembled just a bit as she dropped back into the wicker chair– "made you betray me. *Betray* me. *What on earth have I done to deserve this*," she asked half to herself.

"Well," Gerry drawled, "it was the music, I think."

"The *music.*"

"Yeah, I-I think so. I guess I just ah… got caught up in it."

"*Caught up* in it?"

"Um. Yeah. I guess it just sort of hypnotized me, y'know? I got caught up–"

"I'll tell you what you got caught up in mister. You got caught up in her perfume. You–"

Gerry began to interject, but Shirley cut the air with her hand. "*Shut up*. You got caught up in her bewitching beauty, that's what you got *caught up* in mister. And you probably would have liked to get *caught up* in her pants too."

"That's not fair."

"*Not fair*? I'll tell you what's not fair. Me having to live with this for the rest of my Sunny Glen life! Did you ever stop to think of the consequences? For me? For *us?*"

"Well I just got caught up in the moment and it was kind of… like a reflex, you know honeycakes–"

"*Don't call me honeycakes!* Don't you ever call me by one of those lousy nicknames *ever again!*"

Gerry threw up his arms in exasperation. "Well," he said, "what should I call you then?"

"*Shirley* suits me just fine."

"Okay, I'll tell you what. I-I think I'd better go for a walk. Get some air."

"I thought you had a round of golf."

"Well, I'm not so sure I'm up to it," he said languidly.

"But haven't you already committed to it? Of course, what would Gerry Hagoden *possibly* know about commitment."

Gerry left the room. Hastily, he laced up his tennis shoes and when he stepped outside the day was already warm. The cold snap was over and sandals would have been more in order but he decided against going back inside. He stood a while at the side of the house, studying the bougainvillea that grew wildly up the wall amidst the marigold and petunia that constituted Shirley's garden.

His empty stomach rumbled. He didn't wish to be seen, not by anyone, lurking about like this– unwashed, unshaven, and dressed in yesterday's clothes. Shirley was right– people would be talking. And of course right there across the street was the woman whose reputation he had sullied, or the siren he'd been lucky enough to share a moment with, depending on how you looked at it. So Gerry lingered there at the side of the house by Shirley's garden. He crouched and studied the flowers up close and began to do some weeding. He tugged and managed to pull a few up by the roots, but most of them just broke off at their leaves despite his best efforts. He occupied himself in this manner for a while, raising his head when he saw an emergency paramedic vehicle creeping along Hammersmith. He scratched his head and hoped for a moment that nobody had died. But death, he thought, was inevitable and how could you hope nobody died? If nobody died, we'd all just have an endless ceaseless struggle to live. If nobody died, places would be more crowded than they already were.

He dusted the soil off his hands and started around the house for the garage and the weeding trowel, but the door was closed and the remote wasn't at hand. With a sense of dread and defeat, he trudged back to the side door. He paused a moment, pulling at an earlobe and straining to discern his wife's hushed words beyond the screen.

I mean– he heard her saying in a confidential, muted tone– I guess I can't be mad with *her*, *she* didn't ask for it… what?… no no, I don't think there's anything going on between them… well you know him and his walks, he's gone so much of the time… what?… well I don't know… well I booted him to the couch last night… well, we've got the kids coming down tomorrow and I don't know, I-I just don't know… that man can be so *impossible*… no I'm okay now, I mean as well as can be expected under the circumstances… no, I don't think there's anything going on between them, I mean what could she possibly see in *him*?… well of course I'm jealous, what do you *think*?… well nobody said anything right then and there, but they sure as hell saw it… no I *didn't* have a tantrum, not right there in front of everyone anyway, I had better sense than to do that… no, he walked home… you know what he says Alma? He says the *music* made him do it, the *muuusic*… I know I know… well he can have his daydreaming about boats and about this and that and the other and I've had just about enough of it… and d'you know for the life of me I can't figure out why it's always *me* dragging the recycle bins to the curbside for pickup, d'ya think he could trouble himself to do it? Even the regular trash, by God it's always left to Shirley, I do *every*thing around the place, I've even got to practically push him out the door to do the shopping, if it's not about pleasure he has no time for it, it's like his mind is somewhere else lately... well I hope last night was *real* pleasurable for him, cause he's not gonna get so much as a damn peck from *this* lady again... *what?* I *am* being reasonable... yes, he said he was sorry but... oh Alma...

She went on in this manner and it rang odd to his ears, almost vulgar, hearing his wife refer to him in the third person, *he* this and *he* that, and he hadn't been aware of the long laundry list of complaints Shirley had on him, they were indicated but hadn't been verbally conveyed to him until now, in this odd framing of third person as she unloaded on her sister. It was Alma to whom she was speaking and so he realized with indignation that now it was open information to the family, but he couldn't blame her, she needed to vent and she always vented to Alma.

He pulled on the screen door. Shirley said well I better go now to the phone as he stepped back inside. "Look," he said to Shirley, "I heard some of that. On the phone, I mean. If you want me to do more around here, why not just ask me? Why are you telling her?"

"*Mister*," she said, "I am one bundle of nerves right now, so you'll just have to bear with me, like it or lump it."

"Well," he said, "I can understand your reaction. I can move out, for a while anyway. If it helps any."

"Move out?"

"Yes."

"And just where to, Gerry? Her place, I'll bet."

"Oh sure, I'll just pack my things and hop a plane over to France with a lady I barely even know. Someone I happened to get a little carried away with and, and... pecked on the cheek. Don't be ridiculous."

"On the mouth."

"What?"

"It was on the mouth. You kissed her on the mouth. I was there. I saw it."

"Okay, on the cheek, on the mouth, what's the difference?"

"Oh, there's a mighty *big* difference mister."

"Well it wasn't exactly what you'd call long and lingering."

"Look," said Shirley, "I didn't have a stopwatch. I'm not going to stand here and argue over what constitutes a long or a short kiss. I'm through even discussing the matter."

"I said I was sorry."

After that, they managed only to speak in monosyllables—Gerry fixing himself some breakfast and Shirley pottering around the house saying aloud to herself more than once, I think I'll wait a few days before I go to the pool.

*

The pool was already attracting quite a crowd by nine o'clock. The sun peeked every now and again through an overcast sky, and the air was thick and muggy. Residents and their guests sought relief in the pool's cool, clear water. Among them, Sharon Rutherford and her daughter Melinda. It hadn't been until the crack of dawn before Sharon could drift off to sleep, but it was a heavy sleep, and when her eyes fluttered awake to the sounds of her daughter quietly rummaging around in the guest room, she felt surprisingly rested. She lay listening to the muffled voices from the kitchen, and then she heard the shower start to run just outside the door and she got up and drew her bathrobe on. At the kitchen table, Flora was staring with deep concentration at a check.

"Morning Nana," Sharon said and Flora glanced up, a smile breaking out of her frozen abstraction.

"Hello dear."

Sharon sat across from her great-grandmother and picked up the agenda calendar Melinda had given her yesterday, the one featuring Dali paintings. She fanned the pages abstractedly and said, still paying bills, eh Nana?

"Why," Flora said, stuffing the check into the pocket of her terrycloth bathrobe, "they certainly never stop coming, no matter what your age. Oh yes, your sister Susan called last night. They're not getting in until eight o'clock tonight. Seems the rest of the Philly crowd are all coming down in one bunch."

"Uh huh."

"But it's too late for the last shuttle. If you don't mind, you can fetch them in my old clunker."

"Does it run?"

"I think so. It did the end of last summer anyhow."

"Well… sure. We can test it after breakfast."

Later, when Sharon turned the key in the ignition of the old Monte Carlo, it didn't respond. Mrs. Beasley next door was fetching the newspaper just then, and a moment later she sent her husband over with the jumper cables. Melinda and Mr. Beasley pushed the car out of the garage and into the driveway so that he could pull his Oldsmobile next to it. Once he'd connected the cables, it took just one crank for Nana's car to sputter to life.

"You might wanna try putting some fresh gasoline in that thing," Mr. Beasley said while he gathered up the jumper cables.

"What a huge car," said Melinda. "Big as a boat."

Melinda and Sharon decided to leave the old car and take the golf cart to the pool, and soon they were sprawled out on the chaise lounges, side by side on their stomachs.

"So what did you end up doing last night," Melinda asked.

"None of your beeswax."

"Sounds to me like you're hiding something."

"Me?"

"Yes you."

"Well it's… grown up stuff, I guess."

"Where did you go?"

"Well," said Sharon, propping herself up on one elbow, "if you must know. We crashed a hot tub. Over at the smaller pool."

"Did you smoke pot?"

"Excuse me?"

"Did you get high? I know the Gastons. They get stoned pretty regularly."

"And just how exactly would you come to know *that?*"

"Mom, those were *my* friends you were hanging out with last night."

"Okay…"

"And I know what they get up to."

Sharon bit her lip and said testily, "And I suppose they're doing it in front of you? You've joined in?"

Melinda made a face.

"Don't be ridiculous Mom, of course not. But I've been to their parties. I have eyes. I've seen them. Out back. I can smell the stuff."

The girl turned over onto her back, fetching her beach hat to shield her eyes from the sun. They both lay silent for a while amid the din of conversation from the burgeoning pool crowd.

"So you didn't answer my question," Melinda said at last. "Did you get high? In the hot tub? With the Gastons?"

*

The Gastons were late risers. When the phone rang at ten o'clock, it woke Philip. He staggered into the kitchen to fetch it.

"Hullo," he said groggily.

"Philip."

It was Flora Wheeler's voice that came crackling on the line. "You ought to know better than to throw money at an old lady like me. I might just take a powder, run off to Tahiti or something."

"That'd suit me just fine," he said. "Just don't take a powder without the Gastons, eh?"

"Philip, listen, you really shouldn't have. I can go to the bank myself and draw *something*."

"Nonsense," said Philip. "You need it for a rainy day."

"I'm afraid there's not too many rainy days ahead for me, dear."

"Well, then lots of sunny ones, eh?"

"Really Philip—"

"It's our gift to you."

Silence on the line and then Flora's voice, very hushed. "Thanks. We can pass a hat at the party to reimburse you."

"That won't be necessary."

"No, I thought about it. I'd like to. It's what we used to do in the mountains, when I was just a young thing. Was our way of covering the musicians. And the moonshine."

"*Moon*shine? Now you're talking."

"You're too kind."

"Don't mention it."

"No, you take after your father after all, Mr. Gaston."

"Well, he was a little more civilized than I."

Flora laughed and it got her coughing. "I remember when you and Sugar started visiting them here, right after you two got married. And then your kids. Seems like yesterday. Everything's starting to feel like yesterday."

"Now don't go getting all mushy on me Flora Wheeler."

"Oh well. I can't thank you enough."

"It's our gift. I just want you to relax and enjoy your party. Oh and Flora? Sugar said if you need any help dolling up for it, she's more than happy to have a little hen party beforehand tomorrow, eh? You know, make-up and hair, all that stuff."

Flora laughed herself again into a coughing fit. "I'm a little too old for vanity."

"No woman is too old for vanity," said Philip.

He hung up the phone and lit a cigarette. For a while he leaned against the counter, naked, gazing out beyond the porch windows at his neighbor, who was busily going about picking up the dog poop in his lawn and shooting the occasional menacing glance in the direction of their house. Philip sighed and wondered why the neighbors didn't just leave it there for fertilizer. It wasn't as if anyone would step in it, the neighbors never set foot in their yard anyway. Except to clear the dog poop.

"G'morning honey," Sugar sidled up beside him, yawned and dropped her elbows on the counter. "Watcha watching?"

"Dog excrement removal. Fascinating."

"Well," she said, "he certainly doesn't seem to be enjoying it as much as you."

They both looked on at the neighbor, transfixed.

"What's he picking it up with," Sugar asked.

"Makeshift gloves. Looks like torn bits of trash bags."

"Oh. Should we let them out?"

"Who?"

"The dogs, silly goose."

"Not *now*. Let's wait till this guy's finished the job. I'll take Daisy for a walk."

"What about Joey? What about his royal dogesty?"

"He's all yours, sweetheart."

"Maybe I'll take him for a run. After yoga."

Philip stubbed out his cigarette. "Sounds like a plan."

*

A plan was underway at the Alsatian household, a plan to secure Libby in the house, ostensibly for her own good, while Frank went off to meet Tommy D'Antonio on the golf greens.

192

He'd decided to take D'Antonio's ribbing of the previous night in stride and play one on one with him. He didn't care much for the company of Kenny Fitzroy and he dared not call across the street to Gerry Hagoden, because he was sure Gerry was going to be in the doghouse, be in that old doghouse for a good while. Frank reflected once again at the level of jealousy Gerry Hagoden's bold and very public display of affection had summoned up in himself. Hadn't he felt the strange stirring of emotion for the attractive and exotic woman who appeared to be far less than her years? He hadn't realized the depth of his feelings until his friend took it upon himself to act on similar emotions. He could only imagine the wrath of Shirley Hagoden– his eyes had locked briefly with hers in the frozen moment after The Kiss. Their eyes met in what seemed mutual understanding, a fleeting moment of forlornness, of desolation. Then just like that, Shirley had slammed her plastic beer cup on the table with enough force to spill a good bit of its contents, took a napkin to wipe the beer off her hand, and strode right out of the room in her saddle shoes. Her pronounced exit seemed to mark the premature death of Pub Night.

Frank was hoisting his bag of clubs onto the back of the golf cart when Betty Molnar strode up to him from the sidewalk pulling her terrier around on a leash.

"Hey Frank," she called to him. When she'd gotten close enough to speak in a lower voice, she raised her eyebrows. "Quite a scene last night huh?"

"Yeah, I guess," he replied, shoving at the bag to get it to fit just so.

"They'll be talking about this one for ages."

"Yeah," he said. "I'm sure they will."

"You know how people just love to gossip."

Frank stooped to rub the little terrier's ears a little. Betty looked around in all directions then bent down closer to Frank's ear. "You don't suppose they got something going do ya? I mean between the two of em."

"No. I mean I don't know."

"*Look,*" she hissed, "here he comes now. Coming out of the house."

"Imagine that," said Frank. "In broad daylight."

"Oh now listen, I didn't mean…"

"No," said Frank, "course not. How's your golf Betty?"

Frank turned around, his back to Gerry, pretending to be occupied with his house.

"Oh," Betty said. "Usual stuff. Great drives, great chip shots, lotta trouble with the putting."

"Same here."

"Yeah," she said, "I heard you had a pretty rough go of it last you were out with Tommy. Tommy D'Antonio."

Frank sighed and said, "I better get going."

*

Going to the South Club pool would have been Gerry Hagoden's preference, dressed as he was in his long flowery swim trunks, a towel draped over his shoulders. But instead he found his feet taking him on a long hike to the other side of town, to the North Club's *indoor* pool, because that's what outlaws do, they know when to lay low, and as far away as possible from the scene of the crime.

He and Shirley had been unable to get past speaking in monosyllables. Their son Jimmy, his wife Lisa and their two kids would be arriving tomorrow afternoon and he hoped to be off the couch by then, because the kids always slept on the pullout and any disruption to that routine would be sure to raise a few eyebrows. He knew, too, that his son Jimmy could be a real pain in the ass with the ribbing— he didn't quite know when to kill a joke, and if he gathered anything was amiss between Gerry and Shirley there would be no end to his irksome prying.

The sun was blazing, the air was thick and Gerry was soon out of breath. He tried to look upon all that he passed, the houses, the garden sculptures, the palm trees, the shrubbery, the flowers, all of the scenery with his customary awe and delight, the old comfort in the admiration of the natural world— but it seemed wherever he walked today a dark cloud followed him. What was it had gotten into to him last night? he mused. Was it something to do with out back on the patio at the Gastons just a few nights ago? Had the marijuana somehow served to shake his moral fiber? Had he begun to go soft in the head? While he puzzled at this, cars whizzed by him on Sunset Boulevard. He couldn't hide altogether. He tugged the brim of his baseball cap down a little, adjusted his sunglasses and hunched his shoulders, trying to walk straight and appear purposeful. Just a regular guy out for a regular walk on a sunny day. But his spirits were overcast and there was no getting around it. The North Club came into sight and he picked up his pace. He'd forgot the suntan lotion, but an indoor day was okay by Gerry, he was a villain, a fugitive on the lam.

When he reached the parking lot he saw Elise emerge from the building with a bundle of books under her arm, heading toward the golf carts. He hesitated. He looked in every direction but there didn't seem to be a place to take cover. He crouched beside a car and pretended to check the tires. He waited until he was sure she'd gone. Then he re-emerged and went straight for the building. Close call, he thought as he entered through the sliding doors. Just how many close calls lay ahead of him? He was pretty comfortable here in the North Club, there were more strangers with whom he had no occasion to fraternize with. People from his side of town came here with less frequency, most of the recreational facilities were replicated at the South Club by now. But certain activities remained exclusively here– the billiards club, radio club, model railroad club, lapidary– oddball stuff like that. He thought about spending a little time in the library, then thought the better of it, in case Elise might have forgotten something and needed to return for it. Off he went in the direction of the locker room and the adjacent indoor pool. First he hit the locker room, which was empty. Inside that echo chamber of tiled floors and walls, he shucked his shoes and socks, pulled his shirt over his head and stepped into the shower to rinse off in accordance with the hygiene protocol of the public pool. It wasn't something he normally did, but today he was all for following the rules to the letter. He toweled himself off and was about to head for the door to the pool when the wooden door opposite beckoned. He glanced in the tiny window of the door to the dry sauna. The wooden benches that lined the walls were empty. From the electric heater the sauna rocks glowed orange. He pulled on the door, stepping inside a tremendous and thick heat, then climbed out of his shorts and draped a towel on the bench of the far wall. He lay down naked on his back and clasped his hands over his chest. Maybe this was what he needed most, perhaps this uncomfortable space, the unyielding hardness of the bench surface against his aching joints, the prospective headache lurking at the back of his head. Perhaps the sweat might just purge him of his iniquities, cleanse the transgression right out through the pores, this just might prove to be the penitence so necessary to set everything right again. He lay like that for ten minutes or so until his body glistened with sweat and he couldn't possibly stand it another minute. Then slowly, carefully, Gerry clambered to his feet and, feeling a little light about the head, he sat back down on the hot wooden bench to gather himself. He climbed into his shorts and out of that torrid chamber to the cool waters of the pool. There were just a handful of other swimmers, one lap lane roped off for an ambitious swimmer with earplugs, goggles and swimming cap– the whole getup. Perhaps the heavily chlorinated pool water might serve to wash away his sins and make him worthy of his wife's forgiveness. Gerry floated awhile on his back in the refreshing waters of baptism, considering this possibility. Surely she wouldn't hold it against him for the rest of their married life. But there were a few things that annoyed him, like the thing about the boats. What had she said to her sister, she'd had enough of that? There was a good chance last night's transgression had given his wife the necessary leverage to veto any plans Gerry had for purchasing that extravagant vessel.

He went back and forth from hot tub to pool a few times before finally returning, exhausted, to the locker room, which was now populated with a fair number of residents moving between the wet sauna, the showers, and the locker area. Naked men sat on the tiny wooden benches by the lockers, naked men stepped out of the showers, naked men lounged about on the tiled seating in the wet sauna, men up there in years, a venerable fraternity of those of the sagging balls and developing tits.

Gerry found an empty shower stall and turned the water on cold to try and wake himself up a little. He didn't see anyone he recognized and he was very glad of that, because he was beginning to feel his spirits lift a little and nothing worse to spoil the mood like running into somebody who was privy to his reckless and aberrant behavior with only a couple of drinks in him last night. Nobody, not a soul, knew him here and he was damned glad of it. He dressed, saluted nobody in particular, the room perhaps, and went about his way.

*

"Way back then," Mimi was saying to Elise in French, "that's all we did was read books. It was about all we had to entertain ourselves. I mean besides recreation. Your mother went through them like nobody's business."

"She was a fast reader?"

"Yes. I, on the other hand. Slow and methodical."

"I see. Well then, maybe these books will keep you busy for a good long time."

"Sure," said Mimi, while Marion looked on worriedly. They were seated at the kitchen table amidst the stack of books Elise had brought back from the library. Elise was considering flying back the coming weekend, uneasy about leaving her mother alone to attend to her aunt Mimi. To both of them Mimi looked frail, peaked, her face drained of color. She was awake a lot during the night, and they sometimes woke to hear one of her coughing fits.

"Are you sure you're up to the beach on Sunday?" Marion squeezed Mimi's elbow.

"I'll be okay. The sea air will be good for me."

"Perhaps," said Elise with a sly glance towards her mother, "we should keep my dear mama from wearing a bikini. She's been catching men like flies lately."

This brought a mischievous grin and briefly some color to Mimi's face. Marion *tsk tsked* her daughter and began to clear the teacups from the table. She was about to step outside for a cigarette when Mimi grasped her arm.

"Wait. There's something I need to tell you about."

Marion sat down next to her, and they continued in their native tongue.

"What is it, sister?"

"It's about me. I want you to stay here forever. But I know that's not possible."

Marion took Mimi's hand and squeezed it. "I could never abandon you. Never. You must let me do whatever it is you need me to do."

"Oh dear sister," said Mimi, "I know you're upset, but I have to make a life plan. For my remaining years."

"Is that what it was you were talking to Steve about this morning? You were on the phone a long time."

"Yes. He wants me to sell the house."

"Sell this place?"

"I've discussed it with him. The stroke nearly killed me. It also left me feeling very helpless and alone."

Tears streamed down Mimi's face. "I'm so frightened."

"But it's too soon for you to do it," Marion squeezed their interlocked fingers.

"I think it's best. I was fine with being here, I mean I could be independent, but then last year things changed. I have to face my remaining years."

Marion could sense it was for Elise's sake that Mimi was reining in her fear that Father Time was winning the race and that death was near. Mimi collected herself, withdrew her hand from Marion's and, engaging her hands for emphasis, spoke very softly. "I know a facility that will take me in while I'm still in my right mind and don't need very much in the way of care. Then later if I need it, they'll provide it without an increase. My sons don't have to trouble themselves about a nursing home. Nursing homes can get very expensive. With this place, it's all there in the package. I think it's the best thing right now. I want to go now while they'll still accept me. Steven's trying to get me cleared with the financial board as having enough monies."

Mimi paused to catch her breath.

"Do you *have* enough monies?" Elise asked, fidgeting with the tablecloth.

"Well, there is a little shortfall after my social security and pension annuities– it comes to about a thousand dollars a month. I'll have to draw from my investments. That I feel bad about. I intended to leave my sons an inheritance. It could dwindle down considerably,"– Mimi coughed and brought a hand to her throat– "but I've communicated my regrets about that."

"And what did they tell you," Elise looked at her mother significantly.

"Steve said he never expected or planned his life around an inheritance. Tom is financially troubled of course, but he echoed Steve's sentiments, he said my happiness comes first. It meant a lot to me. To hear that."

"And what happens if you outlive the investments?" Elise asked, fanning the pages of one of the books abstractedly.

"Oh," Mimi stared down at the table, "I doubt that will come to pass."

"But surely,"– Marion took Mimi's hand once again– "there are other options."

But Mimi seemed to have run out of steam, she just fixed her gaze down at the table and shook her head. At last she said with some effort, "I need a life plan for my remaining years."

Marion let the matter rest awhile, they had lunch and then watched the news. Afterwards, they went outside for a cigarette.

"I really am worried about her," Marion told Elise.

"I can see that. *Life* plan. Sounds more to me like a death plan."

"I have to help her."

Elise shook her head. "I don't know Mama. You can't stay here forever."

"Just until she gets well. Then she and I can talk about her coming back home. To France. With me."

"Is that what you want?"

"With all my heart."

They sat and smoked wordlessly awhile and then Elise put her arm around her mother. Marion dropped her head in her hand and she shook a little. When she'd gathered herself she said, "Those sons of hers are beyond reproach."

Elise was unaccustomed to this vitriolic and sharp tone in her mother's voice.

"At least they're looking out for her. Making arrangements. From the sound of it, Steven's practically got the house on the market already– I mean he's even contacted a real estate agent."

Marion dropped her arms in despair. "Oh," she said, "here's my take on it. Roughly translated. Mimi… *I'm just going to get old and die and nobody is going to take care of me, so I guess I'll just have to take care of myself.* Steven and Robert… *that's okay Mom, go ahead, save us the burden of taking care of you in your old age."*

Elise nodded, staring off into space. "Perhaps you're right."

"Anyway," Marion said, "she can sell this place. But I won't have her shut away in a home."

"I can start readying your house when I'm back," suggested Elise. "Then all you have to do is bring her with you."

"Oh my dearest daughter with the purest heart. Can you call the doctor's office and see if we can make an appointment for Monday?"

"Sure mama."

"How does she look to you?"

Elise took a pull from her cigarette, exhaling with a heavy sigh. "Not too good."

"That coughing worries me."

"I know. I'll call the doctor's office now Mama."

"And the beach?"

"Maybe she's right. I think we should go. I'll take some pictures of the two of you. You can lay them side by side with the childhood photos of Biarritz. We can take her out to lunch."

Marion sighed and teased her hair. "Okay," she said. "Okay, we'll go to the beach on Sunday then. We'll go to the beach."

*

The beach was what Flora Wheeler thought of when Mr. Beasley took the hickory cane from her and offered his arm to ease her into the old Monte Carlo, because the car had often been to the beach when her second husband Buddy had purchased it brand new, right off the lot in 1969 down in St. Pete. There was hardly a day they didn't drive it to the beach, her and Buddy, Buddy the companion husband she'd begun to spend time with after Earl passed. Earl's doctor thought the warmer climate and the sea air would add years to his life. Not two weeks after they'd moved into their bungalow in St. Pete, she woke one morning to find her husband on the porch in one of their matching metal patio chairs with his face literally in the newspaper. She knew before she touched his shoulder. She just knew.

Buddy had lived a few bungalows down from them and he'd introduced himself, stopped by to chat while out on one of his walks. He even occasioned to play checkers and sip bourbon with Earl once. Buddy was soft-spoken and easygoing. It was about three weeks after Earl's funeral that he bought the Monte Carlo, and one afternoon he stepped right up to Flora as she was pruning her rosebushes said it'd sure be nice to have someone to take to dinner tonight in this sharp new automobile. It was there that their polite and restrained courtship began. Marriage seemed unnecessary and a little superfluous to them, but Flora's hippie granddaughter Patricia had outright insisted on this during one of her visits, declaring that a beach wedding would be like *wow, far out, y'know, really groovy*. Patty was now retired and settled, but back then she was a hippie from head to toe and Flora still cringed just a little at the photograph of her hippie maid of honor crowning her grandmother with a bridal veil of daisies.

They decided Buddy should rent his house out and move in with Flora. By now he parked the Monte Carlo in her driveway but it didn't sit around much. They drove that car all over the state of Florida, and it seemed she had seen every inch of beach in the state. After Buddy died in 1981, the Monte Carlo idled in the driveway except for quick drives to run errands. Flora got restless. She got lonesome. There were only young people on her street now and they took no interest in a little old lady. Flora heard about a new community on the other side of Tampa Bay that had affordable new housing and lots of amenities for those over fifty-five. It didn't take long for her to put the bungalow on the market and begin readying herself for the seventh move of her life, the one she hoped would turn out to be her last. It's time I settled down, she had joked to her Deadhead hippie wandering great-grandniece Pamela. Pamela rode down with her boyfriend at the time in a Volkswagon mini camper bus with the sweet but naïve notion of moving Flora. Flora had already hired a moving van, but it sure was nice to have company. Pamela drove the Monte Carlo, while Flora rode shotgun in the Volkswagon with Pamela's boyfriend Dootsy– Flora listened to the Grateful Dead, she toyed with the neon-haired troll dolls that hung from the rear view mirror, she said to the long-haired and bearded boyfriend *I guess we was sort of like hippies back in my day.* He said *that is so cool.*

They arrived at the gate, back then a very modest gate absent of security cameras, uniformed guards, or computers. The guard wore a Hawaiian shirt and Bermuda shorts, sat outside a hut on a lawn chair, and kept handwritten activity logs. Into the very first of these notebook logs Flora Wheeler signed her name, then passed the log back, through the hands of the neo hippie at the wheel, who inscribed his name for posterity, Alfred "Dootsy" Hummer. He shook the guard's hand and said *just call me Dootsy, it's what everybody calls me. Or just Doot.* The guard retrieved the clipboard from Dootsy without a word. Then up came Pamela Wheeler in the Monte Carlo and she signed as guest and followed the purple van riddled with flower power stickers along Sunset Boulevard to the first left– into Aberdeen, Section A. This was how Flora

Wheeler arrived to Sunny Glen Palms, way back then, in the spring of '82.

Now the Monte Carlo chugged along Sunset Boulevard and Mr. Beasley suggested they top off the tank with high octane while he had the car out. You can borrow our car, he told Flora, but Flora merely shrugged and said this old clunker could use the exercise. They drove outside the gate and got fuel. Flora said she had an errand to run at the North Club and Mr. Beasley said he'd be glad to run her by. When they arrived at the North Club, Mr. Beasley got out to help Flora out of the car. After he'd helped her to a standing position she asked for her cane.

"I can take it from here," she said.

"You want me to wait here?"

"If you don't mind."

It was a slow walking day for Flora, and it seemed every joint hurt more with each step. It was fifteen minutes before she got from the electric sliding doors and down the hall to the lobby and on past there to the Events office. She gave her name and the receptionist told her Mrs. Everitt was due back from lunch soon. The receptionist came around the desk and helped Flora into one of the chairs in the hallway. Not long after she'd settled herself into the chair, she saw a familiar face approaching. He'd have otherwise passed by her without so much as a nod of ack-nowledgement, his head lowered, eyes shielded by sunglasses and narrowed on his feet in front of him– but Flora called out, "Excuse me. "Don't I know you?"

He stopped and walked backwards a few steps to meet her gaze, lifting the sunglasses and beaming down at her.

"Why, sure. I'm Gerry."

He extended a hand and she took it in hers and held it. "Tell me again, Gerry what?"

"Hagoden. Gerry Hagoden. We live not far from you. My wife Shirley and I. Over there on Tammany Drive. Near Pioneer Greens."

"Yes I know. You're always walking."

"Yes, that's right."

"You must walk in your sleep."

"Keeps me out of trouble."

"I don't know, seems to me it might raise your chances of trouble. Oh well, good for your heart, young man."

"Yes indeed."

Gerry's face flushed a little. Could this wizened old lady see with what a heavy heart he walked right now? Had word of his misdeed reached even the innocent hundred-year-old ears of Flora Wheeler? She released his hand and said, "I hope you and your wife can make the party."

"We will be there," he said. "At least I will."

Flora sensed something amiss.

"Everything alright?"

"Yes," Gerry said, "just out for a little exercise."

Truth was Gerry considered settling himself into the chair beside her to pour his heart out. It wasn't often someone his age had the chance to seek out the advice of elders. He knew behind those blue eyes fading to grey she had accumulated a vast wealth of knowledge and experience not only in practical matters but in matters of the heart, and would that he had the courage to appeal to her to impart some of that wisdom upon his very broken self. Instead he merely saluted her and left her to her business.

However, none of Flora's business would come to pass at the Events office. She riffled through her purse, spilling out its contents onto the chair beside hers, and with a sigh of resignation determined that she had either forgotten or had lost the check. She left a brief note for Mrs. Ellen Everitt and when she returned to the Monte Carlo and Mr. Beasley, she was worn out and her eyelids were getting heavy.

"You're very kind to wait," she said to Mr. Beasley.

"No problem, Flora. I took the car for a quick spin on the highway. Just to see how she behaves at high speed."

"Oh my. And?"

"Like a charm."

"Good. My great granddaughter has a lot of family to fetch and I don't want them getting stuck tonight. You're so kind Mr. Beasley. I mean it, can I give you something for your time and trouble?"

"Really Flora, I don't need it. It's my pleasure. You should be able to rely on your neighbors."

When they got back it was pushing two o'clock and no sooner had she got out of the Monte Carlo than Melinda came flying up the driveway in the golf cart, Sharon scolding her about her erratic and speedy driving.

"I hope you haven't made any dinner plans," Sharon said to Flora. "I'd like to take everyone out to dinner, assuming the car's in order."

"Yes," said Flora, "Running like a top. Unlike your old great, great whatever here."

"Not feeling well Nana?"

"One of those days."

"Oh, well we can do dinner another time."

"Nonsense. No time like the present. I know a really good seafood restaurant out by Manatee Bay, if they're still there. Just let me lay down a minute, and I'll be right as rain."

"You're a wonder."

"I'm an old bag of bones, no more."

Flora thanked Mr. Beasley again.

"Well you sure hit the jackpot on neighbors," Sharon said.

Flora said, "I always seemed to have good fortune that way," and she turned the cane in her hands until Melinda took her arm and guided her towards the house. "Have you shown your mother the paddleball?" Flora asked Melinda.

"We played shuffleboard," said Sharon. "Lotta fun. Then we had lunch at the South Club. Very nice! You've got all of it here Nana. I always loved visiting you as a kid."

"It's built up over time. When your Aunt Pamela drove me down here, back in… oh '82 I guess it was, there was nothing but a few bungalows and sort of swampy land. They were just laying the first golf course. Didn't even have the clubhouse up yet. It's come a long way."

*

A long way from home, Gerry Hagoden was staggering through the underbrush like a drunken lout— wooden, grabbing at the wild brush out in front of him and dancing around to avoid the prickerbushes. He'd lost his way somewhere just east of the North Club pool, where he'd spied a footpath that led into the woods— he thought he'd kill a little more time before returning to the house and its attendant problems. He thought a walk in the woods might be nice. The path had gradually thinned itself into thick foliage and the dead end in which he found himself now. What drew him in were buildings not too far ahead— he thought it might be a section

204

of Sunny Glen Palms he hadn't seen before and he'd taken a notion to explore it. Maybe it was Brunswick, or Clovington, or Devonshire, one of the crude developments from the early 1980s–those simple bungalows that had window unit air conditioners and cute little front porches with flowerboxes. Five minutes later there he was lumbering along, thrashing about in a manner which seemed to him to harken back to the Wolfman, or Frankenstein. *If my grandkids could see me now.* He was making some headway and then he paused a second at an impulse to lower his socks, cursing Frank Alsatian under his breath for causing him, with a single remark, to be so remarkably self-conscious about something as trivial as his damned socks. He forged ahead and right when he saw daylight through the thicket, he felt the ooze gather about his right ankle and realized at once that he'd stepped into a well-camouflaged and muddy creek bed. There was only one way to go, and so in went the other foot and then there wasn't any socks-up-to-his-knees to worry about. Gerry cursed under his breath and plunged ahead like a madman, muttering and high-stepping it through the weeds until at last he came out on the seventeenth hole of Falcon Crest. As he bounded out onto the carefully trimmed green, who stood before him– clubs in hand– but Frank Alsatian and Tommy D'Antonio. They regarded him silently for a good while.

"What are you guys doing here?" he said at last.

Frank looked at Tommy and Tommy shrugged. "Thought we'd get a change of scenery, try another course. You know, spice things up a little."

"Never mind *us*," said Frank, "what the hell are *you* doing?"

"Nothing. I got lost. I just got lost, is all."

"Where's your cart?"

"Back in the garage."

"Where's your car?"

"Same place."

"You mean you're out here walking around, *on foot?*"

"I don't know of any other way to walk."

Frank glanced once again at Tommy, then back to Gerry, who looked utterly disheveled– the wisps of hair he used to cover his bald spot were hassled, dangling over his sideburns. It looked as if something vile and menacing had tried to wrench the clothes off his back– the shirt collar contorted, sleeve torn and frayed, his khaki shorts splattered with mud and grass-stained, his socks and tennis shoes completely soaked and covered in brown guck.

"You okay Gerry? Really. You feeling okay?"

"Look Frank, don't patronize me, please. Been kind of a rough day."

"Sure looks like it," said Tommy. "Can we buy you a beer or something? Look, I'm almost through kicking Frank's ass, just a couple more holes and we can hit the club. There's room on the cart, waddya say?"

Gerry dawdled.

"C'mon Ger," Tommy said, "no way you can go home looking like that. Not sober anyway."

"One of these days, Tommy D'Antonio," Gerry growled, "it's gonna be you who's the butt of the joke. We'll have a good laugh at your expense."

"Don't hold your breath."

*

"Hold your breath, under water, as long as you can, ready?"

Melinda had found a playmate– a cousin she hadn't seen since she was a baby, which was before she could remember. So as far as she was concerned, this was a new friend altogether. Her name was Sherry and she lived in San Diego, one of the Inman clan. They were the far off cousins from Nana's maternal side and after checking in at the La Quinta, they'd swung by to visit Flora, who to them was also Nana. When at last she came up for air, she saw her mother beginning to gather up their belongings while talking to Vanessa Shutmeyer, as the dark clouds looming to the east began to roll in. Melinda looked forlornly at the bleak sky overhead, then slapped at the water, wanting to remain in the company of her new friend. Sharon said c'mon honey, let's beat the rain. Melinda caught herself beginning to pout, decided that was unbecoming in a lady, and instead said, in a little while. To this Sharon pointed up at the sky. Melinda slowly and grudgingly treaded toward the steps in the shallow end. Sherry skittered off to her folks and Melinda accepted a towel from her mother. She stopped herself from complaining that there were still people swimming in the pool and instead dried herself without a word.

"It's getting on for dinner anyway," said Sharon while dodging a lizard on the path to the parking lot. "We've got to wake Nana up."

"Can we run by the library? Only take a second. You ought to see the North Club. They've got everything. Even a lapidary."

Sharon looked from her watch to the ominous sky.

"It'll only take a minute," said the girl. "I just want to pick up a book they've got locked up. There's a librarian there on Friday afternoons and they can release it for me."

"Okay okay then, let's get going," Sharon said, sensing the urgency in her daughter's voice.

When they got to the North Club the sky had gone dark but there were only a few sprinkles. Sharon let Melinda show her the library and before long she was searching the paperbacks for a quick read to take to the pool tomorrow. Melinda chatted with a volunteer who was the consummate librarian– a short stout lady with bifocals and her hair done up in a bun, one for whom books were obviously a passion.

"I am going to be a writer," Melinda confided in her. She held the hardcover book to her chest and shifted back and forth on her heels.

"Oh yes," the demure old woman glanced over her bifocals, sizing up the teenager in front of her. "A noble profession that."

Melinda wondered what made it, in this woman's eyes, a noble profession. But she went on. "My Nana, that's my *great-great-*grandmother, she's the one we're signing out under… anyway, *she* says I've got a writer's temperament."

"Really?" The librarian showed genuine interest. "Have you written anything yet?"

"Just some, like, poems and stuff."

"My heavens," said the lady, "don't say *just* poems. Poems are lovely things to read."

"Not my poems."

"Oh? Why not?"

"Honey," Sharon put a hand on Melinda's shoulder, glanced at the librarian and said, "we really have to get going."

But Melinda just sighed and said, "They're not very happy. But I'm going to write a story. That's what I want to do. Write a story."

"A happy story? A romance, a mystery?"

"No, nothing like that. I want to write about people."

"What kind of people?"

"Regular people. And it won't be a happy story. Because most people aren't happy. I know I'm not happy. Not most of the time anyhow."

"Honey," said Sharon with a little more urgency, "Dinner, remember? Nana? And I have to pick up Aunt Susan and the rest of them from the airport tonight."

"Nice to meet you," said Melinda to the librarian.

"I hope one day it'll be your book on the shelves in here," the old woman said to their backs, and Melinda tossed her a little wave over her shoulder.

On the way to the parking lot Sharon looked inquisitively at her daughter." Do you really want to be a writer, Mel?"

"I can think of nothing else right now."

"Well, like the lady said, it's a noble profession. But not a very practical one."

"Why is it noble? What makes it any more noble than any other profession?"

"Well, you certainly have to do it for the love of it."

"Well I do love it. I love words. I love reading."

"Reading is one thing. Writing's another."

"Well I like them both."

By the time they reached the golf cart, the rain had begun to fall in heavier drops. They spoke to each other from either side of the golf cart as they unfurled and snapped its vinyl cover over the sides.

"Have you thought about school any while you've been here honey? Y'know, what electives you might take next year, your interests, college, that stuff?"

"I already told you. I like writing."

"Well, I can tell you, writing does not pay the bills, per se. Perhaps you could apply your writing skills towards something in the business world, like advertising or marketing, or even human resources–"

"Yuck! Me in the business world? No thanks."

"What do you mean by that?" Sharon said, climbing behind the wheel and setting her pocketbook behind the seats.

"I don't want to end up in some job that I hate just so I can collect a paycheck. I want some adventure in my life."

"Well, believe me, life is full of adventure. You'll find that out as you get older."

"I don't mean the regular shit—"

"Watch your mouth."

"I mean *real* adventure. I wanna do something meaningful."

Sharon backed the cart out of the space and switched on the headlights as Melinda put her feet up on the dashboard and continued. "I don't wanna be stuffed away in some stupid cubicle somewhere like those people we saw at that stupid corporate field trip out at Dupont. Reminded me of caged animals in a zoo."

"I'd say they're just honest hard-working people providing for their families."

"Well good for them."

"Okay, well… so just what is it you want to do then, dear daughter?"

"I wanna travel. Like that guy John who's staying here with his Mom now? He hangs around with the Gastons? Man oh man, he's been everywhere. Even Turkey."

"Yeah and look where that's gotten him. You see yourself living with me when you're a grown adult?"

"Ew, no way."

"Uh-*huh*," Sharon nodded resolutely, taking a sharp turn faster than she intended, causing Melinda to clutch her seat.

"Well," said Melinda, "he's only here for a spell anyhow. I don't mean I want to end up just like *him*. But I want to travel. The Gastons said I could stay with them in Toronto. Philip said he'd take me hunting with his kids."

"You're gonna have to be a little bit older for that my dear. To visit the Gastons."

"They're my friends. I can visit them any time I like."

"Hey now, I don't like your tone, kid. You don't just do whatever it is you please. Not while you're in my custody."

"You make it sound so formal."

"I guess I must pale in comparison to all of your exciting new friends."

"No offense, but I don't want to end up like you."

"Oh? And what's so bad about Sharon Rutherford?"

"All you do is worry about money! Bills! That's your whole life! You never go out and enjoy yourself."

Sharon brought the golf cart to an abrupt stop and then gunned it through the intersection. "Now listen Melinda! Have you ever stopped to consider all the sacrifices I've made just to keep a roof over your head? To provide for you!"

"I will never end up like you. You don't work that job, *it* works *you*—"

"Oh how clever—"

"All those pills you pop! I've seen little brown bottles since as long as I can remember! It's not natural—"

"It's called coping."

"That's no way to cope."

Sharon veered the golf cart off of the slick road and it bumpity-bumped onto the grass. "I'll tell you something, young lady. You've no idea what your mother's been through the last—"

"Fourteen years?"

"Well."

"Go ahead and say it! I'm a burden! I'm just a weight on your shoulders!"

The rain had let up and so there were people about. Their voices were raised and Sharon kept glancing through the clear plastic in every direction, a little anxious about their hashing out personal issues in public. An old woman walking her poodle had stopped to see what all the commotion was about.

"I don't need a fourteen-year-old analyzing my—"

"You are the very picture of boredom!"

"Am not!"

"Are too!"

"Oh, that's great! Nice one Melinda, just keep talking and making your mother feel like dirt. Nice, real nice. Go on."

"When you're not working overtime at home to kiss up to that bitch of a boss of yours, you're watching all that fluff on the television and believing everything they say is true—"

"I do not!"

"You buy everything they sell. You couldn't possibly have an opinion of your own, besides the popular one, because then they'd all look at you funny, all of them corporate clones you try to fit in with every single day! It's just like school! Trying to fit in… getting all worked up about your salary, your job reviews, all that shit drives you to those stupid pills!"

"Watch your mouth, young lady! Must have been your dad, I sure as hell didn't teach you to talk like that—"

"The same stupid pills you pushed on me!"

A small crowd had gathered, people coming out of the neighboring houses, but Sharon was now so engulfed in the rage that lay in that small space between them in the tiny golf cart, the onlookers may as well have been invisible. *"Now you listen to me—"*

"Okay, I'll be polite and restrained. Sure Mom, I'll just get in line and shut up and pay bills and be the robot you seem to—"

"Shut up."

"Don't tell me to shut up."

"Shut the hell up."

"Well now isn't this nice. What sweet words for your only daughter in the world."

"I worked my ass off for you, I toiled and tried my best to do right by you through all the mess I've been through, and what do I get in return. Biting sarcasm and a smug analysis of my—"

"I think we're drawing a crowd."

Sharon glanced over at the lady with the poodle and the crowd of about half a dozen others that had congregated on the sidewalk in front of them. She met the gaze of a tall thin man in a jogging suit who called out, everything alright?

"Of course everything's alright. Just mother and daughter stuff," Sharon's voice came muted from inside the plastic bubble, her remark garbled by Melinda's simultaneous response— "What does it look like to you? No, everything's *not* alright! Everything's *never* alright!"

"Hey," the bystander said, spreading his palms in apology. "I was only asking."

"Well, move along and mind your own—"

"Shut up," Sharon slapped her daughter on the shoulder.

"Physical abuse!" Melinda unzipped the golf cart cover a bit and stuck her head out at the bystanders. *"Did you see that?"*

"Oh shut up," said Sharon. "Sorry folks, show's over." She n reversed the cart back onto the street. The old lady with the poodle looked on wordlessly and a stout woman behind her wearing an apron smiled and waved as they drove off.

Neither of them said a word for the rest of the way back to Nana's. There was, however, no alteration in plans for dinner. Their Nana was having a catnap in the recliner and sprung to life when they walked in the door. Before long they all climbed into the Monte Carlo. The restaurant Nana had in mind was by the water and they were seated outside. There were puddles on the patio from the afternoon rain, but the sky was now clear in every direction and they had a perfect view of the sunset on Manatee Bay. The whole affair was strained. The tension between the two of them was obvious to Flora, who acted as a conduit, and the only means of preventing a dinner held in total silence. They both talked to Flora and she engaged one and then the other. By the time dessert arrived she was every bit as exhausted as she was before her nap.

It was a long drive home with an awkward silence broken periodically by Flora pointing out this place or that. When they returned to the house, there were several messages on Flora's machine and she returned calls, thrumming the Gastons' check in her lap. Sharon flipped absent-mindedly through the pages of magazines and Melinda flopped in front of the television and surfed through the channels, unable to settle on anything.

*

Anything Frank Alsatian might have been thinking about dinner plans would quickly be snuffed out because there was a surprise waiting for him when he got home from the Club after a few drinks with the guys. He sensed something was amiss the minute he turned the key in the double lock and pushed the door open from the garage. The house was dead quiet. He set his keys on the counter and called out for his wife.

"Honey?"

He walked on through the living room to see about the guestroom, the bedroom, the bathrooms. When he stepped down into the screened porch there was broken glass on the floor. One of the window panes had been busted out and the screen lay on the floor, its cloth torn and the frame mangled.

The first thing he did was comb the neighborhood in the golf cart. Along the way, he saw Gerry Hagoden rolling up the garden hose and he didn't go out of his way to avoid him this time. Gerry had by now traded his squishy socks and tennis shoes for sandals.

"What's wrong, Frank?"

"It's Libby. I can't find my wife. She got away. She got away again."

"Man I sure wish I had your problem," Gerry nodded at the house. "You got any idea what it's like dealing with *her* when she's in one of her funks?"

"C'mon Gerry, this isn't the time for jokes."

"Who's joking?"

"Can you help me look for her?"

"Look, Frank, I'd love to. But I've been gone all day and now she's watching me like a hawk."

"I heard that."

Shirley appeared from the side of the house and Gerry spun around sharply to see a familiar speaker greatly transformed in appearance. His wife had been to the hairdressers for a cut and perm and he considered this new visage about her with a vague uneasiness, as if he'd be dealing from now on with a completely different person in trying to resolve their difficulties. She looked from one to the other and said, "What's the matter Frank?"

When he hesitated to answer Shirley said, "C'mon inside the house a minute." Frank followed her and sat down on the sofa, accepting with two hands the glass of filtered water Shirley had drawn from the fridge. She settled herself across from him.

"Okay, tell me what's going on."

"Libby's gone missing."

Frank's voice cracked. Gerry entered the room and stood tentatively by the matching chair across from him.

"I just need a search party before dark."

The Hagodens could tell it was an effort for him to regain command in his voice.

"Look Frank," Shirley said. "I know this has got to be very tough. Got to be very hard on you. We're here to help, any way we can. We'll help you find her again, but after that hon, you're gonna have to make some tough choices."

Frank clasped his hands in front of him, shaking his head gravely. "I can't."

His shoulders were shaking and his chest heaved and then there were tears. "I-I can't just... just... put her away... in- in a home somewhere. Christ she's my goddamned wife! I can't, I just can't."

Shirley got up and sat next to him, patting his shoulder.

"I'm not saying that's the only option. But you can't just go on hiding her and locking her up and expecting it to solve the problem."

It was quiet for a good while. Shirley wrung her hands, glancing up at Gerry. "Well," she said, "you gonna sit down or what? You're making me nervous standing there like that."

"Waddya want me to do?"

"Sit down, for a start."

A figure appeared at the screen door and tapped lightly on it. When Gerry saw that it was Marion Legrand, he looked to his wife imploringly. Shirley looked from the door to him and nodded. Gerry pushed the screen door and held it open. Marion squeezed past– at such close proximity there was no way to avoid their bodies brushing lightly and then he caught a whiff of her perfume as he indicated one of the chairs across from the sofa.

"Can I get you something?" he asked.

"No, no thank you." Marion was fidgeting and looking everywhere but at Frank as he gathered himself, stood up and excused himself to the restroom. Then Marion looked at Shirley and said, "I come to say I'm sorry. To you. Mrs. Hah-goh-den."

"No need to apologize."

"I just–"

"No," said Shirley, getting up to place a hand on Marion's shoulder. She spoke methodically, squeezing Marion's shoulder as she enunciated each word. "Look, a man... asks you to dance... there's nothing wrong in that."

Marion stared straight ahead, her face expressionless.

"A man kisses you, what? You didn't ask him to," Shirley shrugged. "You. Did not. Ask him to."

"I know," Gerry started, "It's my fault and–"

"*Shut up*," Shirley snapped. "Now listen, Marion. This is between me and my clown of a husband and you have no reason to worry or fuss about it. You have enough on your hands to worry about, d'you understand?"

"I think I do."

"You just don't worry, let Shirley do all the worrying."

Frank came back into the room, his shoulders reared and composed. He cleared his throat. "How's Mimi, how's she doing?"

"Oh," said Marion, "she's not well. We make appointment with doctor for Monday."

"Well," said Shirley, clasping her hands, "you let us know if we can do anything."

"Oh, you are veree kind but–"

"Nonsense." said Shirley, "I'm not very kind. But at least I have a heart."

With these words she glared over at Gerry, who dug his hands in his pockets, shuffled his feet and started to say something before Shirley cut the air with her hand.

"Just call us if you need us," she smiled at Marion and then Marion got up to leave. Shirley showed her to the door, waving and hollering after her, "I mean it. Call on us. Anytime."

"Now," she said, turning to face the others, "let's get down to business. I'll tool around on my golf cart and let's make sure we all got our cell phones."

"Okay then," said Frank. "Let's not lose another minute of daylight."

But the sun was already escaping.

*

Escaping from one issue only to meet another, Marion thought, as she opened the screen door and met the expectant gazes of both sister and daughter. She drew a chair and sat herself between them. At least here she could impart all that was on her mind in her native tongue. Before they could query her about the Hagodens however, she broached the subject of Saturday's gala event. They agreed Mimi wasn't going to make it to Flora's party. It was too soon after the stroke to be around such a big crowd and all that excitement. Mimi didn't protest, but when Marion suggested they might hold off on Sunday's outing, she made it clear she wouldn't concede about the beach.

"I think the weather will be perfect," she said, "and besides, we won't have Elise around much longer to enjoy it. Who'll take the photographs?"

She made an effort to laugh but could only accomplish a withered smile. "Still," she said, "I'd like to send flowers and a card with you to the party. I'm glad she invited you both."

"But we'll take turns going, sister," said Marion.

"No no," Mimi had said. "I'll be just fine. I'm just happy she invited the both of you."

"Well," said Elise, "maybe it's better if we go together. That way I can keep an eye on our home wrecker."

She winked at her mother.

"Oh really," Marion rolled her eyes, "I've already apologized to Shirley for the unintended consequences of my incalculable beauty on that poor man."

"And?"

"She did not accept my apology."

"Huh?"

"No," Marion sighed, "she is a most gracious and admirable woman, our Shirley is. The apology, she said, is not mine to give. The fact that it was her husband that kissed *me* was not lost on her. And I can tell you I am more than a little relieved to know that we are not going to be mortal enemies. Because you know something, I like that woman. I like that woman very much."

"Did you know," Mimi said to Elise, "your mother could catch them like flies when she was young."

"How would you know," asked Marion. "You left when you were sixteen."

"You caught me up quite a bit later on, you old hussy. And Martin told me more than once that he fretted about all the boys lining up from the moment he met you, through the engagement right on up to the wedding day."

"Oh nonsense."

"You," said Mimi, "always looked younger and prettier than I. It's a matter of fact."

Mimi noticed with no small amazement how her French had come back to her slowly over the last week, especially in light of how many other things she was forgetting. Maybe, she mused, her brain was making room for the French.

Mimi certainly remembered Flora Wheeler well enough. The crafts room had been their meeting ground. A few years back, Mimi decided to take a course in quilting. She kept passing by the crafts room at the North Club and peering through the glass at the array of colorful patterns and she thought it would be a good way to get out and meet people. At that time she was new to Sunny Glen Palms– bereaved, grieving, and feeling sorry for herself. She'd done some quilting in the seventies, so she had an inkling of what she was getting into the day she ventured past the glass and into that room where a few glanced up from what they were doing and resumed their precision work. There were rows of tables with metal folding chairs and one wall was lined with shelves stocked with yarns, thread, fabric, and needles. A frail old woman was busily stitching at one table, and for an instant Mimi thought to turn away and forget the whole thing. These ladies were elderly to her, and seemed as delicate as the thread they worked with, and their hair resembled the white batting spread out on the tables. She was really quite young by comparison, just over sixty. Perhaps she'd be better off joining the book club.

But the old woman looked up sharply and her smile was captivating. 'Well hello,' she said, 'what's your name?'

'I'm Mimi. Mimi Brooks.'

'You're new here.'

'Yes. I am. Relatively speaking, that is, yes. Moved in a few months ago.'

It had actually been over a year, but she kept to the few months ago reply because at that time she hadn't got out much. It had been a year of indoor grieving and she preferred to think of it in months, not an entire year, not a whole awful year sitting inside waiting for Steve or Tom to call and feeling sorry for herself.

The woman stood up and leaned on an old hickory cane with one hand. With the other she clasped Mimi's hand, gazing up at her searchingly with eyes a delicate and fine blue.

'Well now,' she said. 'Mimi, that's one special name. Pretty name I think, yes. I'm Flora.'

'It's nice to meet you Flora.'

She neither released Mimi from her firm bony grip or the gentle gaze of her bright blue eyes. Eye contact of such duration would normally have put Mimi off, but not right then and there. They talked a little and she felt a glow from the frail old woman. Flora had that facial tic old people sometimes have of dancing their jaw around a little while they listen.

'What is it you wish to do, Mimi Brooks?' Flora asked.

'I thought I'd join the quilting class.'

'Well,' Flora patted her hand and released it, pointing Mimi towards the table. They sat across from one another. 'I teach a class for beginners.'

'You do?'

'Why do you look surprised? These nimble hands still got some fire in them.'

'Oh, I didn't mean to…'

'Pshaw. I'm eighty-seven years old and here I am teaching people how to quilt. Call me crazy.'

'Judging by all the beautiful creations that line these walls, I wouldn't say you're crazy,' said Mimi.

'Oh, pshaw,' said Flora, 'we'll have you making one every bit as nice as these sooner than you think.'

Flora introduced her to the other two ladies in the room and then she walked with her to the door. 'I'm going for a coffee break in that new restaurant by the lobby. Would you care to join me, Mimi?'

'I'd like that very much.'

It was a cup of coffee that Mimi wouldn't forget, because Flora Wheeler plied her with questions. She wasn't nosy or asking just for gossip-hunting purposes. Flora Wheeler was genuinely interested in the whole backstory– Mimi as a child in her native France, Mimi the war bride, Mimi the mother of two, even Mimi the peak-time bank teller. Flora Wheeler was the first person she'd met in Sunny Glen Palms who was genuinely interested.

When they'd finished their coffee and had got up to leave, Flora looked Mimi in the eye again. 'You know Mimi, my mother used to tell me the eyes are the windows to the soul. You,' she patted Mimi's hand, 'are an old soul. You are a good soul, you have a lot to bring to your friends and neighbors, and you will do fine here. It took me a while when I lost my Buddy to come out of my shell, believe me. But you are going to love it here, I promise. Welcome to Sunny Glen Palms.'

This welcome greeting was not a first– she'd heard those same words uttered by that manager at Windmere Properties when she arrived over a year ago to pick up the keys and do a walk through. But from that stiff and saccharinely polite manager, they hardly carried the same openhearted goodwill that Flora now exuded. Not long after that Flora became less and less mobile but her words would prove themselves true– Mimi made herself a nest of friends, lost some and gained some as she stayed on at Sunny Glen Palms. The mention of Flora's party brought on this vivid recollection of the lady who way back then had managed so effortlessly to crack her shell. She thought she was doing a pretty good job of hiding the fact that it was absolutely killing her not to be able to attend the party.

The party was well underway with the Gastons in Ybor City, known as Tampa's Latin Quarter. After decades of neglect, a portion of the original neighborhood had reignited itself into a nightclub and entertainment district back in the early 1980s. Our Gastons and Shutmeyers had ensconced themselves comfortably into wicker armchairs on the balcony of one of the fine dining establishments, amid the fancy ironwork in the style of French Creole. Philip pulled on his cigar and blew a plume of smoke in front of him. He was in an expansive mood. He was doing his level best to describe the pirate-themed Gasparilla parade that was on for tomorrow in that same place, for which there were now several pre-parties underway.

"It's kind of like a mini Mardi Gras," he was saying. "Except the women don't flash their tits."

Ron Shutmeyer studied his cigar as if he were looking at a curious artifact and flicked the ashes off the end. He glanced over at his wife.

"Man, we gotta get out of the gate a little more often."

The gate he referred to was of course, that gate from which one entered and exited Sunny Glen Palms.

"Well," said Vanessa, "I don't see why not. Though you gotta admit," she said, glancing around her, "there's nowhere you can just up and skinny dip around here."

"Point well taken," said Ron, gulping down the rest of one of those fancy cocktails from its wide-brimmed glass. "But you still can't beat the ocean for a good old skinny dip."

Ron jiggled the ice his glass while Philip ordered another round. "What the hell am I drinking, anyway?" he asked.

The drink was fuzzy blue and red, served with a slice of lime and a plastic umbrella stirrer and had a fancy name he kept forgetting, even after three rounds of it. Shutmeyer wasn't exactly cut out for these foo-foo drinks– Ron was a beer man, tried and true. His forays into the spirits world were bound to those rare instances when he'd get a hankering for Jim Beam shots or Jack and Cokes, and those drinks could really get him in trouble with his wife. "Well," he slurred, "I'll have another one anyway."

Vanessa, still nursing her first alongside a glass of water, gave him a sideways glance and patted his thigh. "Better go easy on them," she said.

"Ah," he demurred, "let's let ole Ronny enjoy himself a little tonight,"– he spread his arms at the table– "here among our new friends."

"Sounds *real* good to me," Sugar said, stirring her drink and giving Ron the eye. Philip was picking at the appetizer tray. He shot her a knowing glance and winked. Their waitress returned and they ordered entrees.

"Now," Ron said, "I'd like to raise a little toastie, to the all-time champion old fogey dancers, the Gastons."

Everyone brought their glasses up as Ron continued. "But," he said, "how about my ole GM buddy? He sure as hell won the kissing contest. Just goes and kisses that French woman. Right in front of the room. Right on the mouth."

Ron shook his head and sighed. "Sure takes balls."

"Uh-uhh," Sugar quipped, "you're thinking of something else entirely."

Philip clinked his glass all around the table and said, "Once again my lovely wife hits the nail on the head. There's not that much there to talk about anyway, Ron. Hardly rates, compared to what we get up to on our nude cruises, eh honey?"

Sugar ran her hand along Vanessa's sleeveless arm. "If you haven't guessed, we're swingers. It's a way of life."

Vanessa smiled politely and shifted in her seat.

"Now honey," said Philip, exercising practiced social graces, "no need to go spilling the beans all over a lovely marble table."

Sugar swirled her drink. "I thought for sure they could tell by now."

"So," he continued, "when are you two going to maximize your disposable time and join us on one of these lovely cruises?"

"Not our style," Vanessa replied a little too abruptly to even her own ears. "I mean, um, you know, Ron and I are just getting settled and all that."

"How about a weekend in Daytona," said Ron, "I heard all about a biker fest–"

"Oh," said Sugar, "it's heavenly."

"Just looking at all of those incredible tattoos is worth it in itself," said Philip.

"Let's go," Ron said, "waddya say honey?"

Vanessa shrugged. In recent years, it was aging that had propelled her into a new world of holistic approaches to health, spawned an interest in new approaches to physical well-being that quickly extended to that of a more spiritual realm. Vanessa would rather have heard a proposal to attend a weekend of nutritional counseling, or Reiki, or a folk music festival, or perhaps a Native American crafts fair– not a weekend prowling around drunk from one beer tent to another, out in the hot sun amidst leather-clad chrome rollers comparing tattoos and hollering to one another to be heard above the din. Vanessa, beginning to embark on a long-deferred spiritual awakening, could lately sense her husband was meanwhile headed for a second adolescence. She felt the weight of his hangovers– she was a practicing Catholic and getting him out of bed for Sunday mass at the Spanish church in Lithia was beginning to prove a difficult task. They could play volleyball together, they could share the phone and talk to their daughters, they could curl up snugly together on the sofa and watch a little television. But lately she sensed more and more, with a certain twinge of dread, a burgeoning gap in their mutual interests.

When they'd finished their dinner, the men relit their cigars. Vanessa had her purse out and groped around for a credit card but Philip insisted on covering the check. They went club hopping, everyone doing shots and beers while Vanessa sipped cranberry juice. It was well after midnight when they traipsed off to the parking lot, arm in arm, Sugar and Philip singing some tawdry Irish drinking song, *As I went home on Monday night as drunk as drunk could be, I saw a horse outside the door where my old horse should be, Well I called me wife and I said to her, will you kindly tell to me, who owns that horse outside the door where my old horse should be?* They replaced words with the f-bomb when so inclined, shaking with laughter at each line.

"Man," said Philip, "this place is goin to be one hell of a badass party tomorrow. All those great big floats winding their way along Seventh Avenue, all the pretty ladies in their skimpy outfits throwing beads at everyone?"

"Can we throw beads at them," Ron wanted to know.

"Suuuuure," said Philip. "Goddamn shame Flora had to pick Gasparilla to have her fucking party. I don't know about this double duty shit tomorrow, my dear."

"Oh nonsense," said Sugar, "you're purrrrfectly suited to the mission."

They started up their song once again. *Ah, you're drunk, you're drunk you silly old fool, so drunk you cannot see, that's a baby boy that me mother sent to me! Well, it's many a day I've travelled a hundred miles or more, but a baby boy with his whiskers on sure I never saw before...*

Vanessa took the wheel of the jeep and Philip began to guide her back to the highway, turn here quick he said, balancing a cup of beer in his lap, and she almost missed the entrance to the Selmon Expressway, but she cut the wheel and Ron went flying into Sugar's lap in the backseat and there he remained, his head cradled in her lap, and she stroked his hair as he passed out. Vanessa glanced intermittently at the rear view mirror to make sure no kisses were taken or given, because this swinger stuff didn't sit too well with her, she had embraced the Gastons, hugely embraced them, but an open marriage didn't sit well with her– she neither condemned nor praised it, it was fine for others, but it was *not our style*, as she'd so forcefully remarked to Sugar previously and now as she drove she hoped to God that that statement had settled the matter, put the whole thing to rest, but she wasn't so sure as she watched Sugar run her fingers gently through her husband's pepper gray hair in the backseat of the jeep, Philip Gaston sitting beside her singing that silly old Irish drinking song *And as I went home on Saturday night as drunk as drunk could be, I saw two hands upon her breasts where my old hands should be, Well, I called me wife and I said to her, will you kindly tell to me, who owns them hands upon your breasts where my old hands should be,* Philip Gaston, not a care in the world, not caring one way or the other about what might develop back there behind him between his wife and another man in the jeep's backseat, as it rolled on down the interstate and back to the gate, the gate– and beyond it the confines of ineffable, enigmatic, and majestic Sunny Glen Palms.

7

Edna Norton, you may recall, was next-door neighbor to the Hagodens, and just across the street from the Alsatians. Edna Norton was introverted by nature, a recluse, a homebody- despite Shirley Hagoden's and (for a brief spell before her slide into dementia) Libby Alsatian's best efforts to draw her out socially. She did Bridge night, at Shirley's prompting and then prodding, at the North Club on Wednesdays and occasionally Saturdays. She sometimes went to the pool. But for the most part Edna Norton dwelt among her memories. This was clearly evidenced in her choice of radio station. WTMB Tampa's programming bespoke antiquity, it was Lawrence Welk fare, with a good measure of the World War II-era Big Band music of Jimmy and Tommy Dorsey. In a more contemporary vein, you might hear a bit of Frank Sinatra and Doris Day. The commercial advertising was clearly geared to the aged— pain relief medications, Medicare supplement plans and reverse mortgages. WTMB's target demographic was the over-seventies crowd, and since people were living longer due to the many advances in medical science, this was a large and vital market in retiree-swamped Florida.

Edna's exodus to Florida was at the prompting and then prodding of her sister Charlotte. Edna Norton was a caretaker of the first order. Edna bore two children, first a daughter who was diagnosed with multiple sclerosis at a very early age. Her second was a son who was killed in action in the Korean Conflict, leaving behind a young widow and newborn daughter. After her second child, the doctors informed her that she would no longer be capable of child-bearing. But she was capable enough of child-*rearing* and she doted on her MS-riddled daughter every minute of every waking day, right on through to the girl's premature death at the age of nineteen. Then her own ailing mother came to live with the Nortons and Edna saw to her mother's every whim for three years. Her final performance as caretaker, her swan song, came in response to her husband's three-year long struggle with cancer of the colon and then lymph nodes. After the battle was over, Edna stuck to the house and seldom went anywhere. She had three siblings, but only Charlotte could manage to tease out a relationship of sorts. With a wary vigilance that sister took notice of Edna's tendency to hoard in the years after the husband passed— the modest Cape Cod house had become overstuffed with old newspapers, empty milk cartons, canned goods that would remain unopened, all manner of items which would ordinarily be discarded hung around that house along with the ancient furniture and the time-worn framed photographs that hung on walls or sat on tables. Charlotte intervened, she was the only one who could and so she did. Charlotte said you must get away from this old museum of a house, this tomb of the dead. Charlotte said you need a fresh start. Charlotte and her husband said we're packing you off for Florida, and we're not far behind.

All the same, when he entered the domain of Edna's dwelling there on Tammany Drive, Frank Alsatian had the sense that he'd stepped profoundly and categorically into the past— from the Victorian furniture to the burgundy crushed velvet floor-to-ceiling drapes. From a prominent place in the living room where a television might have been, easy listening music issued from an old Zenith tombstone black-dial radio. An heirloom from Edna's parents, the radio had been preserved and retained for several years. It was that same radio which Edna and her late husband had danced in front of way back when, there in Dad's living room. That radio had been witness to their first kiss.

Into this preserve of yesteryear Frank Alsatian arrived early Saturday morning. He was up and about early after a restless sleep. His wife had gone missing again last night and he wanted her found before the sun went down, because last time the dispatch at the Hillsborough County Sheriff's office told him wait twenty-four hours before phoning in a missing person case and he sure wanted this resolved without police intervention, without involving even Sunny Glen Palms security if he could help it. He was there to launch a neighborhood watch campaign for Libby, he was there ostensibly to obtain another pair of eyes in the search for his estranged and cognitively-challenged wife. But when he sat down somewhat self-consciously on the pristine and plastic-covered Victorian sofa of carved walnut, he realized with resignation that the true impetus for his unprecedented call on Edna Norton was a chance to spill his guts, and for Frank it was easier to unburden a heavy heart on the ears of a stranger, and that is what Edna Norton was to everyone on Tammany Drive and a scattered few in the larger community of Sunny Glen Palms– a reluctant spectator, an unremarkable participant, a perfect stranger.

The curtains were drawn against the Florida sun, the room dimly lit by the antique stained glass table lamps. From the radio The Sandpipers crooned cushy muzak harmonies. Edna brought him a fresh cup of coffee from... yes– the old percolator. Frank wasn't sure exactly where to start and they sat wordlessly among relics while he gathered his thoughts. At last he cleared his throat. "I, ah, just wanted to alert... er *inform* you that my wife has gone missing."

"Oh *my*," said Edna, bringing a hand to her mouth.

Frank nodded sagely, leaning forward and wringing his hands.

"When did this happen?"

"Y-yesterday. Sometime in the afternoon."

"Have you called the police?"

"Well, I- I can't do that. Not until twenty-four hours have elapsed."

"Eh?"

"You have to wait until she's been missing for twenty-four hours."

"Oh my goodness." Edna fidgeted with her nightgown. The radio now sang the Benny Goodman Orchestra's rendition of Sing, Sing, Sing.

Frank heaved a sigh, settling himself into the sofa's deep burgundy fabric cushions. "I don't know what to do anymore."

"I've been wondering how Libby was," said Edna. "Is she not feeling okay?"

"She's ah, she's... she's losing it, Edna."

"Oh my word."

"She keeps forgetting things. It all started a few months ago. Well, maybe as far back as a year I guess is when I started noticing things. Last fall we had my sister-in-law and her husband down for company. She starts pouring a glass of wine, a glass of wine for her sister, and suddenly..."

Frank was miming the act of pouring, and he dropped his hands.

"All over the place. All over the goddamn table, all over the goddamn white linen. Excuse me."

Edna dismissed the apology with her hand, and Frank gathered himself and continued.

225

"She started talking crazy– talking crazy at me and it– it got worse. I came home one day a few weeks back and a whole bottle of Scotch, *good* Scotch, was emptied. I thought my God, she's really gone on a bender. But all it was… you know what it was? She just emptied the damned bottle into the fucking washing machine with the laundry. I'm sorry, I–"

Edna would have preferred that the immutable tranquility of her sanctuary be left undisturbed by Frank Alsatian's crude profanity, but she merely shrugged.

"I'll try to stop sounding vulgar," said Frank, "I'll try real hard. Anyway, that's how it is."

"It must be a terrific burden to you."

"I'll manage." said Frank, "She's my wife. In sickness and in health. I'm a man of my word."

"That's very kind. Well, if I can be of any help, surely… you know, I had to watch my husband suffer. Three years."

"What was it?"

"Cancer."

Frank grunted and took a sip of coffee.

So I know," Edna said, "I know what you're going through. He started losing his faculties. Very much, toward the end."

"But surely he didn't keep going missing. Escaping I mean."

"No, I'm afraid he didn't have strength enough for that. They wanted us to get a home health aid. The doctors. But I said no, I'll take care of him myself. And I did. To the very end."

"Well that's what *I'm* trying to do. Manage it myself."

"I'm not so sure you can, Mr. Alsatian."

"Please call me Frank. Why not?"

"Oh, from what you're describing, it sounds to me like Alzheimer's. And I read a book once, yes it was a very good story it was… anyway, in this story was a man with, with Alzheimer's. And he kept having, I don't know, unpredictable and, and… rash behavior. And it was too much for his family, why they just couldn't, it- it became like rearing a child again, an infant… I'm sorry Mr. Alsatian."

"Frank."

"Frank. Yes. I don't know quite what else to say."

"Well," said Frank, getting to his feet, "I just wanted to let you know. And if you don't mind, I'd appreciate if you could be on the lookout."

"Why of course. *My*, but if a neighbor can't help another neighbor, what—"

"I'll give you my phone number."

"I've got it. I mean it's listed in the directory."

"Well," he said, "let me give you my cell number. I'll be out and about searching today."

Edna fetched a pen and Frank scrawled the number on a notepad. She followed him to the door and stood for a moment watching him trudge back down the driveway, a man captive to an uncertain world and a very perilous situation, and then she closed the door, entombing herself once again in the safety of artifacts.

Frank hit the street. He'd not gone far past the Hagodens when he heard Gerry calling after him. Gerry did a hurry-up walk and caught up with Frank at the corner of Hammermill and Tammany.

"Any sign of her yet?"

"What's it look like? You think I'm walking around for my health?"

Gerry shrugged. "Tell you what, how about a little golf?"

"Golf?"

"Yeah, sure, y'know, just nine holes or something. Take your mind off things."

Frank looked him squarely in the eye.

"Listen," he said, "I don't need to take my mind *off* things, I need to keep it *on* things. My wife is missing, in case you forgot."

"Sure. Sure, Frank. I know."

"Now if you'll excuse me I'll get back to the matter at hand."

Their voices were at conversational level, which Gerry hoped might suggest that Frank was making some headway on whatever it was that kept him forever going to such great lengths to try and keep a lid on this thing with his wife. What was it Shirley'd said to him last night, something about *denial*. Frank walked on towards Normandy and Gerry walked back, somewhat forlorn, to his house.

Last night when the three of them had rendezvoused at the South Club parking lot, Shirley said something about denial alright, and then she went on about accepting things even if you don't like them, and when she said that she looked significantly at her husband and he feared what she might say next. But then she glanced at her wristwatch and said it was late and she had family coming tomorrow and there were things to get ready. Shirley stepped back into her fun machine and that was that. Gerry had held out hope that their mutual mission of mercy, shared support of Frank Alsatian, might turn out to be just the thing to revive Shirley, get her talking again, finagle her out of that damnable sulking. Afterwards when the three of them stood in the driveway she even tried to cheer Frank up a little. Perhaps caught up in the detective nature of their exhaustive two-hour search, Shirley had dubbed the three of them *The Mod Squad*. Gerry kicked in and said if that were the case, then Shirley was clearly the Linc Hayes of the trio.

'Oh *really*,' she said, 'and just why is that?'

'*You know*,' Gerry said, waving his hands around his head, 'the afro. Your perm?'

That one didn't go over too well. Where Shirley might have normally just pulled a face, she'd stared daggers at Gerry. After they'd waved goodnight to Frank, Gerry trailed behind his wife to the side door with a sense of dread, she keyed the lock and walked inside with an indifference that suggested Gerry may as well have been a stranger, that he could come in or not and it was all the same to her. Gerry knew there was to be no lightening of mood in this house that night, no lifting of spirits, Gerry knew their storm wasn't over, not by a long shot.

Shirley'd gone right to the master bedroom and Gerry could hear her drawing a bath while he paced the living room and wondered if he should make up the couch again. This was silly. It was silly and he continued pacing a while and then turned on the television to the local news to see if an unidentified confused woman had turned up anywhere. He switched to basketball and watched the Detroit Pistons in a close battle late in the fourth quarter, and where he'd normally have an emotional stake in the outcome, tonight it didn't matter to him one way or the other. By the time he heard the bathroom door click as Shirley came out, he didn't even know the score. He sure as hell didn't know the score between he and his wife when she announced to him she was going to bed. 'Where should I camp out tonight,' he said.

'Suit yourself,' was all she replied.

So Gerry pulled a blanket and pillow from the stack she'd piled on the living room chair for the guests and curled up, once again, on the sofa.

This morning as he walked back to 1168 Tammany Drive, there were but a few minutes before he'd have to go and fetch his son Jimmy and his lot from Tampa airport.

"Hey hon," he called out with an affected joviality.

"Yes," his wife replied curtly.

"I'm thinking we'd better get going. To the airport."

"You go," she said, "I've still got cleaning up to do."

Gerry heard the whoosh of the vacuum. He paused. First he paused in the living room, then he paused outside by the side door and Shirley's garden, then he paused in the car, and at last he pulled over and paused by the side of the road, by Normandy.

"Anything wrong?"

It was that girl Melinda, calling as she rode up beside him from the golf cart, with the lady he guessed to be her mom sitting beside her.

"No," Gerry waved, "just stopped to take a call. Talk on my cell phone. I-I don't like to drive and talk at the same time."

With a wave to him, Melinda and Sharon drove on. When they reached Sunset Boulevard, the sky began to cloud up. "I hope the weather holds out for the party," Sharon said.

"It always clouds up and then brightens up," said Melinda. Their conversation was somewhat strained this morning and they were sticking to trivialities like the weather.

"I just hope nobody gets lost trying to get here," Sharon said, drumming her fingers on the roof of the cart.

"They won't. Nana put directions with the invitations she mailed. And we blasted an email to Uncle Pete, Aunt Susan and a few others. They can chain it from there."

"That was very thoughtful of you."

Melinda shrugged. She was and would remain Melinda Jane Rutherford today– she wouldn't *play* at being a grownup, she *was* a grownup today and that was that. Grownups helped their family plan a party after all, what was the big deal?

"I'm so glad you're getting to spend time here with Nana," Sharon said. "I think it's been good for you."

Melinda pulled into the parking lot and they climbed out and entered the North Club. Sharon hit the computer lounge to check her email. Melinda said she had to go check on something. When she arrived at the Events Office the door was open but it was dark inside, save for a ray of light from a room at the end of the hall.

She called out hello and a middle-aged woman with choppy blonde hair appeared from her lit office into the hall, in the informal Saturday attire of jeans and a tee shirt.

"Melinda Jane Rutherford," she announced to the woman.

"Oh yes. Come on in honey," she tapped out an invitation on the doorframe. Melinda followed her and the woman pointed to the chairs in front of her expansive desk. "I'm Ellen Everitt."

"I can see that," said Melinda evenly. "It's there," she pointed. "On your name plate."

"Yes of course it is. Just call me Ellen."

They regarded each other wordlessly a while, then Ellen yielded a polite and measured smile. "Everything is going to be good and ready for tonight. The staff are moving chairs into the auditorium right now. I'm sure you all are just as excited as you can be."

"You had my poor Nana scared half out of her wits."

This remark seemed to take a little wind out of Ellen Everitt's sails.

"Oh, I'm sorry. I really am. That's the last thing I intended. It's just, well we have employees to pay, and contractors, caterers and musicians, honey, and it's just a matter of course. I didn't mean to—"

"That's quite understandable. I was just saying."

"Well again I do apologize, I do realize that the last thing we want to do is worry a sweet old woman about money matters."

Ellen Everitt replaced her designer glasses to the bridge of her nose, shuffled some papers in front of her and said, "Do you have something for me?"

"I do indeed."

The girl fished around in her D&G purse, drew the check out and slid it across the desk.

"The Gastons," Melinda said, "are good friends of ours. Very good friends. They have been so kind as to cover the expenses. At least until we might find a way to repay their... really cool and, like, awesome generosity."

Ellen eyeballed the check over the rim of her glasses.

Melinda said, "I do appreciate your patience. I mean with all the trouble."

Ellen didn't say anything, she just collapsed back into the cushiony leather office chair and swiveled around.

"I'll approve this," she said at last. "Our verification system's down on the weekend, but I know the Gastons alright. I know they're good for it."

Melinda nodded.

"Here," said Mrs. Everitt, "take one of my cards. If there's anything you need, you can reach me on my cell. I'll be here until the party starts and from there you've got the building manager at your disposal. I must again express my... regret about the last minute complications with the bill."

"I'm sorry about all the trouble. My uncle Nathan's kind of a mess right now. Like so many grownups. Not a bad guy really, just took his eyes off the prize."

Melinda began to push herself up from the chair. Ellen Everitt looked sharply over the rim of her designer eyewear. "The prize?"

Just before she reached the door Melinda turned to face Mrs. Everitt. "I'm not sure I know exactly what the prize is," she said, "but I guess it's different for everybody."

She hastened to the lounge to find her mother surfing the web. Sharon turned around. "Ready?" she asked Melinda.

"Sure."

"Then let's hit the lobby and have some lunch. There's music in there today. A jazz trio."

"Yeah, I saw them, pretty cool." Melinda bit her bottom lip. "Hey Mom?"

"Yeah?"

"Let me show you something. Just across the way."

Sharon signed out and followed Melinda out into the hall. There was a Windmere Properties representative giving a guided tour of the building. They could overhear the enthusiastic tone of the young man leading an elderly man and his family towards the lobby and the auditorium and saying, *why tonight we've got a big party on, they're going to have a full bluegrass band, a big dinner, the whole works. One of our favorite members of the community is turning no less than a hundred years old tonight. We're going to celebrate in big style.*

"What time's the party," the teenager wanted to know.

"Well," said the man, "it's a private affair of course. But we have regular pub nights and big events for holidays and ..."

The man's voice trailed off as himself and the prospective family drifted away down the hall towards the lobby. Sharon said, "So what is it you wanted to show me?"

Melinda led her to the glass windows of the Lapidary, and on the shelves lay all the hand-made creations sculpted of golden and silver wire and precious gemstones, polished and gleaming in the bright overhead display lights. Amid common necklaces and bracelets there were flowers, there was an alligator, there was an elaborate castle with king and queen figurines standing in front of the drawbridge, there was a calico cat– all white and black and coffee brown stones and two pretty emeralds for the eyes. And there it was– every bit as striking to Melinda as the first time she saw it, the beautiful tree of petrified wood with emeralds and jade for leaves, the faeries in an explosion of bright colors still frozen in their dance. Melinda pointed from one objet d'art to the next.

"Aren't they beautiful, aren't they cool Mom?"

Sharon nodded. "Let's go inside."

They did, milling around a good bit before Sharon sidled up next to Melinda, who stood mesmerized before the elaborate and exquisite tree with all the faeries. "You're really taken with that one, aren't you?"

"The way I feel right now, just looking at it? Makes me feel glad I stopped taking them."

"Stopped taking what, hon?" Sharon put an arm around her daughter and the girl didn't draw away as she ordinarily would.

"The *drugs*," Melinda whispered.

"You mean your prescriptions?"

"Ssssh." Melinda tilted her head toward a woman sitting at one of the tables, engrossed in her work. Sharon squeezed her shoulder. "What? When did this happen? I thought we had filled your prescriptions with enough–"

"No. I just stopped taking them."

"When was this?" Sharon whispered with some urgency.

"A week ago, two weeks, I don't remember exactly."

"We'll discuss this later."

"Mom?"

"Yeah."

"I really want to get this one. For Nana. I-I mean… I don't have a gift for her."

Sharon looked at the price tag. A hundred and sixty-five bucks. One of the more expensive pieces. She released her grip on Melinda and sighed. "It certainly is marvelous to look at."

"I can pay you back," the girl said. "I just don't have any money right now."

Sharon pushed Melinda's shoulder playfully. "Nonsense," she said. "Let's get it."

"Really?"

"Let's do it."

"You sure?"

"C'mon," Sharon squeezed Melinda's hand and at first she shrank away, then followed her mother over to the lady at the table. "Excuse me," Sharon said.

"Why hello," the woman looked up from her handiwork, "aren't they all beautiful?"

"They most certainly are."

"They're made by Sunny Glen residents, all of them."

"That certainly makes them extra special."

"Precious. See anything you like?"

"Yes! Yes, we sure do and my daughter won't let us leave without it."

Melinda shrugged and began picking up and studying the raw materials that lay on the table in front of the old woman.

"Which one is it honey," the woman asked Sharon.

"That incredible tree. With the faeries."

"Oh that's a lovely one. I'm surprised it's hung around as long as it has. I've got a box to put it in."

"My Nana's turning a hundred years old," said Melinda.

"Oh," the woman's eyes lit up. "Flora Wheeler's family. Your grandmother –"

"Great great-grandmother," Melinda corrected her.

"Your great great-grandmother and I quilted together a good while back."

"Oh," said Sharon, "are you coming to the party tonight? At the main hall?"

The woman got up to retrieve the piece from the shelf on the window. "My husband and I have dancing tonight, you know, Big Band orchestra, all that. In Seashell Point. At the community center. But you tell her happy birthday from Peggy Waterson."

"We certainly will." Sharon fumbled around in her handbag, "Do you take a credit card?"

"I'm sorry, cash or checks only."

"Let me hit the ATM machine in the lobby then," said Sharon. Melinda made as if to protest but Sharon waved her off.

"Well," Alice said, "it'll make a wonderful birthday present anyway. Shall I gift wrap it for you?"

"Oh-okay. Sure. That'd be great."

Sharon went to fetch the money and when they'd finished their business, they went to the lobby and the jazz trio played away while they had sandwiches at the restaurant. As much as the girl was tempted to spill the beans about all the business stuff and the party, she reminded herself over and over that she was Melinda Jane Rutherford today and grownups didn't go around yacking about every little thing they did, that was unbecoming. So she kept a tight lip. For her part, Sharon's mind was racing about Melinda and her prescriptions, but she decided to leave that for another time– it seemed they were finally enjoying one another's company and she didn't want to spoil it. And she didn't want to spoil the party either.

When they'd finished it was nearly two o'clock and there they were still in shorts, tee shirts and sandals with only a few hours until the party began. They scurried back to the golf cart. Melinda got there first and climbed behind the wheel.

"Now don't go driving this thing like a maniac," Sharon said climbing in beside her.

"Get in," Melinda said.

"Excuse me?"

"Oh sorry. I mean welcome aboard the Flora Flyer, fasten your seat belts, and thank you for choosing to fly with us."

"That's better."

"Here at Flora Flyer, we're aware you have many golf carts to choose among in your travel decision–"

"Come on," Sharon urged, "we better get moving."

Melinda backed the cart out and when she reached Sunset Boulevard she gunned it to top speed, roughly twenty-five miles per hour.

"Guess we can't make this thing go any faster," said Sharon.

"I'm sure working on it."

When they got off of Sunset Boulevard, Melinda kept the pace, flying around corners sharp enough to have her mother clutching onto the frame.

"Is Nana really okay with you tooling around on this thing?"

"Sure, why not? She's mellow."

"I'm not sure she's seen you in action."

They whizzed by the corner of Normandy and Chaplin with enough velocity to startle Alice McLaughlin, who was out pruning her rosebushes and she turned around, shook her head and went back about her business with the shears. The big Buick came upon them quickly and Melinda had to swerve to avoid it, Sharon clutching the gift in her hands, and the cart ended up on the strip of grass between the sidewalk and the street in front of Alice's house. Alice turned, lowered her shears, and casually approached the golf cart.

"That's it, young lady!" Sharon clambered out of the cart and in her white shorts, white shirt and white sneakers she looked like an angry tennis umpire defending a call.

Melinda raised her palms in a guilty posture. Meanwhile the Buick stopped, the reverse lights came on and back came the car. Melinda instantly recognized the woman behind the wheel, recalling the commotion that'd occurred in front of Nana's house a little over a week ago.

"Oh shit," she said, looking past her mother. An enraged Sharon glanced over her shoulder to see what it was that drew her daughter's attention away from her scolding.

"Excuse me," the woman barked at Melinda from the car, her eyes both piercing and threatening, glancing over her bifocals. "Just how *old* are you young lady?"

Melinda glanced at the car and brought a forefinger to her chest with a quizzical glance.

"Yes, I mean *you*, you brat! You damn kids racing around on golf carts! There's an age limit here!"

Before Melinda could respond, Sharon had come around her and got right up on the Buick. She planted her fists on her hips and said evenly, "She wasn't driving the cart, mam. I was. You got something to say to me?"

"Why that's a bunch of hooey!"

The woman hollered over at Alice McLaughlin. "Miss! Oh *Miss!* You saw what happened here."

The irate driver fumbled about the car looking for a pen and paper. "Please," she said, pointing at the golf cart and looking to Alice McLaughlin expectantly. "Tell this guest that you saw her stupid brat driving that cart."

"How dare you refer to *my daughter* like that!" Sharon took a battle stance in the middle of the street.

Alice raised a hand to shield her eyes from the bright sun, holding the shears at her side. She shrugged, "I didn't see anything. And it's really not my business."

"What's that?"

"Now if you'll excuse me I'll just get back to my gardening."

The woman shook her head, cursed under her breath and turned her attention back to Melinda.

"I'm going to report you," she sneered. "I want your name and address."

Sharon said, "Nothing doing. Move on."

"*What?*"

"You heard me. *Move on.*"

"Why the impudence!"

"She's *my* daughter and I'll be the one to scold her when she needs it. Now please leave us alone."

"Beat it," Melinda added for embellishment.

"Now see here, you are *guests*. Like it or not this is a street and there are rules of the road."

"I know it's a street," said Sharon evenly, "now hit it."

"I'll follow you home, that's what I'll do."

"How do you know we're going home?"

"I can wait."

Sharon grabbed Melinda's elbow and when her daughter resisted she grabbed her by the ear and said, *come on you*, and just like that they settled themselves on the grass next to the golf cart.

"We can wait you out," Sharon said, "we've got all day."

The woman harrumphed and then there was a car behind her. She hesitated, then grudgingly drove on. They watched the Buick troll along down Normandy, tailed by an impatient Honda CRV. Sharon called over to Mrs. McLaughlin, but she kept her back turned, she was back to her pruning and wasn't fielding any further questions.

Sharon took the wheel and, with no paucity of grumbling, drove the rest of the way. There were a few cars and the Gastons' jeep filling up the driveway. She pulled the cart up onto the grass. "Are you gonna stay mad at me," asked Melinda.

"I doubt it." Sharon said, "Not too mad anyway. That lady was a little over the top."

"She's a grump alright. But I was sure as hell proud of you."

"What?"

"You really gave it to her. Pretty ssshweet."

"Did I? Really?"

"Sure. Saw it with my own two eyes."

"Hmmn," Sharon massaged her chin.

"But," Melinda said, "you're not pissed off at me, are you?"

"Maybe just a little bit," Sharon shrugged. "But not to worry." She patted her daughter on the knee. "I feel it wearing off already."

There were a few women and a lot of commotion in the house— traffic in and out of Flora's bedroom, where Sugar held court— she and the girls flitting about with makeup cases, eyeliner brushes, all manner of beauty implements. Sharon stuck her head inside the doorway and there in front of the vanity, Sugar Gaston primping and spraying at her white wispy tufts, sat Flora. She looked up in the mirror, and when her eyes met Sharon's a look of exasperation came over her face.

Sugar stood back admiring her handiwork and said, "I'm definitely seeing a hair extension. Definitely an extension in this picture," she said, making a frame with her hands.

Vanessa Shutmeyer tugged at Sharon's sleeve. "You two are just in time for the hen party. Where have you been?"

"Tooling around Sunny Glen Palms with my lunatic golf cart driver."

"Eh, what's that," Flora said over her shoulder.

"Nothing, Nana. Nothing you need to know about. Not today."

Flora turned back around, rolling her eyes at the sight of herself in the mirror. For one thing, she hadn't worn lipstick in years. The rouge was too much, her hair was beyond thinning and she'd have much preferred to have it pulled back in a hair band than suffer Sugar's attempts to rejuvenate it with mousse and hairspray. Flora once again caught Sharon's doleful gaze in the mirror, to which she shrugged, frowned, winked. Melinda started tugging on Sharon's sleeve, then led her by the elbow to the guest room where she said in a hushed voice, "I have *nothing* to wear to the party. I didn't pack any fancy clothes."

"*You* didn't," said Sharon, "but your overworked boring old mother sure did."

"What?"

"Go over there to the closet. Over there. No, all the way in the back. Behind my black velvet dress... there you go, bingo."

Melinda held a bright red knee length dress with a fancy collar her mother had bought for her over a year ago. "I hope I still fit in it."

"You'll fit in that dress if we have to cram you into it."

"You want me to pull yours out?"

"Please."

"How's Nana?"

"I don't know. I'm still not convinced that's really Nana in there."

They changed and when they came out of the guest room there was a hullaballoo about a dress. Sharon went to see what all the fuss was about as Vanessa Shutmeyer, in a snazzy black velvet dress, began to gush over Melinda, *look at you, you're all grown up,* pinching the fabric of the red dress, standing back to admire it.

"Okay okay, just don't pinch my cheeks, okay?"

Melinda smoothed out the pleats and picked at lint. It was just after three o'clock and the others had finished dressing and making up and left. Sharon stood in the doorway looking on with arms folded as Sugar stood behind Flora, holding a silver sequin dress against her body and saying to the mirror, "It's *divine!* The hottest little number I ever picked off the rack."

"Where did you get it," Sharon asked.

"The Saturday flea market. Behind the strip mall over off Coral Beach Boulevard."

Sharon could see that her great-grandmother didn't share Sugar's enthusiasm for the garment. Sugar excused herself and dashed off to fetch some straight pins from the jeep, leaving Sharon alone with Flora.

"So how we doin Nana."

She walked to the vanity and laid her hands upon frail shoulders, studying her great-grandmother in the mirror. "Havin fun yet?"

"Fun? I wouldn't exactly call this *fun,*" she pouted, the effect exaggerated greatly by the bright red lipstick. "Did you see that glittery thing?"

"Yeah. Kinda hard to miss. I have a hunch you don't like it."

"*Like it?* It's it's... *gaudy.* I'm just a simple old country girl. We're having a bluegrass band, not Liberace."

"Well, try it on. You only turn a hundred once."

"I can't dance in that thing."

"You couldn't dance in *any*thing," Melinda called from just outside the door.

"I heard that," Flora snapped.

"Don't talk to your Nana like that Mel," Sharon said. "Maybe we'll let her borrow *your* dress and you can wear this showy little number."

Melinda made a face and said, "No way I'd go anywhere in *that* glittery mess."

"Glittery mess my eye," said Sharon. "It's a bona fide man magnet."

Sugar reappeared, having caught only that last bit of the conversation. "*Man magnet*," she echoed, then ruffled Melinda's hair and said, "How'd you like to be at your great great great—"

"That's a few too many," Flora snapped.

"—grandmother's wedding the next time we have to doll her up? Now be a good girl and move along and let us move on to wardrobe. My oh my, but isn't that a gorgeous red dress on you."

"Yeah," said Melinda, "No complaints *here* anyway."

Sugar stared blankly, and then went to fetch the dress. Flora was trying her best to convey in a most subtle manner her misgivings about Sugar's gift— but no amount of frowns, doubtful glances to Sharon, or head shaking registered to Sugar, who was too caught up in the excitement of the occasion. At last taking the dress from Sugar with resignation, Flora said help me up, all this get up and sit down is getting tiresome, worse than a church service— and so they each took an elbow to hoist her up and she took the hickory cane and told them to wait a minute and let her try it on, with special emphasis on *try*. Sugar stood at the ready, straight pins clenched between her teeth.

After a few minutes Flora called out for Sharon. Sharon gingerly cracked the door, stepped inside and closed it fast behind her. Flora had the glittery thing caught around her head, she had on her only knee-high hose with large cotton underpants whose utilitarian appearance clashed with the glamorous veneer of the garment she was attempting to layer over them. She suddenly appeared very tiny to Sharon, all bones and wrinkled skin riddled with age spots. It was remarkable to look at and for a moment

Sharon stood transfixed in that intimate space so proximate to the diminutive effects of old age, right up close against it.

"C'mon, help me out of this thing," came Flora's muffled voice through the fabric, snapping Sharon out of her reverie.

"You want it on or off?"

"I want it *off*, but I guess that's not gonna happen."

Sharon pulled tentatively.

"Come on, give it all you got," Flora wiggled impatiently.

So Sharon tugged harder and then the dress was hung on Flora, the spaghetti straps leaving her bare shoulders exposed. She looked in the mirror and grunted, teasing at her hair with her bony fingers.

"Good thing you're not wearing a bra," said Sharon.

"There's nothing to hold up," Flora sighed. "Anyway, what's the verdict?"

"Actually," Sharon whispered, "wait, turn around. Actually, I think it's not so bad."

"*Not so bad?* Well thanks for the vote of confidence. What's the matter with *you look like a million bucks?*"

Sharon began to brush distractedly at the dress and said, "No really, I mean—"

"I know perfectly well what you mean."

"Let's go see what Sugar thinks."

"Oh now *there's* a good idea, let's go see what Sugar thinks."

Sugar's face lit up when she saw Flora in the dress. "*Look* at you! Glamour, total glamour. You are all over that dress young lady. Why you'd be a smash at Oscar night."

"That's what *I* was just telling her," said Sharon, pinching Flora's side lightly.

"Sugar," said Flora, "I have to tell you… I'm not so sure about this."

"Nonsense," Sugar gushed, "you look mah-ve-lous!"

"But it's too loose."

"That's alright, we can cinch it."

"It doesn't feel comfortable. It makes me itch."

But her words appeared not to have the slightest effect on Sugar— she pranced around Flora, clenching a few straight pins between her teeth, sticking one here and one there until at last she stood back to evaluate the outcome. She cocked her head one way then the other and said, that'll do.

"That'll do?" Flora looked at her imploringly.

"It fits you like a glove. You look divine."

Sharon said, "That's quite a makeover."

"What I need," said Flora, "is a *do* over."

But Sugar was already flitting about and she spun around and said, oh my look it's time for me to run along and doll myself up. She started for the door, and Sharon took Flora's elbow and whispered, "What are we going to do with you? Have you got anything else to wear?"

"'Course I do." Flora frowned at her reflection in the vanity, "But that girl's just as sweet as her name and it'd only break her heart if I undid her... whatever you call this."

At the door, Melinda met Sugar, gave her a halfhearted smile, and walked her out to the driveway. "What's eating *you*," asked Sugar. "You look the perfect lady in that pretty red dress."

"It's not *me* I'm worried about."

"Well, don't worry your pretty little head thinking Sugar's going to show up looking like this," she splayed her palms in front of her, "I'm going to fix myself up right now. Toodaloo!"

Sugar Gaston hastened to the jeep and backed out of the driveway without so much as a glance over her shoulder. She seldom chanced to drive the jeep and she fought once again with the old clutch as the jeep lurched between gearshifts.

When Sugar pulled into the Gastons' driveway, the dogs sprung to life from the garage. They went as far as their chains would allow and she petted them both and said sorry guys, you'll just have to go without a walk, this girl's running a little late.

"That's right," Philip called from the screen door inside the garage, shaking a clump of colorful strung beads. "We're running late and we got us some partying to do."

The Gasparilla parade was a beloved annual tradition to the Gastons but in strictly party terms a warm up, a precursor, a mere practice session to the more exorbitant Mardi Gras in New Orleans. "Got the cooler ready," said Philip, letting the dogs off their chains and saying, "now go run a little and do your business. Just don't let old grumpyface see you conducting it on his lawn."

He kissed his wife and patted her playfully on the ass. He said, "Our daughter Olivia called. She and our Adam are coming. Our kids are coming down. I told her to remind her brother to leave the pot at home rather than meet the border patrol with it. He can score some when he gets here. Kid's got a nose for it."

"When are they coming?"

"I dunno. Sometime next week. Or the weekend, I forget."

They dressed for the party and after Philip rounded up the dogs, he backed the double cab pickup out of the driveway. They were meant to fetch the D'Antonios, the Shutmeyers, and then John, for the excursion. Sugar, dressed in a gold sequin pullover, a set of pearls and a black miniskirt, plucked at Philip's loose Hawaian shirt, then the gray khaki pants that were too long to be shorts and too short to be trousers. Rounding off the casual outfit were a pair of open toed sandals. Sugar regarded him from head to toe.

"I'd say you're just a little underdressed for the occasion."

"I didn't want to have to change for the parade."

He'd also had his wife buzz the side of his head outside on the patio that morning, rendering a Mohawk, to which he'd applied a temporary purple dye, just the right festive touch for the parade. Sugar shook her head.

"What?"

"Nothing," she said.

When the Gastons pulled up at the D'Antonio residence on Crescent Moon Drive in the Oakwood development, Tommy was out in the driveway talking to a man in a golf cart, an elbow propped up on the roof and one foot resting on the floorboard. Philip pulled the truck next to it and noticed with a start the man in the golf cart was that nasty bugger from the Pub Night. The man turned at the sound of the jeep but his face remained taught in what seemed a skeptical regard for everything around him. Philip put the truck in park as Debbie appeared at the front door, waved to them and stepped out, locking the door behind her.

"We're going to run with these wildcats for a while," Tommy said to Frank Alsatian and then waved him off. "Let me know if you hear anything."

"You got enough room in there," Debbie D'Antonio asked.

Sugar said, "We can squeeze."

Frank backed the cart out without so much as a wave. He made for home somewhat disconsolately, feeling very much like an outsider. When he'd reached his driveway he watched Gerry Hagoden washing his car, turning the hose on his grandkid to the

242

boy's shrieks, equal torment and delight. "Pop," he heard Gerry's son call from the house, "come and show Amelia how to work the television, she wants to hook up her Gameboy."

"One thing at a time," Gerry said, and went back to rinsing the car.

Frank left the golf cart there in the driveway and went to check the answering machine. There was a big red zero. He went to draw a glass of filtered water from the door of the fridge, then pulled it open and drew a beer instead. He dropped into the Lazy Boy and stared a good while at the blank TV screen. There was nothing on that he cared to watch and this seemed to him a lot like life, there was nothing on to watch. It was a Saturday and he knew the D'Antonios were going to that birthday bash for the old lady who was turning one hundred. They were invited and he wasn't. He could've sworn Gerry mentioned the Hagodens had also been invited. Gerry with his family of snowbirds down for their annual visit, Gerry going about his chores uncomplainingly, Gerry with a wife coherent enough to feel the pangs of jealousy.

And Mimi Brooks and the French ladies never did call on him for anything, he hadn't seen hide nor hair of them, had he? Fact was nobody called on Frank Alsatian for anything and there was nothing he could do about it. Because down here in Sunny Glen Palms nobody needed anybody, everybody had insurance for contingencies. Nobody needed anybody and he was too tired to look for his wife anymore, he'd just sit there and wait until she turned up. Someone would find her and identify her soon. It was Saturday and people were out and about doing things, it seemed to him everyone around him were leading happy and fulfilled lives except him. Everybody else had nice families, everybody else had plans and events, things going on. The only thing going for Frank Alsatian today was a pity party.

He got out of the chair and walked into the garage. The German Messerschmitt model plane lay cradled on the wooden horses and he switched the light on to study it. The sharp teeth painted onto the nose took on an eerie visage today– the fighter plane seemed to leer at him menacingly. He stood regarding it with a very critical eye. The cockpit glass had glue smears on it. The wings were a little uneven. A great wave of frustration came over him and then he had an urge to dismantle it– rip the wings off and not even bother to buy another and try again. He looked across the street at Edna Norton's and there was nothing doing. Further down the street in the Hagodens driveway Gerry finished rolling up the garden hose and then walked through the garage and back into the house with his little grandson in tow.

When Gerry cracked open the door onto the utility room he nearly collided with his wife.

"Going to the party?" he asked her.

"What party?"

"*What* party? You know, Flora Wheeler… one hundred years–"

"Oh that. We've got company, in case you hadn't noticed."

"Oh Jesus. Thanks for pointing out the obvious."

They stood facing each other silently amidst the blaring television set, their pillow throwing grandkids, a singing daughter-in-law and their son who had a nagging habit of talking to his laptop. "Well," Gerry said at last, "I'm going to show my face for at least a little while."

"Well you go do that. I wanted to cook lobster for the kids tonight."

"That's great Shirl, that's great. I can lend a hand, then we can run over to the North Club for a little–"

"I'm staying put."

"Well then," Gerry said, "I'll go now."

"What?"

"I'll go now. Get it over with."

"You make it sound like an awful obligation."

"No. I'm sure it'll be fun."

"Yeah," Shirley said. "Fun. Just don't go kissing any strange women."

He made as if to backhand her, staying his hand, leaving it suspended in midair– merely glaring at his wife. He made for the bedroom and stepped hurriedly into a pair of dress pants, a short-sleeve button down shirt and a pair of penny loafers.

"You going somewhere pop?" His son Jim glanced up from his laptop in the living room.

"He's going to a party." said Shirley, "He's leaving us to go to a party."

"Actually," Gerry said, fastening his belt, "if anyone cares to join me, we have a standing invitation."

His daughter-in-law Lisa suspended her singing. "What's this now?"

"It's a party for… hey get this Amelia, hey Amelia? Amelia, you got a second?"

"Amelia, listen to your grandfather," Jim said curtly. "It's like the darn kid's hypnotized with that Gameboy."

"How did you manage to hook it up?" Gerry asked.

"I figured it out," his granddaughter was getting impatient at having to pause the game. "What is it?"

"We have a lady here who's turning a hundred years old."

"Wow," said Amelia blandly, "that's *old*."

"You betcha." said Gerry, "And she's even got a great great-granddaughter. Staying with her. Can you imagine it? That's like your child's child to us. Can you imagine it?"

"Wow," said Jim while scrolling email, "isn't that something Amelia? Imagine your old grandpop in forty years."

"He'd have no teeth," Jim Junior giggled.

"How do you know," said Gerry.

"I'll tell you what," said Shirley, "he keeps up with his shenanigans, he sure *won't* have any teeth left."

"What's all this about?" asked Lisa.

Gerry shot a warning glance over at Shirley.

"He's just driving your poor mother nuts, she said. Same as usual."

"Pop, what are you doing to the poor old gal?" Jim quipped.

"Believe me," said Gerry, "she thinks I'm winding her up. I haven't even started yet."

"He's messing with my dinner plans."

"Go on," said Gerry, "and eat without me. Anybody coming along?"

"I don't want to go to a party," Amelia said, "I want to go to the pool." She seemed to speak for everybody except Gerry, who backed the car out of the driveway and drove off for the North Club. When he got there, the parking lot near the auditorium was full. He swung the car around and headed for the front but it was convoluted, you had to go through the gate, U-turns were illegal and so he found himself crawling down Coral Beach Boulevard to the next traffic light to turn around and come back in the gate. He stood in line three cars back while a car he imagined without a resident sticker or guest pass held up progress. He glanced at his watch, going on five-thirty. He cursed under his breath and then, making sure all the windows were rolled up, out loud. He sat. At last he got out of the car and went to see what the holdup was. Two cars up and directly behind the cause of the delay was the big Buick. The woman rolled down her window and said to him in a commanding tone, *go and see what on earth they're doing up there.*

"What the hell does it look like I'm doing," he sneered.

"Well well, look at mister *wise guy* here," she remarked.

"I'll be darn sure to give you a full report when I find out," he said, shaking his head while approaching the guard.

"What seems to be the holdup?"

"Just waiting for someone to verify a guest. Another one for that Wheeler party."

"Well here's a thought," said Gerry. "Anybody says they're here for a one hundredth birthday party, why don't you just let them through?"

"You trying to be funny?"

"Uh uh," said Gerry, raising his palms, "just practical." The guard waved the shiny new rental car through and Gerry turned without a pause and when he caught the glare of the lady in the Buick, he stuck his tongue out at her. I hope, he thought, she's not going to the party. She'd be the death of it.

He parked the car, switched off the ignition and sat a while, with a feeling akin to stage fright, butterflies. He'd have preferred not to show up unaccompanied. He wondered if he'd be the object of gossiping. He stalled. Then he took the sidewalk to the rear of the North Club and approached the double doors with some trepidation. Stepping out of the bright sunlight, the North Club seemed ominously dark and quiet to Gerry. As he headed down the hallway in the direction of the auditorium, he recalled the last party he'd had occasion to attend there. That was New Year's Eve and the place was packed– Shirley'd had the foresight to secure their seats well in advance as the event was gaining in popularity. A full Big Band orchestra was on order and there was a big buffet and an open bar included in the price of the ticket. There was often no room to spare on the dance floor for the big steppers.

When Gerry entered the auditorium for this party, those memories were quickly dispelled. There was a scarce amount of people– their kids had an overabundance of room to run around in. An open bar with buffet serving tables lined the right wall. In front of him, folding tables were set up all the way to the far end of the room near the stage. On the stage, a five-piece bluegrass band was playing not so loud as to disable conversations. Gerry recognized the banjo player, a stout fellow with a neatly trimmed gray beard, from the Michigan Club dinner Shirley had drug him out to last year. Gathered around him was a woman on mandolin, a heavy set fellow in overalls with a guitar, a frail old man bent over a fiddle, and a buxom old woman on the upright bass. It came back to Gerry from his conversation with the banjo player they were known collectively as the Front Porch Pickers, and had sprung from a folk music club that met regularly for barbecues and picking tunes. They were now picking away at a reel as Gerry stepped among a crowd far below capacity. The first familiar face he recognized was Kenny Fitzroy. Kenny was standing alone near the bar in his standard getup— old jeans, tennis shirt and sneakers. Among the well-dressed crowd around him, he kind of stuck out. Gerry strode up to him and extended a hand.

"Kenny old boy."

"Hey Gerry."

Fitzroy fidgeted. Kenny Fitzroy was always fidgeting.

"Listen," Gerry said, "sorry about the other night. I mean Frank. He's been real upset lately, kind of has a lot going on."

Kenny shrugged and said, "It's all good."

Gerry knew he'd have to try and avoid becoming captive to Kenny's running monologue. He wanted to get a drink but he thought the better of it. Would it display a lack of social graces, he wondered, to start drinking at an open bar before you took the opportunity to greet the host? He excused himself and headed for the tables to check in. Lining the stage behind the tables were streamers in the romantic colors of pink, red and white. Gerry saw the same thing over his head under the faux chandeliers. He dodged young kids chasing each other around as they do at such gatherings, the little boys' ties already slackening and the little girls having shed their shoes and sliding around in their frilly white socks. Young parents held cocktails with one eye on those with whom they engaged and one on their meandering prodigy. Beyond the cluster of people at the main table, he spied Flora. She'd have been hard to miss in her glittery outfit, ensconced in a cushioned armchair, her old hickory cane leaning up against it. Her appearance had been modified by Sharon just before they'd left the house– makeup, lipstick and rouge were removed then modestly re-applied and her hair combed straight back and held with a broad hair band. Now Flora could smile. She recognized Gerry and broke off her conversation to greet him. "I'm so happy you could make it, tell me your name again?"

He did and she grasped his hands and said, "Where's that pretty little wife of yours?" Gerry said they had family visiting and he thought he could only stay a little while and then Flora said, "Well get yourself a plate, there's loads of food over there. I'd like you to meet my great-nephew from California."

He shook hands with a guy who looked to be about his own age and the guy iron-gripped him, wouldn't let go and said, "Every time she says her *great* nephew I think she's paying me a compliment. Do you live here?"

"Yes, I do."

"Well that's swell. Good of you to come out and celebrate with this young lady."

"Oh pshaw," said Flora, "flattery will get you nowhere with this old bag of bones."

Gerry left them to their conversation. At the end of the main table lay a pile of gifts and he immediately regretted having shown up empty-handed. He walked through a sea of strangers to the bar for a drink to take the edge off a little. Kenny Fitzroy leaned against the bar staring absently at a bottle of beer in front of him, and Gerry switched gears for the buffet table. As much as he felt like a heel, he just wasn't sure he was up to Kenny Fitzroy today. He was scooping mashed potatoes onto a red plastic plate when he saw them enter the auditorium– the Shutmeyers, then the D'Antonios and behind them the Gastons with yet another couple and some young fellow he didn't recognize. The revelers served to inject new life into the party and immediately caused a very sparsely populated room to look a little less empty. Purple-haired Gaston led his entourage to the throne of the queen and Gerry wandered over to shake Ron Shutmeyer's hand, perhaps engage in a little banter with some locals.

Flora started to push herself out of her chair to greet Philip, who fluttered his hands and said don't get up, save it for the dancing.

Gerry felt a tug at his elbow and there beside him was the girl. He didn't recognize her at first, all dolled up as she was in a bright red dress, her dyed hair pulled up in braids. "Hey you'd never guess what," she said.

"What?"

"Ran into that old windbag in the big car. My mom and I."

"That's funny," Gerry said, "I just gave her a piece of my mind a minute ago at the gate."

"Good for you!" said Melinda, brightening. "My ma told her off pretty good. I don't know what makes that lady think she can just go and boss everybody around. Like she owns the joint."

"Well, she can't be very happy can she," Gerry mused.

"No. I just wish she'd stop taking it out on the rest of the world. Are you good friends with my Nana?"

Gerry paused to ruminate over this. "I guess," he said, "you couldn't really say good friends. But I guess we'd be fast friends if she could... we-we just moved down here, my wife and I..."

"Somebody told me you've been here a few years. Where's your wife? What's her name again?"

Gerry fidgeted, he couldn't help feeling just a little ill-at-ease with this barrage of inquiries from a teenager just a few years ahead of his own granddaughter. The girl merely blinked her eyes, waiting for answers.

He smiled and said, "Maybe we'll see her later. We've got family visiting."

"Oh." said the girl, "Well come on over and meet some of *our* family. I want them to meet as many of the residents as possible. Just trying to get some backstory on you."

"Well, that's very kind of you."

The girl reached a hand out and soon she was pulling Gerry around the party and he reluctantly obliged. There ensued a flurry of introductions and he forgot each and every name. While he heard them give the details of their relationship to the guest of honor, his thoughts strayed to Libby Alsatian and he thought he'd step away from the noise at some point and call Frank for any bit of news. He was self-conscious of Shirley's absenteeism and he wondered if there would be many more opportunities such as this for he and his wife to avail themselves of. Had his blunder at Pub Night put their Sunny Glen social future in peril? He wondered about these things while he nodded and smiled, shaking hands with complete strangers.

Melinda was jerked away, with a measure of indignation, by one of the children and then propelled into whatever game was in progress in another corner of the room. Flora by now was up and dancing, albeit slowly, deliberately– with Philip Gaston, much to the delight of the Front Porch Pickers, who knew all too well from experience that once you got the first one up to dance, the rest would follow and then you had a dance floor.

So when Gerry turned around to fetch another cocktail from the bar, it was a very different room his eyes met– it was now filling up with some new arrivals and among them were Marion Legrand, her daughter Elise bearing a birthday gift, and to his surprise– withered, hunched over, walking with the aid of her niece's elbow and a cane– Mimi Brooks.

He was a little shocked at this new version of his nearby neighbor. She'd lost both weight and color since he last saw her. Perhaps it was more obvious to him with her standing up than when she sat across from him at the dinner table just a few nights ago. It sure was a far cry from a few months ago. He approached them with some trepidation. "Can I get you something from the bar," he asked, avoiding Marion's eyes.

Mimi said a glass of sparkling water and so Gerry and Elise went to fetch drinks while Marion took the gift and led her sister towards the guest of honor's table. The musicians now had dancers. Philip, having delivered Flora back to the armchair with perfect chivalry, made a bow and headed for the bar.

Flora's face brightened at the sight of Mimi, and Tommy D'Antonio pulled a chair over next to hers and patted it, helping Marion seat her sister. Flora brushed at Mimi's shoulder, regarded her. "How are you, young lady? Been a while. Don't get out like I used to."

"Well," said Mimi, "rough go of it myself lately."

"Ah," Flora patted her shoulder, "you'll get around it."

Mimi thought, *most everybody goes through things, Flora Wheeler just seems to go around them. Perhaps that's the secret, just dodge them altogether.*

Flora saw Marion and reached for her hand. "Well look at this pretty lady all dolled up. Glad you could make it."

"Oh…" Mimi laughed herself into a cough, batting a hand in front of her. "I'm sorry. This is my sister Marion. She's wonderful and she's visiting from France."

Flora pursed her lips in mock astonishment. She slapped playfully at Mimi's hand. "Of course. We've already met, silly."

"Oh dear," said Mimi. "I keep forgetting things."

"Believe me, you'll get used to it," said Flora.

"Joyeux anniversaire." Marion beamed.

"She's wishing you a happy birthday."

"Happy birthday," Marion repeated.

"Shoo-wee," Flora said, "look at all that beauty multiply by ten when she smiles."

Then Flora patted Elise's hand, looked past them at the large hall and said, "All my brothers and sisters are long gone by now. But there are many manifestations of them in this room." Mimi conveyed this sentiment to Marion in their native tongue. Marion smiled, looked adoringly around the room then back upon Flora and Flora repeated, *she's so pretty, she's so darn pretty,* squeezing Mimi's skeletal arm, saying, "I can really see the resemblance."

The staff, in their black and white uniforms, had begun to prowl among the guests with trays of champagne in plastic flutes. The music and the dancing ceased and an impeccably dressed and well-groomed man with the distinguished features of middle age stepped onto the stage and took the microphone. He tapped it, blew on it and said, *may I have everyone's attention please.* He stooped to accept a glass of champagne at the foot of the stage. "I'll only be a second and then we'll get back to the hootenanny," he said, turning to acknowledge the band with a smile.

"For those of you for whom I haven't had the pleasure of acquaintance, I'm Rodney Webb and my grandmother, God rest her soul, was the last of our guest of honor's children. I think we can all say we are honored to be here today, in the Sunshine State to honor such a sunny, special, wonderful, loyal, caring, faithful, wise, loving and I daresay I didn't foresee this one… *glamorous* lady."

That drew a good bit of applause, and he waited for it to subside. And for some of us the very well from which we sprung.

There was another outburst of applause and the man on the microphone nodded at Flora affectionately while it abated.

"As you draw to a close your first century and embark on a new one, we all wish you, Nana, the very best. May we continue to comfort you as you comfort us. I know of so many of us in this room, including myself, who have called on you many a time over the years, called upon you for your wisdom and counsel. A wisdom that only expands with the years. I know I can speak for many when I say you are truly the loveliest, most gracious and outstanding woman I've ever known. And I say that at the risk of my wonderful wife giving me a good boot in the butt, or worse."

Another round of laughter and applause.

"So let's raise a glass, everyone." He raised the champagne flute above his head, exposing gold cufflinks and a very posh wristwatch. "To Flora Jane Boothe Wheeler. Your hundred years have been a blessing to everyone with whom you have bestowed your presence, and that's a lot of lucky folks."

Everyone applauded and then Flora, with the aid of a few of the young men and the old hickory cane, got up from her seat. At the same time Mr. Webb, the toaster, with the aid of the banjo player, negotiated slack on the microphone's cable so as to allow it to be passed down to Flora. From the microphone came a brief squelch of feedback and then Flora had the floor.

"Welcome everybody, and thank you for coming."

Her hand was shaking the microphone. Melinda stepped forward, taking the microphone and holding it in front of Flora.

"As I was saying just the other day to this dear sweet great great-granddaughter of mine…"– Melinda blushed and Flora reached around the girl's waist to pull her in close– "I was tellin her that in them olden days, them hard, hard times under the cold mountain air under the stars we'd have many a hootenanny with musicians such as these,"– she glanced over her shoulder at the group behind her on the stage– "and many a time the men brought something down from the mountains to pass around and sip.

With a mischievous glance she brought a finger to her lips to much laughter. "Well," she continued, "we had us a little tradition I guess you'd call it, little thing we did way back then, and I guess it'd make an old girl happy to see it done today. We had a notion to pass a hat for the band and I guess we could do that today for old times sake, and so give em what you can, let em know you 'preciate em."

From the stage a woven basket was passed down to Melinda.

"Well my good kinfolk, before my head swells up with all the praise or my special great great-grandbaby's hand cramps up, I'd just like to thank y'all for coming and let's get back to dancin and carryin on and havin a good time."

Melinda handed over the microphone and then began to canvas the room toting the basket, ostensibly to collect donations for the band, but with a few closer relations she expounded on the real impetus, that glitch in the financing. "But don't tell mom," she said to Aunt Susan, "she'd freak out."

Flora had been hoodwinked into a dance as soon as the band started up. Her company was a middle-aged man of some girth who was family by marriage. He wasn't much of a dancer but he sure could talk up a storm. She pretended to be interested by nodding occasionally and echoing some of his words back to him. "How is it you can hear everything," he asked.

"Well you see, I've got these little things called ears. On my head. Right here, see?"

"No I only mean—"

"I know perfectly well what you mean. How is it the old lady can hear a durn thing. Well it's all in the hearing aids. *Good* hearing aids, so small you can hardly see em. And more expensive than any fancy diamond earrings. My great-grandson Nathan gave them to me."

"Oh, which one is he?"

"He's not here."

The staff had begun to busy themselves unfolding more tables for the burgeoning crowd. Marion and Mimi had taken some remaining seats at a table near the front and upon Elise's insistence Gerry joined them, mindful to draw the empty chair beside Marion for Elise. The ladies rose to head for the buffet line and Gerry, deciding on a second helping, joined them. On the way he spied Kenny Fitzroy standing off by himself watching the band amid the dancers. He shook Kenny's elbow and said, c'mon buddy pull up a chair and join us.

Melinda was having quite a good time ferrying the basket around, deeming herself an integral part of the events, too old to be giggling and screeching and sliding around the floor dirtying up her pretty red dress— she was Melinda Jane Rutherford after all, and grown-ups didn't behave as such. A lady just might ruin her hair around such reckless folly. Ms. Rutherford was most at home amidst a great deal of books but today it was a collection of adults she surrounded herself with, and for the moment that was just fine by her. She chatted away at her elders, drawing long and impressive adjectives from her arsenal and then she overheard Philip Gaston's young friend saying, I can sum up tonight in three words– drink, drank, drunk.

By now Gerry was enjoying another dinner plate and the company of Elise, who'd gone to great lengths to put him at ease. Elise also seemed to have the effect of snake charmer on Kenny Fitzroy, who sat uncharacteristically mute. She even asked Kenny to dance. He merely shook his head and said he was dangerous on the dance floor, and not in a flattering sense. So she looked to Gerry and what could he do but oblige. The Front Porch Pickers were really laying into it now, the collective stomp of their feet providing a natural pulse for the dancers. What Gerry and Elise encountered was a square dance in full swing, with four sets of partners. They stood on the sidelines and clapped in rhythm with the other onlookers. Flora was still up and about, leaning on the old hickory cane, returning the many gazes that fell on her in her glittering attire to match the bright look on her face. Gerry felt the pulse of his cell phone in his front pocket and when he took it out and flipped it open, he could see it was his own number ringing, and then he had a pang of hope it was Shirley with good news about something or just wanting to hear his voice the way she used to. But when he clicked on he met with only sharp anxiety at the other end.

"Hold on," he said, "let me get away from the noise." He left the room and stood in the hallway outside the double doors. "Hello? That's better."

"I thought I better call you."

"What's up?"

"Coming back from the club. The pool. With the kids. It was terrible. I've never seen him like that."

"Who?"

"Frank."

"What's he doing?"

"Walking around in a drunken stupor. Right in front of the kids."

"Oh shit."

"Yeah. We helped him home. Me and Jim. I gotta tell ya, it was a little embarrassing."

"Yeah."

"Well, are you coming back or what?"

"I'll be back soon. They're just getting ready to present the gifts. I feel bad I didn't bring anything. Not even a card."

"Well, see you when you get back."

Gerry clicked off and returned to the auditorium, nearly colliding on the way with Ron Shutmeyer and the Gastons' young hangabout John. Shutmeyer clapped Gerry on the back and said boy isn't this one helluva party. Gerry didn't relish the thought of leaving such a festive atmosphere for the doldrums of the house.

The girl had by now made the rounds with the basket and she placed it behind Flora's throne at the front, heaved a sigh and flopped down into the cushiony chair. She was a little pooped from all of the activity and the people overload. She got up and drifted through the throng towards the opposite end of the room. When she stepped outside the auditorium and the doors closed behind her the din of music and voices faded just a little and then there was another party in progress, smaller in scale, in one of the conference rooms. She walked past that one and then down the hallway, further out of earshot. By the time she reached the library, the noise had become very distant and faint, and when she closed the door behind her it was quiet, it would be just her and the books and that was just fine by her, a little time out among her favorite companions, those bound volumes that bore the heart and soul of those who'd troubled themselves to fill the pages with words. Melinda leaned against the door and closed her eyes, drawing a deep breath and gathering herself in the silence.

The silence was broken by the sound of the sharp flipping of pages. Melinda passed the line of bookshelves to her left and when she got to the magazine rack by the front desk, there at one of the tables, hunched over a book, head resting in the heel of her hand, sat a woman. Her dark hair was matted and she remained motionless a good while. When at last she showed her face, it was splotchy and there were bags under the eyes. Melinda clasped her hands together.

"So," the girl said, "it's you again. What ever are we going to do with you?"

There was no response to this and when the girl stepped nearer she met the foul odor of the un-bathed, the woman reeked badly and Melinda went queasy and dropped into the chair beside her. The woman remained mute. Melinda, trying to regulate her breathing said, "Whatcha reading?"

Libby fixed her eyes on the girl with a vacant stare from behind the loose strands of hair that dangled like a veil in front of her face. The unbroken stare seemed to bore right into the very core of the girl's being. Then Libby's countenance softened and she looked imploringly at the girl. She said, "Do you like books?"

"Oh yeah," Melinda glanced at the bookshelves, "I sure do."

"That's *good!*" Libby smacked her hand on the table. "That's good," she repeated with a whisper.

"What's your favorite book," Melinda asked.

"There was nothing I could do." The woman appeared not to have heard the question. "Nothing I *could do*. D'you wanna know what it was?"

She clutched Melinda's arm. *"It was all a farce."*

Melinda stared down at the table, playing with her fingers.

"Oh," Libby spread her arms in a gesture of exasperation and flopped back into her chair listless as a rag doll, *"what's the use?"*

The room returned to silence. Melinda was about to say something when Libby suddenly sprang back to life as if she were a marionette with some invisible puppeteer pulling the strings. "D'you know what I used to read? Cosmopolitan. I got Cosmo."

"The magazine?"

"I got Cosmo. I got Family Circle. I got Woman's Day. That's what I would read."

"Do they have those here?"

Libby clawed at the sleeve of Melinda's dress in another burst of energy. "I want to read but I can't. I-I can't concentrate. I want to understand but it's too late."

"It's never too late—"

"Do you think... do you think I could have learned something? *Could I have learned anything?"*

"Sure." Melinda patted her arm, "There's always something to learn in books."

"I got Cosmo," Libby wailed, "all that time and I get *Cosmo!"*

"Ssshhh." Melinda wished she could pinch her nose to shut out the musky odor. She said, "Are you with anybody?"

"I used to read books when I was a little girl. That counts, doesn't it?"

"Sure."

"Oh I have to get out of here!"

"Is anyone with you? Anyone looking after you?"

"Oh I've wasted my mind don't you see. I've *killed* my mind and I have to fix it. *Right here!"*

Libby got up and started pacing this way and that among the bookshelves.

"Um, I think we should get you somewhere now."

"Killed it!"

"I can bring you some books–"

"It's *too late!"* she shrieked and Melinda was now growing very anxious.

"Too late!!!"

"We should go now, I think we should go."

Libby seemed to run out of steam again and Melinda took the opportunity of this lapse to take her by the arm, gently, so as to lead her to the door and then once out in the hallway gently prod her right– in the direction of the auditorium, past the party and towards the lobby where there was a manned security office and the staff could take it from there, she had a party to get back to and this woman stunk something awful to be at any gathering, least of all Nana's hundredth birthday bash.

When she reached the end of the hall and turned right past the auditorium doors there was a commotion in progress just outside the door of the conference room. Another private party was going on in there. A trim and fit man of considerable years in blue khakis and a polo shirt was very red in the face and he had Ron Shutmeyer by the forearm in a vise grip. "What the hell were you doing standing in *our* food line if you're a guest of *that* party?"

He glared at the double doors of the auditorium.

"C'mon buddy," Ron had his other hand up in apology. "We were just trying to be friendly."

"Friendly? You consider stealing people's food *friendly?"*

The elder fellow released Ron and then crouched low as if making ready to karate chop. John smirked and glanced around for somewhere to dispose of a paper plate of chicken wings he clutched in his hands. But before he could do so, another man emerged from the conference room, snatching it away from him. The man nodded at the double doors to the auditorium and said, "Let's make sure they're not gate crashing *that* one too."

In all the commotion, Libby had wandered into *that* one, Melinda having loosened her grip on her just as somebody was making their exit through the double doors. Now Libby Alsatian

257

found herself in the dimly lit environs among the revelers and she made a mad dash for the buffet table, dodging children at play, bumping into a few startled guests in the way. Libby was hungry.

Gerry first noticed her, in profile, piling a plate high with country ham, then building a mashed potato mountain with the large serving spoon. He was at that moment doing his darnedest to hear the music above Kenny Fitzroy's treatise on the influence of country music on the Stones. He saw her and did a double take.

The French ladies were animatedly engaged in their native tongue when Gerry got up from the table and left Kenny Fitzroy speaking to the air. He started towards Libby at a leisurely gait, politely negotiating his way through the crowd so as to prevent scaring her off. He approached and tapped her shoulder lightly. She turned and Gerry met with a foul odor.

"Libby." he said glancing around for a far off table, "Would you like to sit down?"

"I don't want to go back to that house."

"No," said Gerry, "we'll stay here."

He took her elbow. "Let's sit over there."

Gerry's smooth voice seemed to calm her somewhat, and she carried her plate to the table Gerry indicated by way of a nod. He fished his cell phone from his pocket as he followed her. The Gastons and their gang bid their farewells and he watched them saunter out. He speed dialed Frank's number. It rang four times and then the answering machine. Libby had seated herself in the meantime and commenced to gouge herself in a very undignified manner from the abundant serving of food on her plate. Gerry sat down next to her and dialed his own number. Shirley's voice boomed. "Where the hell are you?"

"At the party. Listen I—"

"At the *party*? Listen mister, we've finished lobster, we're just getting the kids ready for bed you have family here, in case you forgot."

"I only—"

"Let me tell you, you're cruisin for one mighty big bruisin mister, if you're—"

"—*Shut up.*"

"Ex*cuse* me?"

"Remember that thing we were looking for?"

"*What* thing? What on earth are you talking about?"

Gerry was keeping an eye all this time on Libby and now she glanced up at him sharply.

"I thought you were coming to the party dear."

He knew he was making not one bit of sense to his wife, cupping a hand over the phone and mouthing silently at Libby, *my wife. Shirley*. He rose from the table to quell the agitated voice suggesting a Shirley fit was in the cards. "*Shut up,*" he whispered, "*shut up a second,*" and when he'd got far enough away from Libby he hissed into the phone, "*I found her. I found Libby.*"

The news seemed all at once to rein Shirley in and snuff a full-blown tirade. "What! Where?"

"Where do you think?"

"Hey, don't push your luck wise guy."

"Look, I gotta go. Frank's not answering his phone, can you go on over and check?"

Shirley heaved a sigh.

"Well. *Can* you?" Gerry eyed Libby with a mounting unease.

"He's really got to do something, this situation is really—"

"I know. Look, I gotta run. See you soon."

But Libby had already bolted for the dance floor.

Gerry closed his cell phone and returned it to his pocket, looking on while an easy waltz became disrupted by the frenzied dance of Libby Alsatian. Her arms flapped, she wiggled, and her fidgety legs seemed to have a mind of their own. There was a scene. Oh Jesus, he muttered. He didn't move. He knew building security would be summoned real soon. He knew right then this thing was irrevocably out of his hands.

The band played on, seemingly oblivious to the aberrant dancer in their midst. Gerry watched the attention spread like a wave from those in Libby's immediate vicinity on out until even Flora Wheeler and then the French ladies had their conversations disrupted by the importunate distraction. He sunk deep in his chair, then pulled himself forward and dropped his head into his hands, rubbing at his temples. Were there to be no smooth and easygoing social events, undisturbed by the intrusion of scenes that would have people shaking their heads for months and years afterwards? This place was supposed to be the pastoral haven that Gerald and Geraldine Hagoden had chosen to spend their remaining years in relative rest and relaxation. Yet he idled too long and too often with restless and uneasy thoughts. Was there to be no peace until the final resting place? Gerry, hands clasped and elbows on his knees, looked on. By now they'd made way for Libby, who was cutting quite a rug on the dance floor. The musicians, at a safe distance, had changed gears and upped the tempo with a lively jig to catch up with this new pilot at the eye of their musical storm. The square dancers stood frozen with their hands at their sides, their choreographed movements now overrun by the very random and haphazard gesticulations that comprised Libby's frenzied dance. Gerry looked on with the wary attention one might afford a particularly gruesome scene in a horror film, shaking his head. Security arrived, in blue trousers, white polo shirts and walkie talkies– a young beefy guy with two gray-haired thin fellows. Their presence only served to suffocate the festive mood, the music stopped and for a moment it seemed that Libby's antics would prove to be the death of the party.

Gerry Hagoden had an odd epiphany then, looking on while the security guys tried in vain to avoid drawing attention to themselves or to divert attention from a *scene* in the middle of a celebration, did their level best not to give the appearance they were *manhandling* Libby Alsatian, which in fact they were. Gerry did the math and realized with a pang of wistfulness that he was on the far side of his years and suddenly death wasn't so far away.

Death lurked behind corners at Sunny Glen Palms– death lingered inconspicuously among those relaxing under the bright sunlight by the pool in chaise lounges sipping at drinks spiked with gin, rum or vodka. The Grim Reaper hung around the golf greens, amidst those gathered at folding tables at the crafts clubs, tucked away in the tufts of dense forest, or in the ace of spades in the cards at Bridge nights. There are so many things that might have happened that night that would have involved death, either sudden and unforeseen, or perhaps more inevitable and expected. The Gastons could have had five too many and caused a fatal car crash there on Interstate 75 with seven fatalities. Frank Alsatian, searching frantically, blinded by his own tears, could have been struck by a car on Sunset Boulevard. Libby Alsatian might have turned up lying in a ditch somewhere. Gerry Hagoden might have been murdered by his wife in a fit of jealous rage, and perhaps Shirley may have gotten the noose for the crime of passion. Flora Wheeler may have, with dramatic flair, collapsed into her great great-granddaughter's arms and bought the farm right there in front of everyone at that monumental event to commemorate her hundredth year. Or her great great-granddaughter, having ceased ingesting her prescribed meds to treat anxiety and depression may have lapsed and attempted to inflict the worst possible harm upon herself– or conversely– having returned to said drugs which have rare but possible suicidal tendencies as a side effect, may have become yet another teen casualty. Edna Norton may have passed peacefully in her sleep, sitting upright in that old ancient armchair in front of that old Zenith tombstone radio, no one to discover her corpse for days on end. Or Kenny Fitzroy, having at last been sunk by the heavy weight of a deep depression, may have brought that family heirloom pistol he'd inherited from his mother to the very lips that once suckled at her breast and pulled the trigger.

What did happen that night was this. Once the music had resumed and order was restored to the festivities, Elise deemed it about time to call it a night. Marion had objected to her sister's attending in the first place, but Mimi said she felt cooped up and needed to get out and see people. When did a little socializing ever hurt anybody after all? But they'd stayed, in both Marion and Elise's estimation, a little too long. Mimi's face looked pale and drawn, and her heavy eyes should not have been subjected to that scene with Libby Alsatian. They got up to leave. After bidding their farewells to the guest of honor they got corralled by some old geezer insisting on a dance with Marion. Marion rebuked him, gently but firmly. They nonetheless got caught up in a web of introductions. Mimi leaned on her cane and locked elbows with Elise. Melinda came running to them and Marion first stooped to embrace the girl, then took hold of Mimi's arm so that Elise might do the same. As Elise clutched the girl, rocking back and forth, Marion was supporting her sister and then all at once she felt the weight go, everything happened so fast, the arm squeezed into her own suddenly gone limp and there was nothing she could do but watch her sister crumple and drop to the floor in an instant. She fell to her knees, pulling her sister's head upon them, at the same time looking up imploringly at those who began to cluster around them. "Eau! Eau! *Water!*"

She shifted her legs to sit Indian-style on the auditorium floor, cradling Mimi's head on her lap. Mimi's eyes fluttered then closed, fluttered then closed. Elise scrambled around grabbing at shirts, suits, clinging to dresses, begging someone to summon help. Just as a number of the guests dialed 911 into their cell phones, the same three security guys arrived once again to the party and someone at the bar said to the fellow next to him, round two. The other guy said by way of response, one hell of a party this turned out to be.

The security team went about their business. The beefy guy crouched and felt for a pulse. One of the skinny guys did his best to clear some space— *make room, give the lady some air* he said while the other guard radioed the paramedics on his two-way. It wasn't long until a pair of paramedics arrived at the double doors, oxygen tank and mask, rushing in and attending to Mimi while everyone backed off to afford them space. The team went about their business, one paramedic muttering to the other there were strong indicators of stroke. The Front Porch Pickers were all at once deflated, they plucked absently at their strings, occasionally exchanging a few grave words among themselves. The stretcher arrived, it was lowered and Mimi placed upon it. The paramedics, having hooked up the oxygen and elevated the stretcher, made a dash for the doors, Marion and Elise running along to keep up while Gerry Hagoden looked on in a stupor.

—

Marion loping along beside the stretcher and clutching Mimi's hand all the way to the emergency vehicle, an orange and white square box with flashing yellow lights, while outside it begins to drizzle. Marion kissing Mimi's hand and blowing kisses, as the paramedics bear her into the depths of the compartment. Marion directed by EMT personnel to the vehicle's front cab, Elise guiding and then following her in. Marion glancing over her shoulder at her sister hooked up to the breathing tube. Marion looking straight ahead through the windshield wipers at the beam of headlights on dark wet streets. Marion finding herself praying fervently although she isn't particularly religious and never prays out of habit. Marion wiping the tears with the back of her hand as raindrops pelt the windshield. Marion clutching Elise's hand and Elise squeezing, squeezing as hard as her mother could bear, just knowing the point of pain like she knows the back of her own hand. Marion dreaming of Mimi pulling through, Mimi packing her bags and flying back home with her sister to live out the rest of their years together. Marion berating herself for not coming sooner to fetch her sister from the jaws of death. Marion looking on after the EMT vehicle pulls up at the emergency room entrance of Memorial Hospital and the stretcher is extracted from it. Marion holding Mimi's hand and pleading with her sister not to leave, not now, *it's not supposed to happen this way.* Marion wailing when the attending physician pronounces Mimi dead on arrival.

The auditorium emptying out, the last stragglers gathering around Flora by the double doors, trying to squeeze that one last shared memory into the conversation. The Front Porch Pickers shuffling off with instrument cases. Melinda floating around to summon help for gathering the presents and directing one of her hired hands, a boy around her age, to the last of the boxes. Flora tugging at Sharon's elbow, nodding toward Melinda and winking. The staff folding tables and sweeping floors.

Gerry Hagoden driving home disconsolately on the wet streets. Pulling the car into the driveway, turning off the ignition and sitting there a good while. Shirley appearing at the side of the house, standing there, calling.
Gerry?
Shirley scurrying over. Gerry? *Gerry?*
Tapping on the window.
Gerry cracking the door, throwing a leg out.
What is it Gerry, what's the matter honey?
Gerry climbing out, shutting the door gently behind him and then reaching for his wife. Shirley gathering him in her arms as he shakes, rubbing his back.

Down the street, Libby Alsatian sound asleep and Frank popping a couple of Tylenol PMs, flopping into the recliner and channel surfing, unable to focus on anything that comes up. Dropping the remote into the cushions, climbing out of the chair and pacing around the room. Cracking the door of the bedroom and listening to Libby's soft snoring, watching the rise and fall of her body under the comforter. Willing that all she needs is a good night's rest and he'll have his wife back again, he'll wake up tomorrow and she'll have Sunday morning breakfast warming up in the oven for him, talking about a round of golf while she flips through the pages of Cosmo or Woman's Day. Switching on the garage light and regarding the imperfect model airplane on the wooden horses, suppressing an impulse to smash it to bits.

The last of the floats at the Gasparilla parade long since passed, those in pirate-themed costumes having flung beads upon beads to the revelers who lined the sidewalks of Seventh Avenue in Ybor City. Everyone adjourning to the Gastons' truck for a round of beers from the cooler. Ron Shutmeyer and John having themselves a good laugh about the incident at the private party earlier that evening, Vanessa and Sugar having swooped in on the same party and the same old guy who'd apprehended Ron turning out to be nothing but sweetness personified towards the ladies. The Gastons swathed in beads of every color and swigging beer on the tailgate of the truck. Tommy D'Antonio doing his best to tell them a long and funny story and his wife Debbie yawning and glancing at her watch and wishing they'd taken their own vehicle and might leave on their own terms. Vanessa Shutmeyer watching her husband and knowing full well she'd be pulling out bedding for the couch tonight because Ron always snored a thunderstorm when he'd had a few too many. Wondering aloud whether there'd be a few too many nights like this now that they were retired.

Kenny Fitzroy pulling his mother's old Dodge Dart into Mimi's driveway. Marion and Elise clambering out, thanking him, cheerlessly bidding him goodnight. The house dark, remote. The ladies facing it, arms linked, reluctant to enter. The porch light coming on at the Hagodens. Shirley appearing in pajamas and bunny slippers. Shirley watching them stand wordlessly there in the driveway and then knowing, just knowing. The French ladies hearing her footsteps and turning around. Shirley saying, I'm so sorry. Shirley pulling a shuddering Marion into her pudgy little arms. Melinda and Sharon walking across the tiny lawn from the golf cart, the girl kicking distractedly at the blacktop with thumbs hitched in her jean pockets, at last crumpling into Elise's arms. Sharon stroking her daughter's hair saying, we don't want to intrude and Elise whispering *please*, we would prefer not to enter the house alone.

Flora Wheeler tossing and turning, laying on her back and willing the ceiling fan to hypnotize her, lull her to sleep, but her mind racing nonetheless, a dull ache having settled into her back and her hip. Flora fanning through the many faces that had come before her that night, many for whom age had cruelly played its hand. Some of them having promised to join her at the pool tomorrow, but Flora now reflecting with doleful resignation that tonight would prove to be the last time she would see most if not all of her kinfolk. Flora reckoning that when her number was up, she'd be ready to see whatever there might be to see on the other side. But not wanting to think too much about death, not just yet.

ABOUT THE AUTHOR

Ricko Donovan resides in Nashville Tennessee. When not plying his hands to a variety of stringed instruments, he types away at stories. When not raising his voice to song, he is known to tell stories. He's made some pretty cool records too.
www.rickodonovan.com